MW01620317

ANDREW WYETH, CHRISTINA'S WORLD *and the* OLSON HOUSE

ANDREW WYETH, CHRISTINA'S WORLD *and the* OLSON HOUSE

Michael K. Komanecky *and* Otoyo Nakamura

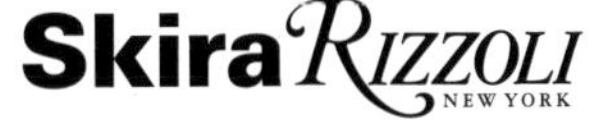

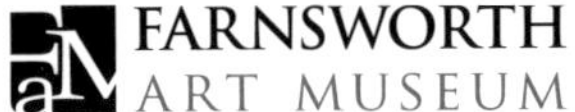

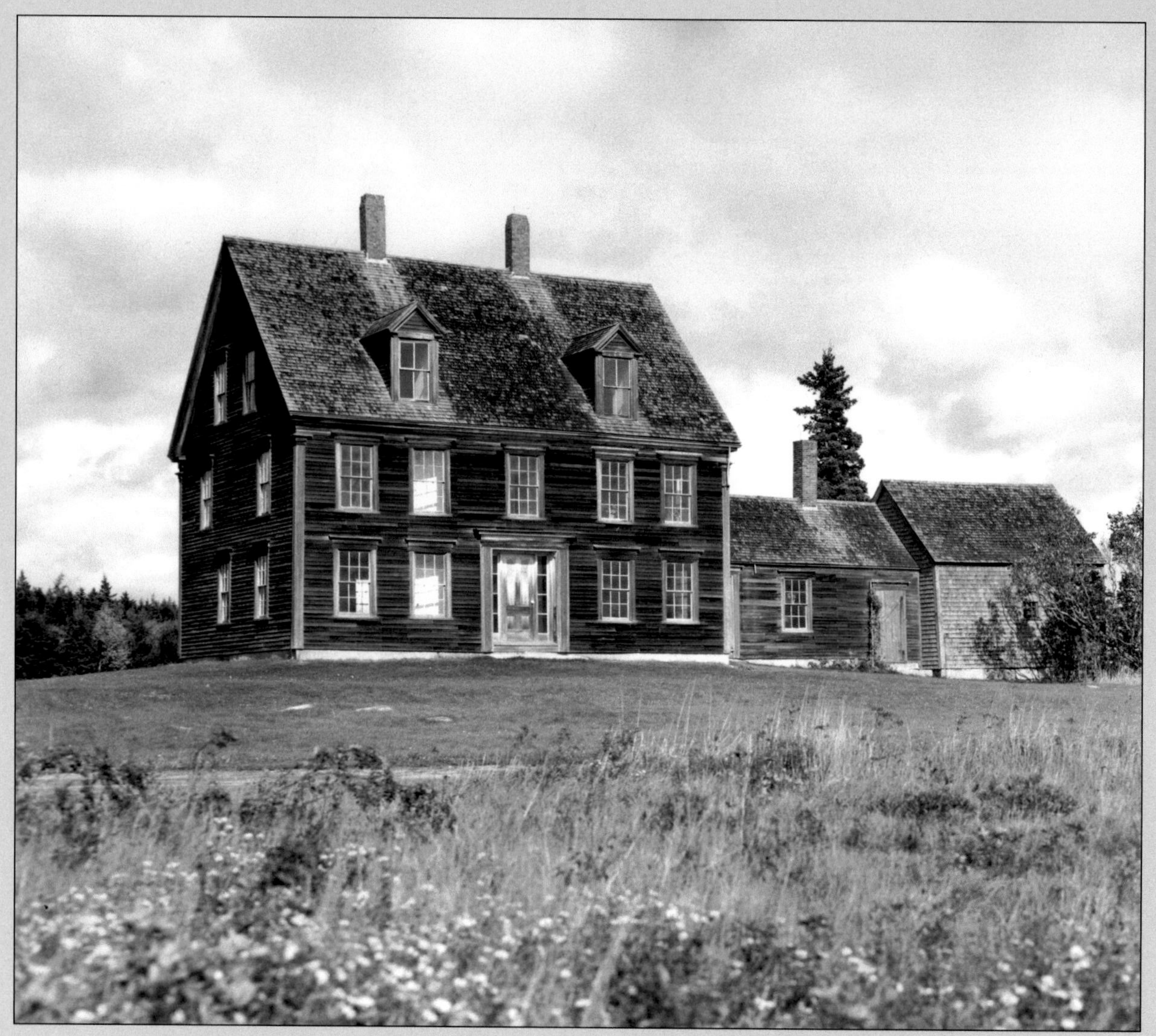

Olson House, c. 1968

TABLE *of* CONTENTS

A Welcome to the Olson House

Director's Foreword
Christopher J. Brownawell — 9

Greetings from Marunuma Art Park
Katsushige Susaki — 11

Guided to Andrew Wyeth's World
Otoyo Nakamura — 13

Christina, Alvaro and Andy
Michael K. Komanecky — 21

Archival Photographs of the Olson House — 31

Plates

Alvaro and Christina — 67

The Olson House — 93

Checklist — 121

A WELCOME *to the* OLSON HOUSE

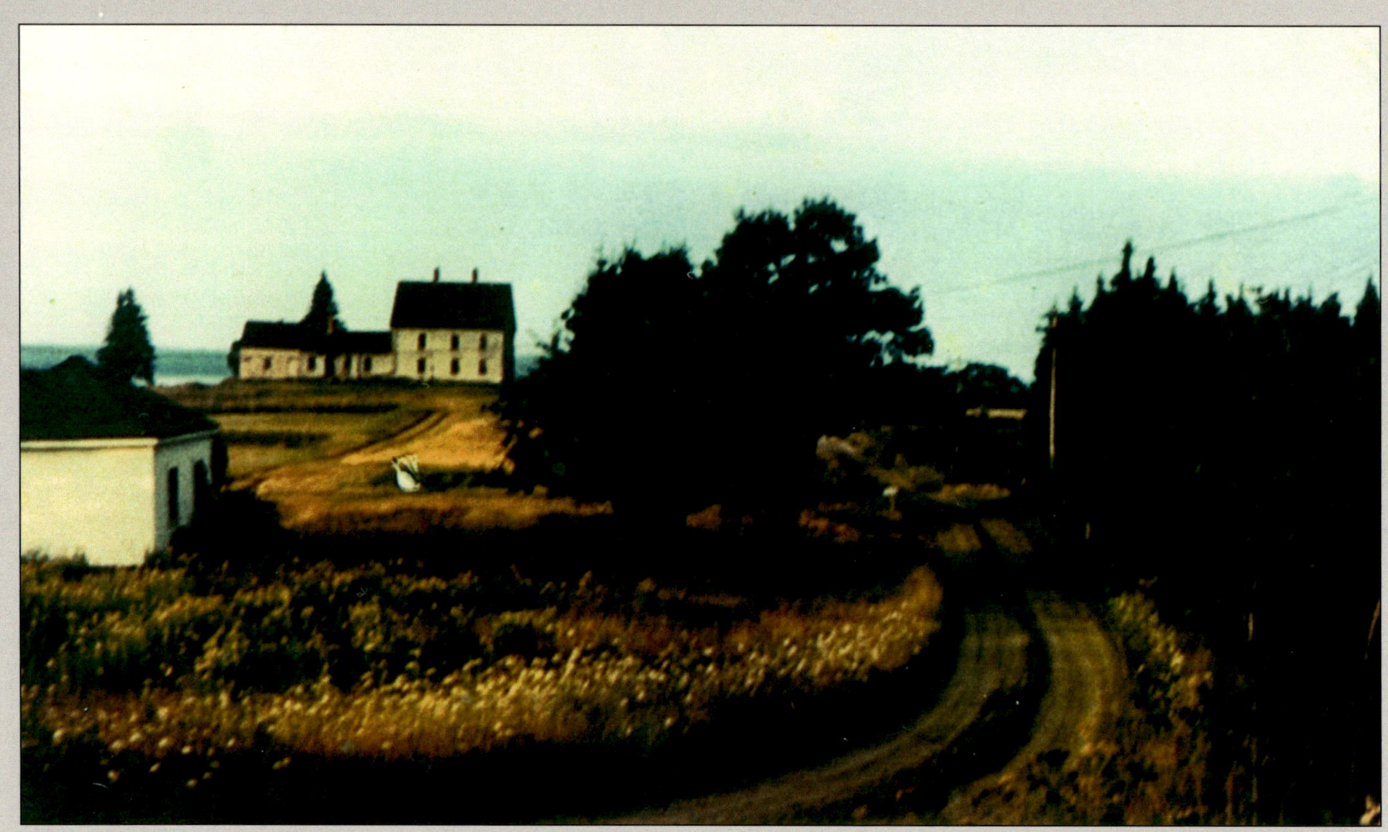

Olson House, 1940s

DIRECTOR'S *foreword*

Christopher J. Brownawell, Director, Farnsworth Art Museum

We commemorate the twentieth anniversary of John and Lee Adams Sculley's gift of the Olson House to the Farnsworth Art Museum with the exhibition *Andrew Wyeth, Christina's World and the Olson House*. Arguably one of the most important objects in the museum's collection, the Olson House is one of Maine's most treasured and identifiable landmarks. It was here that Andrew Wyeth developed his close relationship with Christina Olson and her brother Alvaro, a friendship which spanned more than thirty years. Throughout this period Andrew would return each year to reconnect with his friends, catch up on the important news and celebrate the Olson's simple approach to life on their saltwater farm in Cushing, Maine. While he was visiting, Andy filled countless sketch pads with ideas and notes that would later become finished paintings. Without question he created some of his most compelling and important works of his long and distinguished career at the Olson House. *Christina's World*, painted there in 1948, and purchased that same year by the Museum of Modern Art in New York, is one of the most recognizable and iconic works in American art.

By the time the Olsons died, Alvaro on December, 24, 1967 and Christina just one month later on January 27, 1968, several hundred drawings and paintings had been created by Andy. In 1996 a large part of this body of work was purchased by Mr. Katsushige Susaki from a fellow Japanese collector and added to the Marunuma Art Park's collection in Asaka City, Saitama Prefecture, Japan. This impressive collection of pictures reflects the love and admiration Wyeth had for Christina and Alvaro. From the wonderfully rich works that capture the beauty of the Maine coast and the Olson's saltwater farm, to the intimate interior scenes that reflect the Olsons' quiet and contemplative moments, Wyeth portrayed them with great sensitivity and respect.

The Farnsworth Art Museum extends its sincere appreciation to Mr. Susaki and the Marunuma Art Park for their generosity in lending thirty-eight of these remarkable works of art to the museum for *Andrew Wyeth, Christina's World and the Olson House*. The Farnsworth is the only venue in America where these will be seen and it is a privilege to welcome visitors from throughout the United States and abroad to see this historic exhibition. Because of the generosity of Mr. Susaki, the Sculleys and the Wyeth Family, this exhibition presents a truly rare opportunity. Not only will visitors be treated to these beautiful and inspiring images but they will also have the opportunity to visit the Olson House and to walk through the rooms where the Olsons lived and Andrew Wyeth visited so often—an authentic experience rarely duplicated.

On behalf of the Farnsworth Art Museum, I extend my sincere appreciation and gratitude to Mr. Susaki for making this exhibition possible, the Sculleys for their generosity in donating the Olson House that has become so much a part of the Farnsworth experience and the Wyeth family for their continued generosity and enthusiasm. In addition, I would like to thank Amy Morey and the Wyeth Study Center for their cooperation and encouragement. Special thanks to our lead sponsors, Areté Foundation/ Betsy and Ed Cohen, Tina and Joe Pyne, and additional generous support from Mr. Richard Gilder and Ms. Lois Chiles, Mrs. F. Eugene Dixon and Mr. and Mrs. George Twigg III. The exhibition is also funded in part by a grant from the Maine Arts Commission. Also, sincere thanks to Michael Komanecky, Chief Curator of the Farnsworth Art Museum and his talented staff of Jane Bianco, Angela Waldron, Lorraine DeLaney and Leith MacDonald for their wonderful support and expertise in bringing this exhibition to life. And finally to Mary Margaret Sesak, Art Director, and Joyce Houston, Editor, for creating this beautiful and inspiring book. Additional thanks are due as well to Betsy Bailey and Paula Donovan Olsen of BaileyDonovan LLC for their work on the exhibition catalogue and for their handsome design of the installation materials.

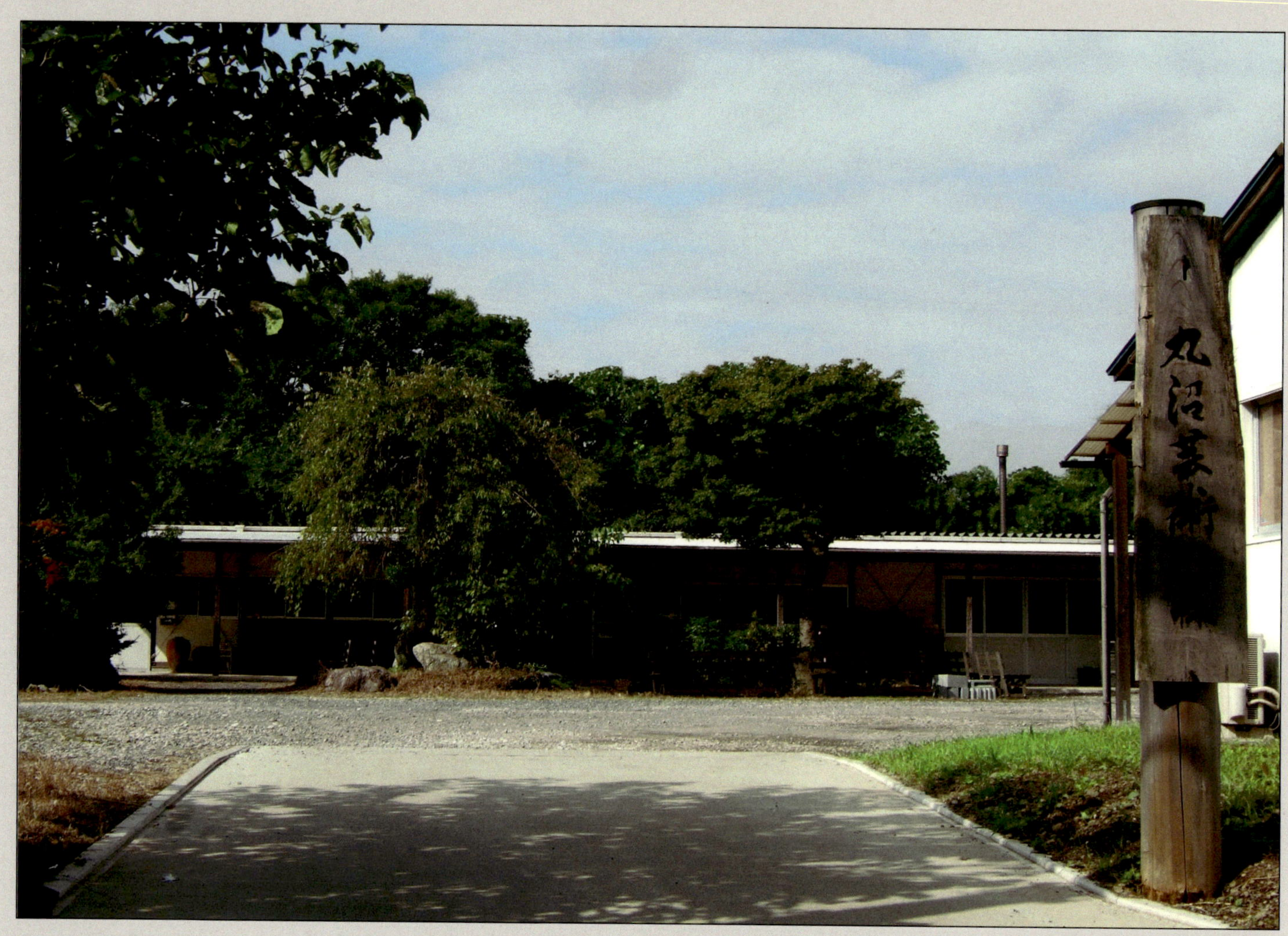

Marunuma Art Park, Asaka, Japan

greetings from MARUNUMA ART PARK

Katsushige Susaki, Director, Marunuma Art Park

I would like to extend my greetings on the opening of *Andrew Wyeth, Christina's World and The Olson House* here at the Farnsworth Art Museum. This exhibition consists mainly of works from the collections of Marunuma Art Park, and I am very honored to lend works from Wyeth's Olson House series. Maine, of course, was the home of the Olsons, whom Andrew Wyeth painted for some thirty years.

Andrew Wyeth was called a master of watercolor. He said, "Watercolor perfectly expresses the free side of my nature." He kept painting until the age of 92 when he passed away. Thus it means a great deal to us holding this exhibition at his home ground, and feel that our efforts are being guided by Wyeth's spirit.

I started Marunuma Art Park in 1985. This is a place dedicated to young artists as their creative ground. I believe that those who aspire to be painters learn more from studies than from completed works because they often offer a glimpse into the artist's intentions and skills. In this regard, I found the studies of Wyeth in particular more notable than any other artist.

In the process of collecting works, as if led by destiny, I encountered Wyeth's productions and met the artist himself at the Olson House in 1996. Mr. Wyeth asked me why I intended to purchase so many of his works and I replied that I was not purchasing them, I was only assuming the role of caretaker. I explained that art belongs to the people, and I would temporarily take care of some of his works so that young people studying to become artists in Japan would have a chance to see them. Upon hearing this, Wyeth cried out, "Great!" and gripped my hand with intense energy. This exchange and that firm handshake are the source of the energy that has driven me from that moment on to expand our activities at Marunuma Art Park. I sincerely hope that many people will come and enjoy this exhibition.

Before I close, I would like to express my deep appreciation to the Director, Christopher J. Brownawell, Chief Curator, Michael K. Komanecky, Registrar, Angela Waldron and all those who made every effort to realize this exhibition.

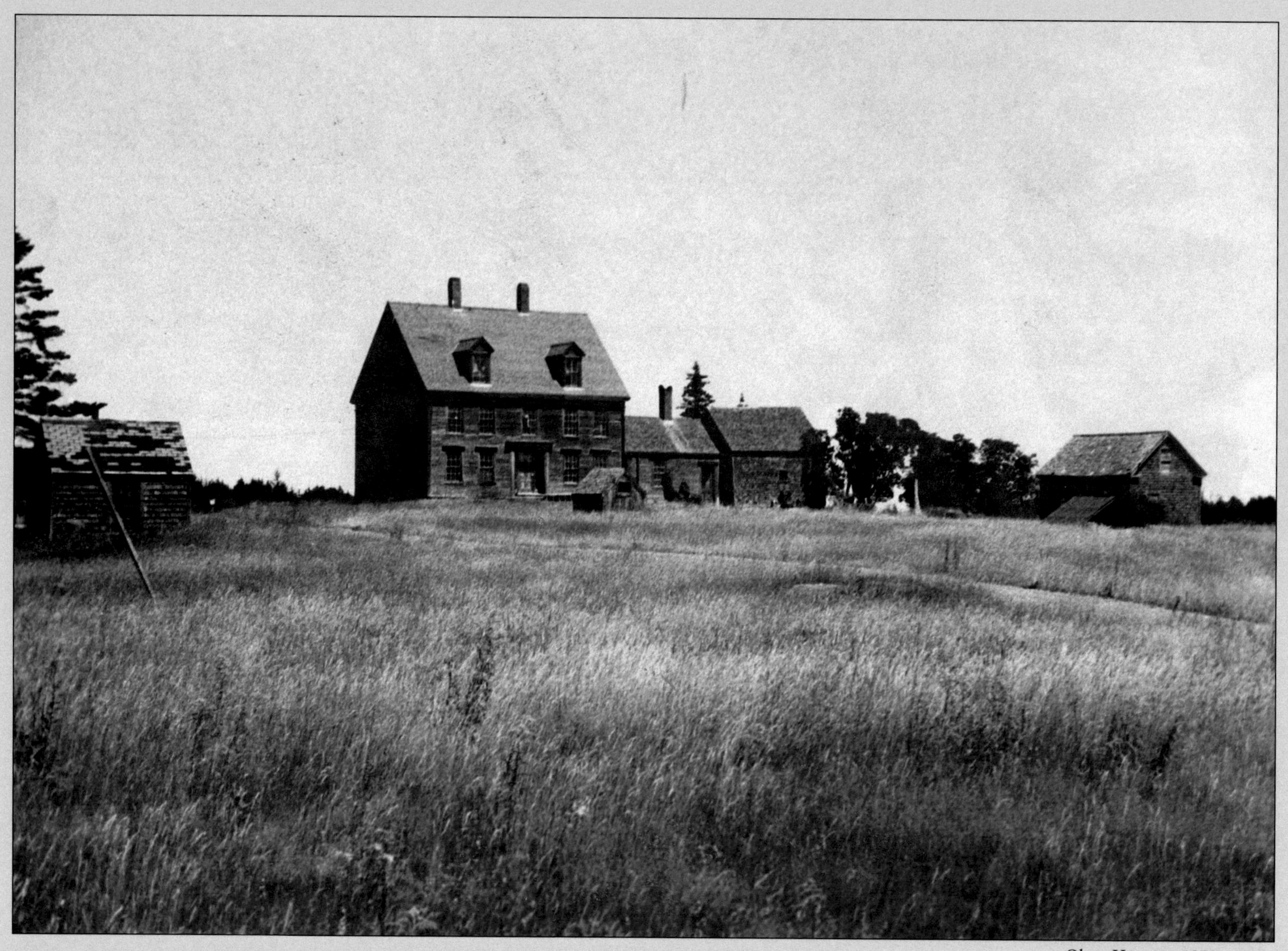

Olson House, c. 1970

guided to ANDREW WYETH'S WORLD

Otoyo Nakamura, Curator, Marunuma Art Park

In 1998 I first encountered the Wyeth collection at the Marunuma Art Park. I believe it was a fortuitous encounter. I do not remember ever seeing a Wyeth painting before then. I like *Nihonga* [Japanese painting] with its lovely depictions of birds, flowers and the many faces of nature, and ink paintings with their subdued palettes. The first Wyeth pictures I saw were a dark painting and a pencil drawing. I was somewhat disheartened; they were nothing like the watercolor paintings I had imagined. But then I saw the reproduction of *Sea Running* and my heart rejoiced. The bell tower was standing on the shore and a rusted anchor in the foreground stood across the sea from the spreading fog that blurred the horizon line. It looked just like a single scene from a movie, surely there was a tale behind that scene. My encounter with that painting made me suddenly appreciate Wyeth.

I empathized with the comment made by the owner of this painting Katsushige Susaki, "I want to educate young artists, I want to share the thrill of seeing Wyeth's paintings with many people," and finally I was able to become one part of Susaki's activities. I volunteered to translate the Wyeth books into Japanese and almost before I knew it I was spending day after day in front of the paintings, taking on work that was essentially that of a curator in charge of the Wyeth paintings. Eventually we organized exhibitions and forums, and as the interest in Wyeth in Japan grew, I took on the role of intermediary between the Wyeth family and the Marunuma Art Park. The following is an introduction to the activities of the Marunuma Art Park, its Wyeth Collection, and the memories with Andrew Wyeth.

Introduction to the Marunuma Art Park

The collection's owner, Katsushige Susaki, heads a warehouse operation in Asaka-shi, Saitama prefecture and, along with his late mother, Hana, supported young artists. In 1985 they used the grounds of an expansive bamboo grove to construct an artist colony named the Marunuma Art Park. Nature is clearly in abundance around the area, including forested areas. The artists in the colony can feel the natural light, wind and atmosphere as they devote themselves to their creative activities. Studios are built in clusters within the compound, which also includes a ceramics classroom, kiln and display rooms. Thus Mr. Susaki has provided a creative site where artists can inspire each other as their art grows.

The grounds of the Art Park are filled with examples of pottery set out to dry, and terracotta works and sculptures that have over-flowed from the indoor studio spaces. These and other elements all add to the creative atmosphere. Today fourteen young artists working in a variety of media are diligently pursuing their creative activities in the Park's studios. Some of these artists also hold exhibitions of their works, teach at universities and travel overseas as their creative realms expand. Takashi Murakami, a resident at the site, is one of the most popular new artists of the contemporary age.

The gallery, built in 1994, holds one Andrew Wyeth exhibition each year and an art appreciation meeting every month in which curators and artists introduce works from the collection. In addition to the presentation of works created in the ceramics classroom, an exhibition featuring works by all resident artists is also held at the end of each year.

Wyeth Exhibition and Wyeth Forum

The *Olson House* series, consisting of 90 watercolors, 147 drawings and one tempera of the interactions between Wyeth and the Olsons, reveals the artist's creative process. Indeed, the group of drawings can be considered an incomparably important group. This series was acquired by Mr. Susaki, who sought to use them to some effect in the art world. This led him to hold a series of ten Wyeth

Forums over the course of the decade beginning in 2001. Mr. Susaki rejoiced, "I want to take responsibility for my collection and present to the public these important Wyeth works, which will become important American cultural relics in the future. Being able to introduce these works to large audiences through exhibitions is the first step to fulfilling my promise to Wyeth." The Forum exhibited the Wyeth works in the galleries, while establishing a study place for young art students, those who study painting, and those who want to learn more about Wyeth. There they are able to study the works together, learn from his techniques and discuss their individual views of Wyeth. The Forum program runs over two days with lectures and media meetings. The speakers at the Forum include Wyeth scholars, art historians, art museum curators, artists and Americans involved in Wyeth studies.

One of the merits of being a participant in these forums is the ability to carefully examine actual art works and then attend lectures on the subject. The workshops give participants an opportunity to directly experience Wyeth's techniques and share their views on Wyeth with other participants. The forums led to a number of interesting episodes. For example, the illustrator whose own painting style changed after an encounter with Wyeth, spoke about the experience of going alone to visit the Olson house and camping in the yard. Or the young woman who stood in the galleries in front of the paintings, sobbing as she said, "I feel a deep sense of prayer in Wyeth's paintings." The young woman had recently lost her mother and she cried as she spoke of Wyeth and thought of her mother.

The various individual reactions to Wyeth glimpsed at the Forum are deeply fascinating. Wyeth fans from all over Japan gather to enjoy these Wyeth Forums. I was amazed at the range of Wyeth fans, young and old.Reading the comments gathered on a survey conducted at the Forum, I came across many heartfelt statements about Wyeth's watercolors and drawings. For example:

> "I could feel the artist's breath, my soul was touched. I felt nostalgic, and cried."

> "I was able to enter into the paintings. I sense the wind, the scents, the atmosphere, all conveyed to my five senses."

> "I felt as if I was witnessing a movie in Wyeth's depiction of the Olsons. These works conveyed the meaning of living, amidst a long unseen rich lifestyle."

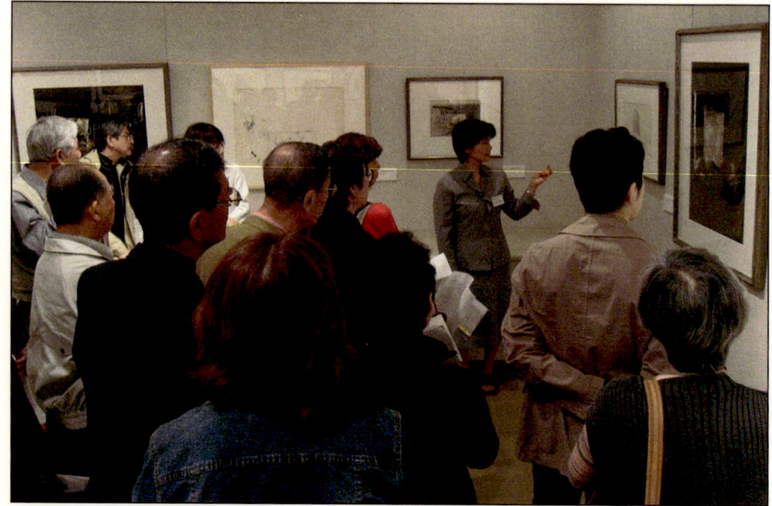

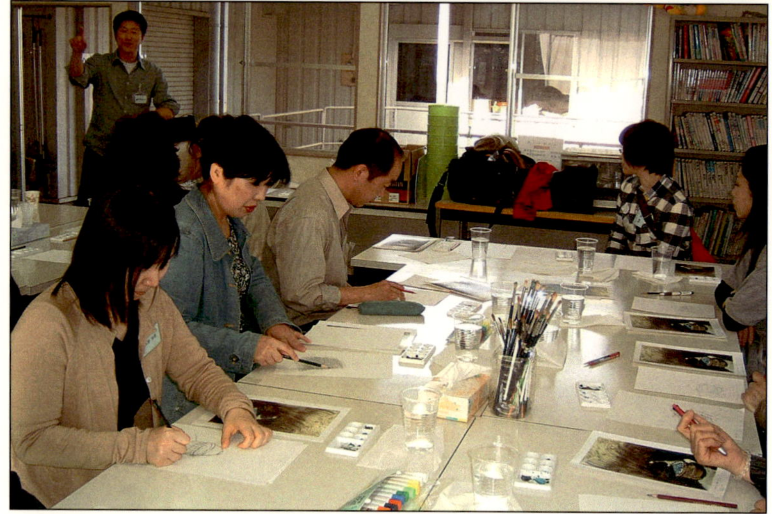

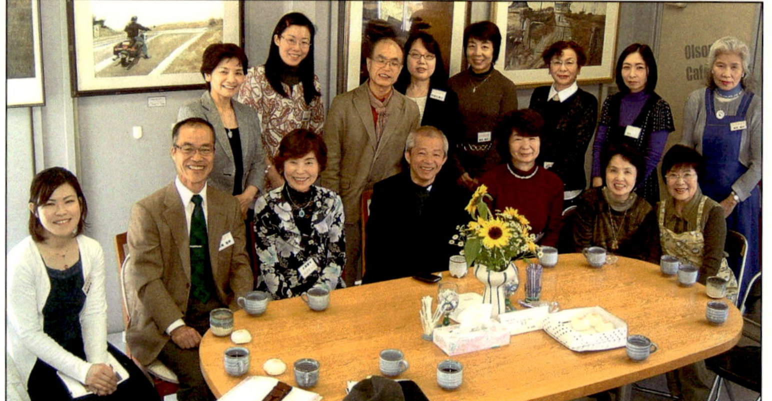

Lectures and classes at Marunuma Art Park with curator Otoyo Nakamura lecturing (top) and director Katsushige Susaki (seated in dark jacket, bottom)

These reactions closely mirrored the feelings of the many people who have enjoyed Wyeth exhibitions both in America and in Japan, clearly reflecting Wyeth's appeal that transcends national boundaries, age or gender.

Multi-venue Wyeth exhibition

The Marunuma Collection Wyeth exhibition traveled to four venues in eastern Japan in 2000, and another touring exhibition was held at four venues in the western part of the country in 2004. An exhibition opened at the Tokoha Museum of Art in October 2006, and then an exhibition from the Marunuma Collection was sent to America in January 2007. This exhibition traveled in America for one year, opening at the Cincinnati Art Museum, Butler Institute of American Art in Youngstown, Ohio, and the Gilcrease Museum of the Americas in Tulsa, Oklahoma.

Regardless of venue, each one of these exhibitions attracted record numbers of visitors. Surprisingly, there were many reactions from Americans that echoed the statement from one visitor, "I had never seen Wyeth's drawings before. Why are these works in a Japanese collection?" The Cincinnati Art Museum was surprised at the response that exceeded all expectations. Three opening parties were held, with violin music adding to the festive atmosphere. In America, Wyeth is said to be a painter who reflects the national spirit, and this feeling was apparent at the Cincinnati openings. All of the gallery walls at all of the venues were painted a moss green color known as Wyeth Green, creating a uniquely dramatic setting for the art works. My greatest joy during this American exhibition was seeing the children who came to see the exhibition, ranging in age from primary school to college. They sketched, listened to gallery talks and fully felt the power of Wyeth.

When 65 works traveled to Sweden in 2010 for an exhibition at the Nordic Watercolor Museum, amazingly they had 130,000 visitors in just four months. The Museum was near Gothenburg where relatives of Maine's Olsons live, and fortunately I was able to meet four of Christina's and Alvaro's relatives. The director of the Nordic Watercolor Museum arranged what was a memorable meeting for us with two young men, their mother, and a cousin who looked much like Christina. They talked about Christina's niece, Jean Olson Brooks, who visited her relatives in Sweden and remains in contact with them. I learned that Andrew Wyeth thought that Christina had tremendous dignity and pride, as did her family members there. I thought Christina and Alvaro might be very happy to know that their relatives came to see them in Andrew Wyeth's works and had a chance to talk about them.

These traveling exhibitions and forums were made possible by the great cooperation of the Wyeth family, including Mary Adam Landa, Curator of Collections for Andrew Wyeth, and Karen Baumgartner, Assistant Curator. Lectures by Andrew Wyeth's granddaughter Victoria Wyeth fascinated audiences and greatly added to the exhibition's success. Mr. Wyeth expressed his appreciation for the Marunuma Art Park activities in a letter to Mr. Susaki. Feeling a connection with Wyeth through his Olson House collection, Mr. Susaki has continued to make donations to support the preservation of the Olson House.

The memorable meeting with Wyeth

Thanks to arrangements made by Mary Landa, we were able to meet again with Andrew Wyeth in Chadds Ford in December in 2007. This was my second meeting with Mr. Wyeth since a meeting at the Farnsworth Art Museum in Maine four summers ago. Ms. Landa met us thirty minutes early and told us the plan for the meeting. Then we waited together for the first glimpse of Mr. Wyeth. He arrived on schedule, driving himself in a Ford van. He was wearing a long down coat with white hood over a dark green suit made up of a high-collared jacket and pants of the same color.

I said, "What an attractive suit, it looks like the suit you wore to the White House to receive your award." He replied, "That suit was the same style, but made in gray cloth. This suit is in the German military fashion, and I like this color. Indeed, it is Wyeth Green!" he said with a smiling face. Mr. Wyeth had the usual mischievous twinkle in his eye. Ms. Landa was surprised, "Even though he always wears jeans and a sweater, today he is dressed in formal wear!" She was thrilled that he had made the effort in honor of their guests who had come all the way from Japan. It was hard to imagine that he was ninety years old, with his bright smiling face and unchanged deep voice. To Mr. Susaki he said, "We haven't met since 1997 in Maine. You told me about your activities with my works in Japan. Thank you very much for those efforts." He then took Mr. Susaki's hand in a firm handshake.

We mentioned his honor of the previous year, when he was awarded the National Medal of Arts (2007) by President Bush at the White House. Mr. Susaki presented Mr. Wyeth with a Wajima lacquer desk box for letters. Mr. Wyeth responded, "This is beautiful! Japanese handicrafts are truly beautiful! I will place my medal in this box." He seemed very pleased.

We also conveyed our thanks to Mr. Wyeth for his cooperation regarding the Wyeth exhibition from the Marunuma Art Park collection, and he was thrilled, responding "I have heard that it has been a great success at each venue. That is wonderful!"

Before parting, Mr. Wyeth pleasantly surprised us with wonderful gifts he had brought with him. They were woolen wrist warmers knitted by Mrs.Wyeth, who couldn't make it that day due to some errand. I remembered that she is good at knitting. Mr. Wyeth said, "My wife made them. Pick whichever you want. Which color do you like?" The white wicker basket was filled with colorful wrist warmers. I picked a pair of wine colored ones, the same color Ms. Landa chose for herself. Mr. Wyeth was wearing dark green ones, same color as his suit. He showed his wrist warmers to me and said, "Look, they're Wyeth green, too!" Mr. Wyeth , walking with a small wicker basket hanging from his forearm, looked just like any other ordinary person, which I found heartwarming and somewhat amusing. It had indeed been a special honor to have met Andrew Wyeth, a great artist.

We were fortunate enough to have a glimpse of Wyeth in a painterly episode. I was surprised to see that beneath his splendid suit he was wearing his paint-splattered work boots. After we had said goodbye, Mr. Wyeth opened the door to his car to get in, and he knocked over a plastic water bottle filled with water. Mr. Susaki, thinking it would harm the car, rushed over and placed it on the grass. Mr. Wyeth laughed and picked up the bottle before returning to the driver's seat. Apparently, that was the water he used for his watercolor paintings. Looking into the car we saw a drafting board covered with drawings. Every morning Mr. Wyeth begins drawing at 8 a.m., and he had been drawing before he came to meet us. This was yet another glimpse of the unassuming, frank personality of this great man.

Conclusion

The past ten years have truly changed me, someone who had not even heard of Andrew Wyeth's paintings. I have done things I would never have imagined, like going to America and meeting a famous painter. Truly I have been introduced to Wyeth's world. I have encountered the Wyeth warmth that embraces people, and the more I learn about the background of his paintings, the more I am fascinated by them. And indeed, these experiences make me want to share that fascination with other people. These works are not only a case of surface beauty, they also reveal a deep-rooted respect for human life, and they resonate in my heart, teaching me about the links between people. We are involved in more and more projects that will involve the ongoing cooperation of the Wyeth family and the Marunuma Art Park.

Although there is no possibility to see Mr. Wyeth again, his world still holds many mysteries to me, and I am endlessly fascinated about where it will lead me in the future.

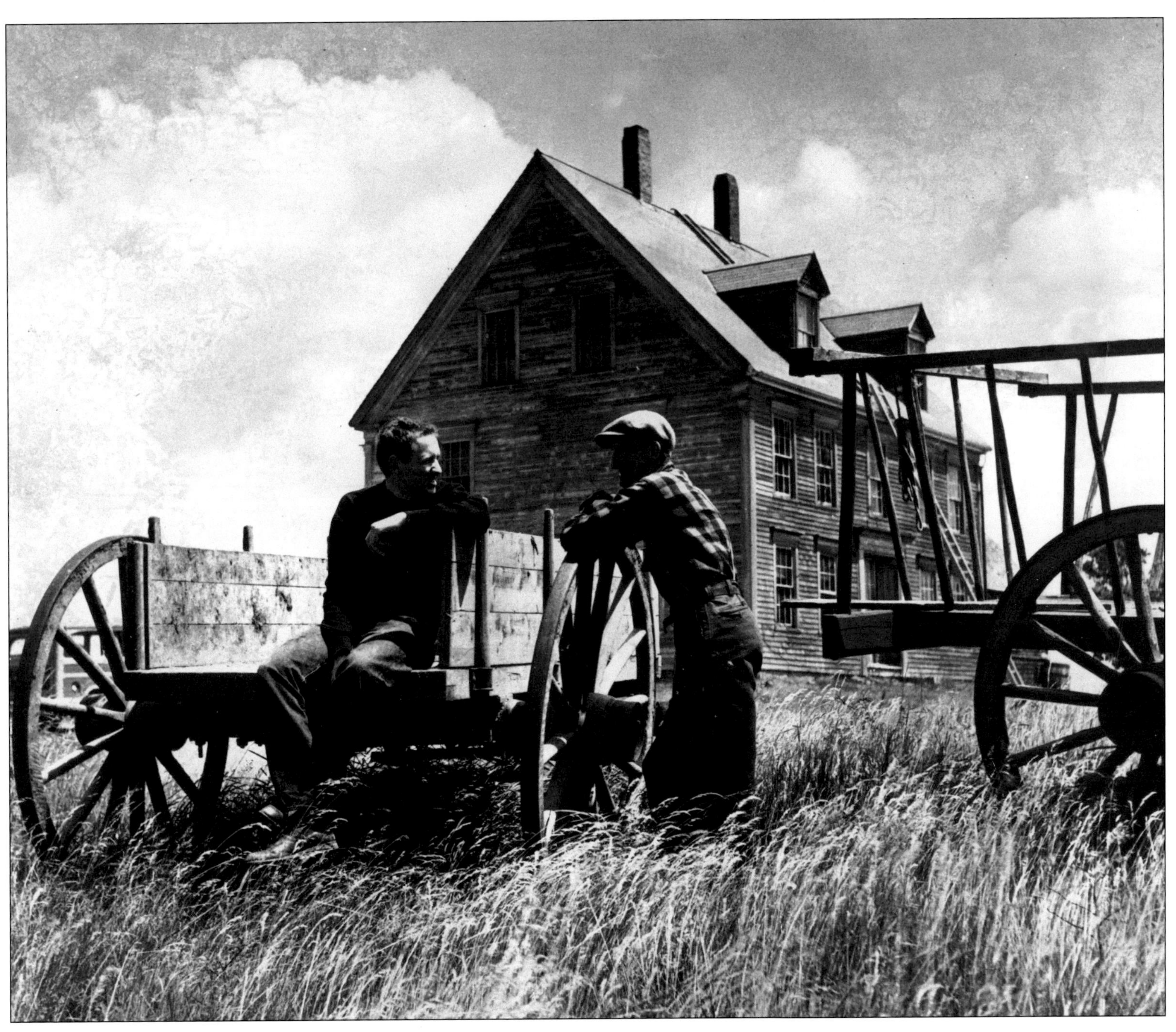

Andrew Wyeth and Alvaro Olson, 1951; photograph by Kosti Ruohomaa, courtesy Black Star Publishing Co., Inc.

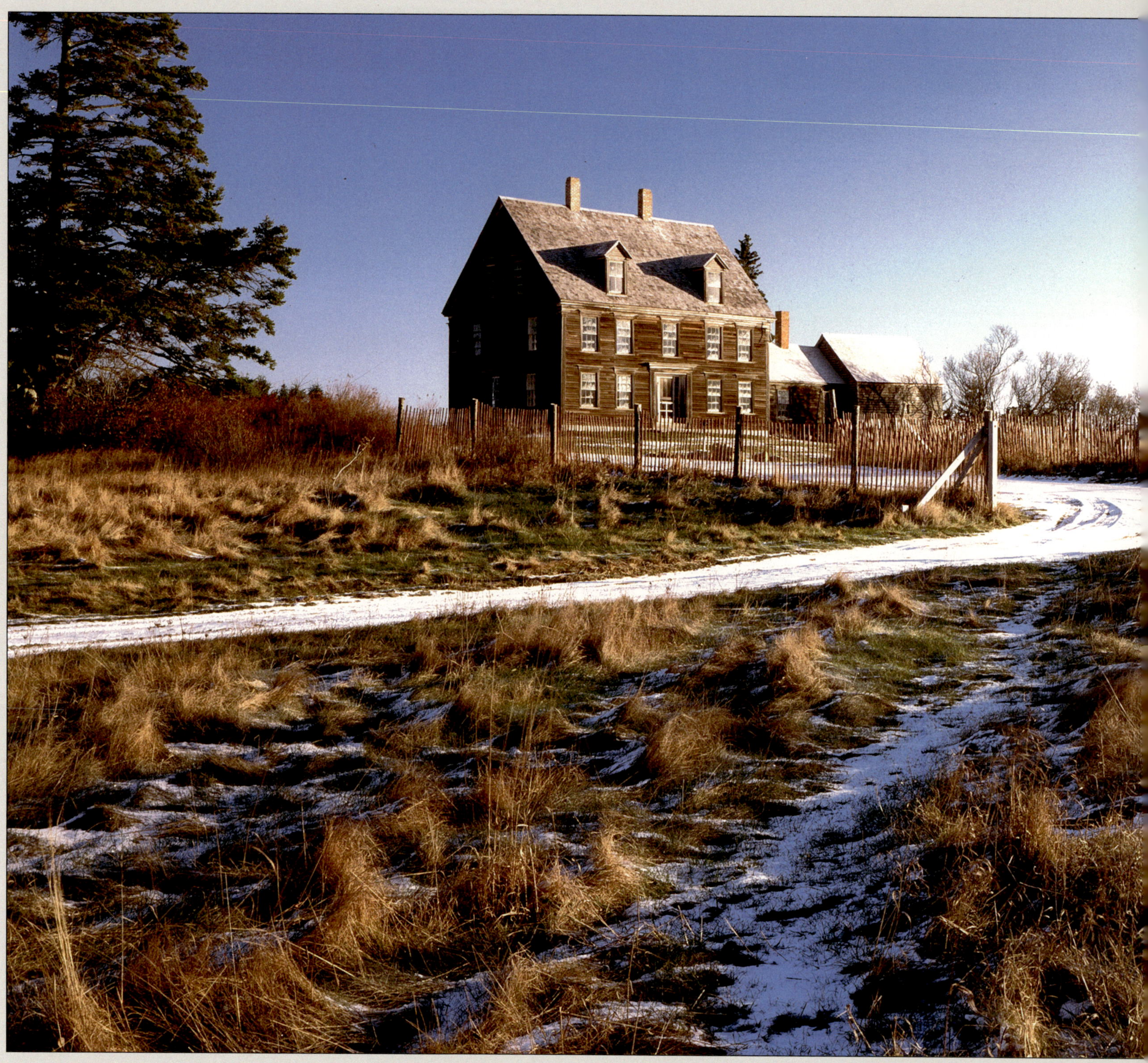

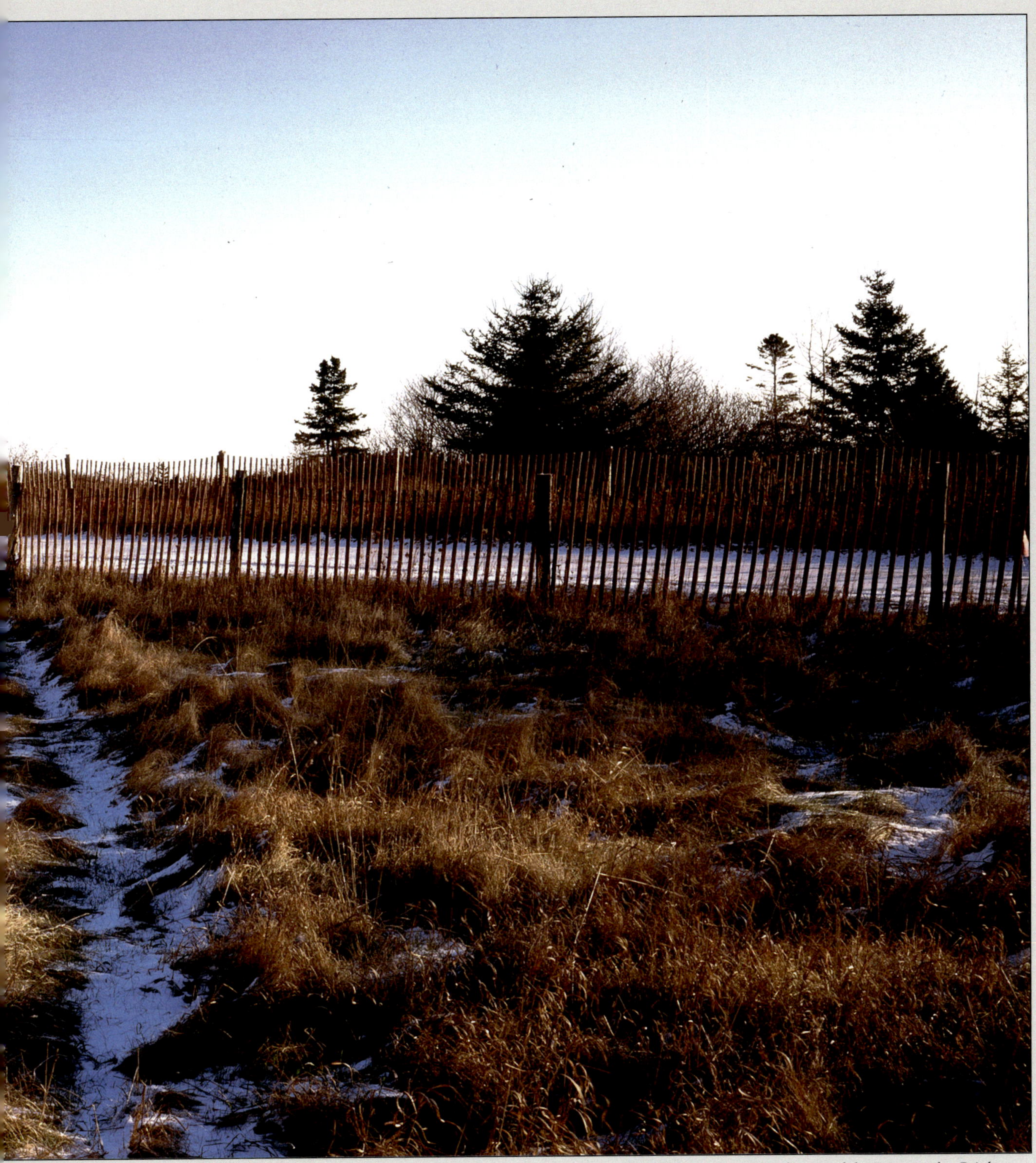

Olson House, 1995; photograph by Brian vanden Brink

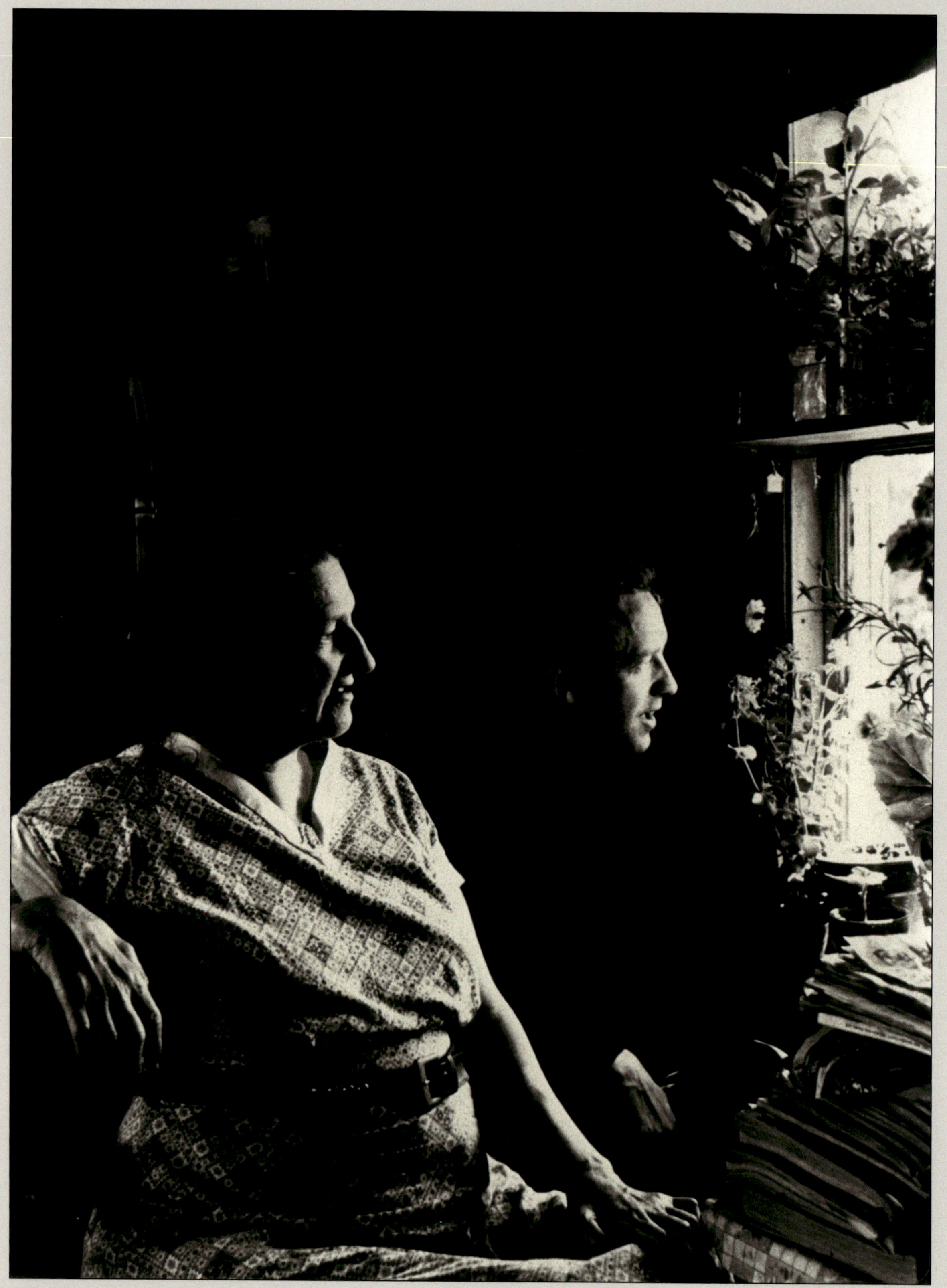

Alvaro and Christina Olson with Andrew Wyeth, c. 1950;
photograph by Kosti Ruohomaa, courtesy
Black Star Publishing Co., Inc.

CHRISTINA, ALVARO *and* ANDY

Michael K. Komanecky, Chief Curator, Farnsworth Art Museum

Introduction

Why has a weathered nineteenth-century saltwater farmhouse (p. 12) located on a quiet midcoast Maine peninsula become a virtual pilgrimage site for thousands of visitors every year? The answer for most is that it is the place that inspired American artist Andrew Wyeth in 1948 to paint his best-known work, *Christina's World* (p. 35). Wyeth's reputation, already bolstered by sellout shows in 1937 and 1939 at New York's Macbeth Gallery, rose still further when the Museum of Modern Art, then the country's foremost proponent of the art of the avant-garde, acquired the painting the very year it was painted. *Christina's World* has become an icon in the history of American art, admired if not revered by the public at large and known to people throughout the world through millions of posters, postcards, note cards and other reproductions. Together the painting and its reproductive stand-ins have led people to visit the place where the painting was made, where its human subject, Christina Olson, lived, and to experience what inspired the artist and the work he made. In the process, the Olson House, too, has become as much an icon as Wyeth's painting

In many respects, Andrew Wyeth was responsible for the Olson House's very survival. Its two final occupants, brother and sister Alvaro and Christina Olson, along with the place in which they spent their entire lives became the focus of Wyeth's work from 1939 until shortly after their deaths in 1968. During that thirty-year period, he did more than 300 drawings, watercolors, dry brush, and tempera paintings of the house, its surroundings, and most of all, Christina and Alvaro. In a fundamental respect, Andy chronicled their lives there and, by extension, the life of the house made famous by his iconic 1948 painting. These works were a creative act of recording, forming a visible memory for something that no longer exists. What most of the world knows of the Olsons and their house lives on through the product of Wyeth's extended devotion to his art making and, in no less a degree, his devotion to his friendships with Christina and Alvaro.

The exhibition *Andrew Wyeth, Christina's World and the Olson House* is drawn from the large body of work by Wyeth featuring the Olson House in the Marunuma Art Park in Asaka, Japan,[1] supplemented by a selection of related works from the Farnsworth Art Museum. While the inclusion of *Christina's World* undeniably would have enriched the exhibition, its absence—due to conservation concerns—nonetheless offers an opportunity to look closely at the rich, diverse range of subjects that Wyeth explored, frankly without being under the large shadow that this painting would understandably have cast. His work in the ten years preceding the painting should not be seen as a build-up to *Christina's World*, and his work in the next twenty should not be seen as some kind of postscript to that one painting for which he is best remembered. As has frequently been the case for Wyeth, there is also the need to go beyond the technical dexterity he so frequently displayed in the media which he employed, and to look more carefully at what he depicted. His iconic painting notwithstanding, Andy's choice of subjects at the Olson House was not exclusively or even primarily Christina, but as much Alvaro and the unrelenting, physically demanding work that was a part of Alvaro's everyday life: fishing, raising crops and livestock, making repairs to the house and surrounding buildings, doing all that was necessary to take care of himself and his sister, to sustain themselves in a challenging environment with limited economic resources. Wyeth's work there was as much about Alvaro's world as it was Christina's, and in more ways than one, it was Alvaro who made Christina's world possible.

The Olsons and their house

What is known today as the Olson House traces its origins not to the Olsons, but to the Hathorn family of Salem, Massachusets, who were probably of Scotch-Irish descent and came to New England from Northern Ireland.[2] In 1743 Boston-born merchant Samuel Waldo gave 100 acres each to Samuel Hathorn I, his brother William Hathorn VII, and William's son Alexander Hathorn. Waldo, one of the largest landowners in the Massachusetts Bay Colony of which Maine was then a part, owned more than 500,000 acres in present-day Knox, Lincoln, Penobscot, and Waldo counties, including all islands located within three miles of the shore.[3] It is not clear what led Waldo to convey the land to the Hathorns, although it is known that another family member made unsuccessful claims to land in this region as early as 1690.[4] Nonetheless, on January 26, 1743, Waldo conveyed lots 59, 60 and 61 to Samuel, William, and Alexander respectively.[5] The land the Hathorns received was located on a point, on the west side of the St. George River, adjacent to Maple Juice Cove in Cushing, Maine (p. 36). William built a log cabin on the site, no evidence of which has been discovered.[6]

In the 1780s or 1790s William's son, Samuel Hathorn II (c. 1750–after 1820) built a two-story, wood-frame structure on the site.[7] A sea captain, Samuel married twice and among his eight children was a son, Aaron (1790–1859), who also became a sea captain. After Aaron's death in 1859, his widow Mary Louisa Hathorn sold the house but in 1865, her son Samuel IV (1822–1892) bought the house, returning it in the Hathorn family.[8] From this early period, no images or descriptions of the house survive, although it is reasonable to assume that the land around it was cleared for farming, and the trees used for fuel and lumber.

Samuel and his wife Tryphena Elwell Hathorn had four children, of which only one, Kate (or Katie, born c. 1857) lived into adulthood.[9] By 1873, Samuel IV, now retired, added a third story and dormers to the house, thus creating bedrooms on the uppermost floor which the family rented out to summer visitors. Following the Civil War, the entire Maine coast, accessible by boat as well as rail, was an increasingly popular getaway for urban visitors from all along the east coast, particularly the stretch from Boston to Washington, and for twenty years the Hathorn family welcomed these summer visitors. The Hathorns' boarding house became known as the Umbrella Roof Inn.[10]

The early 1890s marked two key events in the history of the house. During the winter of 1890, a young Swedish seaman by the name of Johan Olauson (c. 1858–1929) was trapped by an early freeze on the St. George River. Stranded temporarily, he found a place to stay in the Hathorn Point home of Captain John Maloney, on whose schooner Olauson was serving. While there he studied English in the one-room Wing School #4, learned the language and changed his name to John Olson. As he waited for the river to thaw so he could put back to sea, he met the thirty-four-year-old Katie Hathorn and fell in love with her. When he returned to sea, Olson wrote Katie as often as he could, and in 1892 asked her to marry him.[11] Less than a month before their July 1 wedding, however, Kate's father Samuel died, and John Olson, as he was now known, took over the family farm.[12] Kate and her mother continued to operate the boarding house, while Kate's new husband earned his living as a farmer and fisherman.[13] John and Kate Olson had four children, two of whom were to later befriend Andrew Wyeth: Anna Christina, born in 1893, and her brother Alvaro, born in 1894 or 1895; their siblings Samuel and Fred were born in 1900 and 1904. Thus the Olson name became firmly attached to the property that had been in the Hathorn family for nearly a century and a half.

The earliest known image of the house dates from around this time (p. 33), a photograph that shows the family standing in front of the three-story white clapboard structure. The house appears well maintained and, perched on a hilltop overlooking Maple Juice Cove and the St. George River, it is not hard to image why it would have attracted summer visitors in search of a peaceful and rustic interlude on midcoast Maine. The Olson children attended Wing School #4, one of the original seven schoolhouses in Cushing located two miles away from their home.

Christina, Alvaro and Andy

Katie Hathorn Olson died in 1929 and although her husband, John Olson, survived her, he suffered from severe arthritis and was confined to a wheelchair for the last fifteen years of his life. When Katie died, her four children took on the tasks of managing the farm and taking care of their father. When he died in 1935 the children inherited the farm. Sam and Fred had already left the family home to strike out on their own, and their siblings Christina and Alvaro remained.[15]

That they chose to stay in the house in which they grew up together was a decision based on a number of factors. To be sure, keeping the property in the family was a time-worn New England tradition, just as prevalent in Maine as anywhere else in the region. A decision both economic and practical, it was also affected by Christina's physical condition. While still an infant, she was struck by a mysterious illness.[16] As her niece, Jean Olson Brooks, later reported, by the time Christina was three, "she was walking on the outsides of her feet with a clumsy and exhausting gait."[17] Doctors in Rockland were unable to diagnose her condition, and a subsequent trip to specialists in Boston in 1919 was no more successful. By then, "she could walk only three or four steps alone and then she would need to grasp a piece of furniture for support ... Because her hands were misshapen and unsteady due to the worsening of her condition, she practiced using her elbows, knees, and wrists for tasks that her hands once did ..."[18] Eventually, she lost all use of her legs and managed to crawl using what strength remained in her arms and upper body and, at the very end of her life, only reluctantly agreed to use a wheelchair.

Christina's deteriorating condition limited her ability to contribute to the household she and her brother Alvaro shared, though by all accounts she possessed powerful determination and a resilient spirit which she put to use to be as independent as possible and to do as much as she could to support herself and Alvaro. Alvaro had been a fisherman and seaman, but with Christina's disability and the death of their parents, he chose to make his life in company with her on the family farm.

The story of Andrew Wyeth's discovery of the Olsons and their house is well known: The Wyeths began coming to this part of Maine in the late 1910s, and in 1920 N.C., the family patriarch, bought an old sea captain's house in Port Clyde, on the other side of the St. George River from Cushing.[19] On July 12, 1939, his twenty-second birthday, Andy decided to visit Merle James, another summer resident and professionally trained artist whom he had gotten to know. When he knocked at the door of Broad Cove Farm where the James family was staying, James' seventeen-year-old daughter Betsy answered the door. Andy was immediately taken by the striking young woman, and when he said he had never seen Cushing she suggested they go visit her friend, Christina Olson.[20] Two things happened: Andy fell in love with Betsy and married her the following year; and Andy befriended both Christina and Alvaro Olson, struck as much by their fierce independence as by the place in which they lived. That very day, as he sat by his station wagon while Betsy went up to the Olsons' front door, he took out his sketchbook in order to do a watercolor.[21] With that unexpected visit, Andrew Wyeth's thirty-year relationship to Christina, Alvaro and their house began.

The works from the Marunuma Art Park collection selected for the exhibition date from 1940 to 1969, and demonstrate the full range of Wyeth's growing interest and commitment to the artistic possibilities that the Olsons and their house offered.[22] *Olson's Cove* (cat. 1) dates from 1940, the summer after his first visit there. Characteristic of Wyeth's early watercolors, it is vibrant in color and expressively painted, and shows the house from nearby Maple Juice Cove. The house (and in this case, the adjacent barn), which was the first subject Andy explored in these early works, is seen on the horizon, just left of center. The house and its relationship to the surrounding site would occupy Wyeth repeatedly during his time there, most famously in *Christina's World.*

Subsequent watercolors and drawings, however, such as *Alvaro in His Garden* from the same year (cat. 2), show Wyeth turning to what became one of his main themes at the Olson House—the ordinariness of the everyday lives of the brother and sister who lived there. Although at first the scene seems to be dominated by the house and barn, the lone figure of Alvaro can be seen walking between the rows of his vegetable garden in the field that ran from the house down toward the cove. Both raising crops and livestock were an essential part of the Olsons' lives, providing food for themselves and a modest amount of money from selling what was left over. Such self sufficiency was a necessity as much as it was a mark of character. In the 1942 watercolor, *Alvaro and Others, Raking Blueberries*, Alvaro, cap on his head and pipe in his mouth, walks through the blueberry fields in front of the house. The arduous task of gathering berries was not something he took on alone; two white-shirted workers labor beside him. Alvaro is shown repeatedly doing the work to make ends meet on a saltwater farm in midcoast Maine. In one work he is shown raking hay (cat. 8), in another reshingling the roof (cat. 11), and in another painting his dory (cat. 7). Alvaro's often demanding life was not without its occasional respites, though, as seen in *Alvaro on Front Doorstep* and *Stairway and Front Door* (cats. 4 and 9)

Even when Wyeth turns to images that appear at first glance to be vignettes in which neither of the Olsons are seen, there is nonetheless an implication of their commitment to self-sufficiency and what it meant in their everyday lives. *Harness in Olsons' Barn* (cat. 16), *Hitching Post at Olsons* (cat. 15), *Hayloft in Olsons' Barn* (cat. 24), *Alvaro's Hayrack* (cat. 43) *Grain Bag* (cat. 17) and *Beans Drying* (cat. 28) all refer to life on the farm. *Downspout* (cat. 21), easily dismissed as an intriguing and carefully composed rendition of this detail of the house, is a revelation of something more, namely Alvaro's creative and frugal solution to a broken downspout helping keep rainwater away from the house's stone foundation. *Breakfast at Olsons'* (cat. 26) is another work whose subject is somewhat hidden, save for its title. Wyeth depicts a segment of the larger house and the connecting ell, and through the window of the ell, where the kitchen was located, the standing figure of Christina is visible as she makes breakfast for herself and Alvaro, smoke pouring from the chimney above.

Christina, too, was the subject of many of Wyeth's works at the Olson House, the most famous of which was, of course, *Christina's World.* The story behind this iconic work is also well known. In May 1948, Wyeth's tenth summer of drawing and painting at the Olson House, he was on the third floor of the house and through a window happened to see Christina dragging herself on the grassy field down below the house toward Christmas Cove. She had a garden there where she cultivated flowers that she picked and placed on the first floor of the house, and Andy saw her as she was making her way back. Later that afternoon, as he rowed back to his place in Port Clyde, the idea of making a painting of Christina began to occupy him. While at dinner with his wife and her parents that evening, he suddenly left the table, went to his studio in the barn, and made a single drawing outlining the composition: Christina with her back to the viewer, in the field, looking back up toward the house (cat. 33). Over the course of next few months, he made numerous drawings and sketches, using his wife Betsy as a model for Christina's pose, gradually working out the details of what would become a 32 1/2 x 48 inch tempera painting.[23] The six drawings and one watercolor in the exhibition show the care Wyeth took to faithfully render Christina and her pose. Another watercolor (cat. 19) is a study for the Farnsworth's drybrush, *Wood Stove* (cat. 44), in which Christina sits at one of her two favorite places in the kitchen, at a small table looking out a window on the backside of the house where a dirt road then led down to the river. Three other pencil studies (cats. 39, 40 and 41) also demonstrate Wyeth's fastidious preparation, in this case for a portrait of Christina.

With Alvaro's and Christina's deaths within less than a month of each other's in December, 1967, and January, 1968, Wyeth gradually ended his three decades of work at the Olson House, though not without undertaking three signature works. In *Alvaro and Christina* (cat. 44) he symbolically portrayed the two siblings with whom he had been friends for thirty years, Alvaro as the tub and bucket—signs of his never-ending work—and Christina as the blue door that led to the kitchen that was the center of her life in the house the two siblings shared. *Christina's Grave* (cat. 30) places the viewer just behind the black headstone that marks her grave, recalling at the same time one of Wyeth's early views of the house from Christmas Cove and his painting of *Christina's World,* the work that brought fame to both artist and subject. His final work was *End of Olsons* (cat. 31), a view from a third floor window to the ell and shed at the far end of the house—the title thus referring to both the end of a place and the end of two lives so intimately bound together. Through Wyeth's work their lives have become part of an American saga.

The Olson House: 1968 to today

With the acquisition of *Christina's World* by the Museum of Modern Art and the painting's subsequent widespread popularity, the Olson House itself became a destination for visitors. People came to the house to see it and, if they could, meet Christina. Some, unfortunately, left with stolen mementoes of their visit.[24] With Alvaro's and Christina's deaths, however, the Hathorn's and Olson's more than two-century-long hold on the land and house came to an end. Their passing, and especially Christina's, brought national attention. The headline of the brief obituary in the *New York Times* made clear why her passing was newsworthy: "Christina Olson, Whose World Wyeth Immortalized, Dies at 74.[25] As her brother Fred recounted, "When Christina died and Alvaro, just a couple of months apart, well the phone just rang constantly. Reporters calling from just everywhere."[26]

The celebrity of the Olsons and their house continued to grow. In July, 1968, just six months after Christina's death, an auction was held at the Olson House to sell off furniture, farm equipment and implements, basically anything that family heirs did not keep.[27] The house's fame made the auction an event (pp. 37–40). As Christina's brother Fred reported:

> Thousands of people came and they bought everything. One woman arrived late, and she was almost in tears because there was nothing left to buy. Finally she spotted a busted old chair we'd thrown out on the junk pile and drug that up to me. 'How much?' she asked. I didn't know what to say. It was

worthless, not enough left there to repair. 'Four dollars,' I said. She gave me five and went away happy. She'd have paid twenty for it, I'm sure.[28]

Concurrent with the auction and the settling of Christina's estate, her brothers Sam and Fred decided to sell the family homestead, including the house, barn and other outbuildings, along with 70 acres of land which included 4,000 feet of shore frontage on the St. George River. The property was on the market for $180,000.[29] Apparently, the plan changed and the prime shore section of the property was sold first, leaving the house, the barn, other outbuildings, and a surrounding twenty acres to be sold separately.[30] There was reportedly an effort by the Cushing Historical Society to raise the money to acquire the property and to preserve it as a historic site, but it was unsuccessful.[31] Its concern that the site might be put to use in ways that would not acknowledge its significance was well founded. It was reported that a local developer acquired the property, apparently with plans to construct twenty-five ranch houses.[32] The developer's plans apparently didn't include the Olson House itself and a portion of land from the farm, which Fred and Samuel Olson still owned.

An ad in a Boston newspaper attracted the attention of Rosalie Harrison Levine, wife of film producer and distributor Joseph E. Levine, who was visiting her sister while she recovered from heart surgery. Mrs. Levine knew the house's connection to Wyeth. Her husband was a great admirer of the artist, and together, they owned thirty-six Wyeth paintings.[33] She immediately phoned her husband in California and he just as quickly instructed his lawyer to buy the house for $30,000. Thus the famous Hollywood producer and his wife became the new owners of the Olson House, legally under the auspices of the Joseph E. Levine Foundation.[34]

The Levines came to Maine and were given a tour of the Olson House by the Wyeths. Betsy mentioned that she and Andy still had many of the drawings and watercolors from his work at the house, few of which had ever been seen by the public. The idea was hatched to turn the site into a place where these pieces could be shown and made accessible to the public; the reported $100,000 cost was born by the Levines.[35]

What was undertaken was not a restoration, but a renovation, a distinction which is not always understood by those who see the house today. Christina's and Alvaro's lives in the house and on the farm that surrounded it were difficult by any measure, with their efforts and what limited economic resources they had devoted to sustaining themselves. Photographs as well as Wyeth's numerable works done there clearly trace substantial changes that the house had undergone over the years. Insofar as the exterior was concerned, when Andy arrived on the scene, the house was still white (p. 36 and cat. 4), but it gradually lost its paint and almost certainly for reasons of cost was never repainted. (p. 17) By the time the Levines acquired the property, the barn just across the dirt road from the house was all but collapsing,[36] and the henhouse was in equally poor shape.[37] The barn's dilapidated condition can be seen in Wyeth's 1968 drawing, *Christina's Grave* (cat. 30), which also shows the henhouse, an outbuilding in front of the house, and another adjacent to the barn.[38]

The inside of the house was another matter entirely. In relating many years later the story of first meeting Andy and taking him to meet Christina, Betsy wondered if Andy would be able to tolerate the odors inside the house, one of which was that of Christina's urine. As Andy came to discover, Christina could not easily get herself to the rudimentary privy in the shed or, apparently, use a bedpan, and when the urge struck, she succumbed to it wherever she was. Other visitors were not so forgiving as Andy: he once brought the actor Robert Montgomery to the house to meet Christina, and almost as quickly as he entered the house Montgomery retreated, went outside, and vomited.[39] As Wyeth biographer Richard Merryman has described:

> The kitchen ceiling and walls, impregnated with years of dirt, were a scabrous black. The grime was a lighter shade along the lower three feet of one wall, the height Christina could reach during a long-ago attempt at housecleaning. The overheated air was fetid with wood smoke, fuel oil, urine, musty cloth, cats, and tobacco."[40]

From the few published photographs showing the inside of the house during this time, there was also a sense that the house was set up so as to make both Alvaro's and Christina's lives as simple as they could be in the light of her disability. One of these photographs, for example (p. 34), shows wood stacked in the entry hall—close enough to the front door, to Alvaro's bedroom to the left, and to the rest of the first floor rooms where the brother and sister lived in the winter months; heating the second floor was an unnecessary expense of fuel and effort in a place that another of the Olsons described as "like trying to heat a lobster trap."[41]

The inside of the house reflected both the realities of Christina's and Alvaro's circumstances as well as the typical accumulation of objects and artifacts from a family that had so long been there. In addition to the dust and soot, there was fallen plaster and peeling wallpaper (p. 42).[42] The leaking roof contributed to the crumbling plaster inside, especially prevalent on the first floor, and the chimney bricks were badly deteriorated,[43] but the roof was not the only structural shortcoming. Glass was missing from windows whose pine frames and sashes were in poor shape. In short, it was in no way presentable to do what the Levines and Betsy Wyeth had in mind.

What was undertaken was an ambitious and in part necessary refurbishment. Much of the work involved repairs and improvements to the structure. A new wood shingle roof was installed, and the shed stairs and granite stoop (with granite from nearby St. George) were replaced (p. 42). The unpainted pine exterior of the house had suffered over the years, so much so that most of the doors and windows were replaced with wood from other similarly aged houses nearby. When new boards were required, quarter-sawn red cedar was selected—not pine, as was originally used. These new boards were roughened with a steel brush mounted on a radial saw to bring out the grain and then stained with gray Cuprinol so that the new boards would look like the old.[44] In addition the crumbling barn was in such bad shape that it had to be largely rebuilt. New timbers were cut, using traditional methods and tools, and on the inside of the barn the wood was stained gray.[45]

Systems had to be upgraded as well. A new well was dug next to what was the ice house, adjacent to the barn (p. 42). Indoor plumbing was installed, as was new wiring, electric baseboard heating, and a modern pump and hot water heater.[46] On the interior, damaged plaster was either repaired or replaced with "a gray board material used by the masons as a foundation for plaster" (p. 43), and in some cases new steel lathe had to be inserted.[47] Many floor boards were replaced, too, again with materials from old houses in the area.[48]

The most visible changes made during this renovation, however, were those to the interior. The intent of the renovation was to create a place where Andrew Wyeth's works related to the Olson House could be shown, i.e. in a space that would complement those works. The patched and worn walls, ceilings, and floors had to be dealt with, and Betsy Wyeth chose to create an environment that would do justice to her husband's art. She chose generally light and muted colors to paint walls and floors, and painted "a whimsical border of blueberries atop a pale blue wall in the guest room" as well as a stenciled floral pattern on the walls of a second floor room (p. 43).[49] On the floor in entrance foyer a leaf pattern was painted (p. 43). In what was Christina's childhood bedroom, fragments of the original wallpaper were allowed to remain (p. 44). Betsy also selected the curtains with these various color schemes in mind in those few places where curtains were used; most of the house's twenty-six windows had shades, though they typically were left up, allowing views onto the landscape that Andrew Wyeth had captured his works.

The interior was further transformed by Betsy's addition of "early Maine treasures," and, apparently, some items associated with the Olsons. The original wood stove was returned by the Olsons' nephew John to the house's kitchen, where there was also a rocking chair, oil lamp, and pots of crimson geraniums, recalling how the room looked when Andy spent time there talking with Christina and Alvaro (p. 20). The pantry was stocked with "old crocks," John's "old, much-mended felt boots and his long wooden crutch" hung on a wall in what was called the egg room, nearest to the hen-house outside. The dining room was furnished with "an antique corner cupboard and a long, narrow sawbuck table." Also on the first floor, the parlor, which the Olsons had called the "shell room," containing shells collected by their seafaring ancestors, once again held "sea shells of all kinds: sailors' valentines and sewing boxes made of shells; a small white conch which Christina once gave to a small girl named Betsy and which has found its way back home again." The shell room also had an anonymous late nineteenth-century oval portrait of Abraham Lincoln in a shell encrusted frame, another Olson family heirloom that was returned to the house (p. 45).

What Betsy Wyeth had created was not only a sympathetic environment in which her famous husband's works could be properly shown, but also an environment that resembled the spare, evocative interiors that were a hallmark of his work not just of the Olson House but throughout his career. When a *DownEast* reporter wrote of her visit to the house in 1971, the egg room contained studies for Wyeth's *Weatherside* and *Al Saving Wood.* In the dining room were a dry brush of geraniums and "a watercolor of the Olson House after an early autumn snowfall." In the parlor or shell room were pencil studies for *Christina's World* and in the front hall was Andy's painting of a newel post, close to the very subject of his work. Alvaro's second floor bedroom contained a drawing of the room and "a large pencil drawing of a good-looking younger Al."[50] Two drawings of *The Revenant* (a 1949 tempera self-portrait) hung on the second-floor room where Andy was when the idea of the painting came to him. Betsy, in concert with Andy, turned the Olson House into a new kind of art object, part artifact and part stage set, one that reflected his thirty-year relationship with his friends Christina and Alvaro.

With the renovation activities taking much of the spring and summer of 1970, the house opened to the public for two days in August when Cushing celebrated "Early Settlers' Day," and then reopened for the month of October. Not unexpectedly, when the house opened the following summer, it quickly became a popular destination and remained so the following year as well, with reportedly as many as 30,000 tourists a year coming to the house.[51] The sudden influx of visitors onto what had previously been a quiet Cushing peninsula, however, was not met with complete equanimity by the Olson House's Hathorne Point neighbors. There were complaints about traffic and "refuse from picnicking on the grounds." It was reported that a small cemetery near the house (where Christina and Alvaro were buried, on property still in the possession of the Olson family) was used as a toilet by visitors.[52] Others complained that the house's and the Wyeths' fame "indirectly served to inflate taxes" of Cushing property owners.[53]

What then transpired was a classic battle over public access to a private site. In 1973, two lawsuits were filed, around issues evolving from public access to the house. One of Levine's neighbors put up a snow fence around their property, apparently to prevent Olson House visitors from trespassing on their land, and then constructed a mound of dirt on their property which Levine alleged blocked the view from the house to the St. George River.[54] Levine subsequently threatened to sue to have both removed. At the same time, the Foundation obtained an injunction to prevent a New York film company from filming the inside and outside of the house, and the company sued the Foundation to get the injunction lifted.[55]

By the summer of 1974, relations between the Levines and some Cushing residents had become toxic. Many were angry with the sudden influx of visitors and their cars, and did not want to see the house opened again. The conflict was suddenly a national story. *The New York Time*s reported in June that Levine was contemplating moving the house to Waterloo Village, a restored nineteenth-century canal town in Stanhope in northwestern New Jersey (p. 46). "Right now I feel like I just want to get rid of it. I feel betrayed, like they spit on my face," he told the *Times*.[56] Moreover, it was reported the Wyeths were not only fully behind Levine, but were themselves considering leaving as well. "Moving the home is the only solution Mr. Levine, my husband and I can think of," Betsy stated. "Not one person gave us a vote of confidence, not one. I had a hard time convincing Andrew to come back to Cushing this summer, and we're thinking of leaving permanently."[57] The story gained momentum, appearing in the *Boston Globe* and the *Boston Herald American*, *Philadelphia's Evening Bulletin*, and as the public acrimony continued, in Portland, Bangor, and other Maine newspapers. CBS News reporter Charles Osgood came to Cushing with a film crew to interview Wyeth and Levine, preparing a story "on the latest episode in the nationally publicized brouhaha."[58]

Careful reading of the news reports, however, suggests that opinions of residents about visitation were not one-sided. Some residents stated that the traffic problem was overblown and that it had become less of a problem than when the house first opened. The Cushing town clerk was reported to have said that the majority of complaints came from new residents, not natives: "They have come here for a retreat and don't like the tourists."[59] As is often the case in such community controversies involving public access in an otherwise peaceful rural setting, there was a fair amount of hyperbole. The *Portland Press Herald* reported that the Olson House "attracted a horde of tourists who turned quiet Cushing roads into Hollywood-style freeways," in what seems an obvious jab at Levine.[60] And even the move the Wyeths were considering was not as drastic as many reports suggested: their deliberation was about leaving a home they had in Cushing to retreat to Port Clyde, just on the other side of the St. George peninsula.

Behind the scenes, unexpected efforts were quickly underway to find a way to address the neighbors' concerns and to keep the Olson House open to the public. The *Bangor Daily News* reported on July 9 that Maine Governor Kenneth M. Curtis had contacted Levine and the Wyeths. Dr. Donaldson Koons, Commissioner of the Maine Department of Conservation spoke with both Levine and the Wyeths, and "told them the state is willing to either buy it or to take it over (Fig. 23)."[61] Curtis's reasoning was simple:

> I think Andrew Wyeth's association with Maine is something the state should be extremely proud of, and this will last far beyond his lifetime…I think the benefit to the state from the

historical and arts and humanities standpoint in this will far outweigh the inconvenience which I'm sure will eventually blow over.[62]

This venture was not necessarily met with universal support, either; a little more than a week after the *Bangor Daily News* reported the state's interest in buying the Olson House, its own editorial page argued that:

> For all his gift, skill and sensitivity, Mr. Wyeth is still just a man who lives in Cushing. ... Perhaps Mr. Wyeth could persuade his outspoken associate, Mr. Levine, to dismiss the New Jersey idea, and move the old place six miles down the road to the 140-acre Wyeth homestead. With all the river frontage there, Mr. Levine ought to be able to find a site that would both accommodate the Olson museum, and provide a good view, to boot. ... Best of all, the people of Cushing might get some peace and quiet (p. 47).[63]

As negotiations continued between the state and Levine, the proposed arrangement began to be shaped. Koons indicated that the house would become a "historical monument" under the auspices of the Maine Museum Bureau and the grounds as a state park. There were also discussions about Levine lending a number of works from his collection to the house, thus continuing its function as a kind of Wyeth museum (p. 50).[64] The talks moved quickly, and the state announced on July 18, 1974, that Levine had agreed to donate the house to the state, "only on the condition that it be maintained as a museum to Andrew Wyeth, that it be run with simplicity, and that no admission will ever be charged."[65] An adjoining seventeen acres that contained the Olson family cemetery, also part of the Levine property, would be leased to the state for a dollar a year.[66] Tentative plans were laid for creating a parking lot in the field across the road from the house, and landscaping and a fence that would help address an abutting neighbor's complaints.[67]

Perhaps not unexpectedly, what to some was a sound solution was not so to everyone. Rockland's newspaper editorialized that "We strongly suspect that little thought has yet been given by Governor Curtis to developing ways to protect the rights of adjacent and nearby property owners from thoughtless curiosity seekers." More ominously, the editorial went on to say that:

> As much as we admire the work of Andrew Wyeth, we fail to see the urgency of the need to preserve a building which was merely a model for some of his work ... we feel that a more fitting tribute to this man's talent would be an addition to the Farnsworth Museum. There not only could more people see his [work], but also the work of other talented people suitably displayed.[68]

Whether this statement reflected principled position or a veiled attempt to have Rockland rather than Cushing benefit from the controversy is impossible to know.

Once again, the Olson House story was big news (p. 50). At the governor's announcement:

> More than forty reporters and cameramen—including ABC and NBC News—trailed after (Andrew) Wyeth and Levine, jostling for camera angles, competing for questions and barking at startled tourists who kept getting enmeshed in yards of trailing wires and audio cables.[69]

Andrew Wyeth's increased visibility in the press may have had an unintended consequence, for in the same edition of the paper that announced the happy resolution to the Olson House controversy, it was also reported that in late May three men broke into the Monmouth, Maine, home of Fred Woolworth, one of Wyeth's dealers and collectors, and stole one work by Andrew and four by his father N.C., only to be arrested soon after by the FBI.[70]

Meanwhile, as letters to the editor in various newspapers continued to give life to the controversy over the Olson House's fate, the actual mechanism by which the state would acquire and operate the property began to be developed. As government officials began to scrutinize the proposed arrangement, however, not everyone was on board. The state's Executive Council, whose agreement was required for the deal with Levine to go through, expressed its concerns (p. 53). Council member Howard W. Mayo from Bath was quoted as saying:

> I'm leaning against it. I don't feel it warrants the expense to the taxpayers to set up the facilities it would require [costs he estimated at $25,000]. The building is not a historical monument as such. I think we may be opening a Pandora's box in which they'd be trying to save every little landmark in the state.[71]

Mayo's concerns also included the fact the Levine was reportedly not offering to donate the house, but offering instead a five-year lease.[72] What may have prompted Levine to alter his offer is not known, but its impact was that for the state to qualify for federal assistance to construct parking and toilet facilities, a twenty-five year lease was required, as Commissioner Koons reported to the Executive Council in early September.[73] There was nonetheless strong support for the arrangement among the council members, and after a brief delay it was approved on a five-to-one vote on September 18 (p. 54).[74]

The next task was to prepare and get approval from both Levine and the state in the form of a legal agreement that stipulated the various conditions of the donation. As negotiations continued into the next year, however, prospects of an agreement fell apart over financial matters. Levine apparently wanted no more than a five-year lease while the state sought twenty years and, Levine also complained of "an inadequate proposed state budget to maintain and preserve the property." The state's plans to open the house on July 1 were hence summarily scuttled.[75]

So the Olson House and its surrounding property remained in Levine's hands, no longer a museum of Andrew Wyeth's works and no longer accessible to the public. In April 1977 Levine announced he was going to sell the property through a New York gallery, claiming Maine's refusal to come up with sufficient funding to run the house —and the fact that he had put more than $400,000 into the house—left him no choice. Levine claimed, too, that the Westchester, New York, Chamber of Commerce was trying to persuade him to sell the house to them, offering to provide a fifty-acre park for the house if Levine would pay to get it there.[76] Levine's reputation for generating publicity makes it hard to assess the accuracy of statements attributed to him in newspaper accounts, but there's little doubt that there was still intense public interest in the Olson House's fate.

As it turned out, the house lay fallow until 1986, when Levine put the property up for sale through Sotheby Parke Bernet International Realty Corporation. Advertised as a fifteen-room, 3,000-square-foot house with "no modern bath facilities" and 220-volt wiring for electric heat, it also included the 40 x 45-foot barn, a caretaker cottage, and two storage sheds, all on twenty-two acres. Its new owner, John Sculley, had as much visibility as Levine. Sculley, former president of PepsiCo and then CEO of Apple, had been an architecture student at Brown University before getting his MBA from Wharton School of Business at the University of Pennsylvania. His wife, Carol Lee Adams Sculley, was an avid rider and the couple planned to keep their horses at the house during the summers. The sale was formalized in September 1986,[77] the Sculleys reportedly paying $200,000 for the house.[78]

In yet another unexpected turn of events, the Sculleys used the house less than they originally thought they would, and in 1989 put the house and its twenty-plus acres up for sale through Sotheby's International Realty, with an asking price of $1,250,000 (pp. 55-57).[79] There were apparently little serious interest in the house and it was still on the market in 1991 when the Farnsworth Art Museum approached the Sculleys about possibly donating the house to the museum, noting that beneficial tax regulations currently in place might not be renewed. The Farnsworth by then had a nearly fifty-year-long relationship with the Wyeths, having purchased several of Andrew's watercolors even before it opened its doors to the public in 1948. And, for nearly every year since then, it had shown Andrew's work either in exhibitions or in displays of its own collection. In fact, the museum had early on shown interest in the work of all three generations of the Wyeth family of artists. It organized a major show of N.C.'s works in 1966, and in the summer of 1969 opened a show of the young Jamie Wyeth's oils, watercolors and drawings, still one of the most popular shows the museum has ever had. The art of the Wyeths were an integral and regular part of the museum's programs, incorporated into its larger mission to celebrate Maine's role in American art—in which the Olson House could clearly play a major role. That the museum complex also included the 1850 Greek Revival home of its founder, Lucy Copeland Farnsworth, listed on the National Register of Historic Places and by Lucy's will open to the public, demonstrated its expertise as a steward of historic properties.

The Sculleys agreed to the museum's proposal and, on September 19, 1991, the museum formally accepted the gift of the house (p. 58). The museum's plan at that time was to focus its efforts on preserving the house as an important artifact in the history of American art, and not to open it to the public. Instead, after upgrading its mechanical systems, it thought of renting it to an artist or other suitable tenant, and to apply to place the house on the National Register of Historic Places, which it subsequently did. The museum promised not to construct any permanent structures on the property for the next twenty-five years, and that it would not be used for any commercial purpose. In light of the house's prominence and public popularity, however, the museum recognized how important it would be to allow public access to the site. Over the next year, the museum's staff devoted itself to assessing the structure's condition and determining the house's needs in accordance with the museum's stated plans. In the summer of 1993 the Olson House opened to the public, and has continued to be a virtual pilgrimage site for admirers of Andrew Wyeth's work from all over the world.

Preserving a landmark

In 1995 the Olson House was listed on the National Register of Historic Properties. With Andrew Wyeth's passing in 2009, the property became eligible for National Landmark status, which it expects to receive in 2011. Each of these designations requires a high level of commitment to preserving what are recognized as nationally significant sites.

When the museum acquired the house, it immediately undertook a thorough study of the property. The museum engaged Pamela Hawkes of Ann Beha Associates (now Ann Beha Architects), the highly respected architecture and architectural preservation firm in Boston to prepare a conservation assessment of the Olson House. By this time, all the outbuildings except for the barn (which was not part of the museum's property), had disappeared. In the 1992 Beha report was an outline of the tasks necessary to preserve the exterior and interior. A major challenge was, and continues to be, how to preserve an unpainted wood frame house in the extremes experienced in the midcoast Maine climate.[80] The goal was to maintain as much as possible the weathered appearance of the house so often depicted in Wyeth's work. When Levine acquired the house, many of the house's original pine clapboards and trim had to be replaced. By the time the museum acquired it only some of the original clapboards, mostly on the north side, remained. Sooner or later, almost all of the house's original exterior fabric may have to be replaced. In addition, much of the interior was altered during the Levine renovation, with the loss of much of the original wallpapers and large sections of plaster walls and ceilings, as well as replacement of original floorboards.

Changes to the site have taken place as well. The large tract of land that was formerly part of the Olson farm has been broken up over the years, with a number of plots now owned privately, some owned by other members of the Olson family, and what was formerly the Olson House's barn and field across the road now owned by Up East, Inc., an entity created by Betsy Wyeth to preserve that part of the site made famous by her husband's work. One of the most visible changes to the original farm site has been the growth of trees and other foliage, thus blocking what was in Christina's and Alvaro's time an almost unimpeded view to the cove and river. With the transfer of parts of the site to new owners, it is unlikely that those views can be recaptured. Christina's flower garden, and the blueberry and other fields Alvaro tended are gone, though part of the Olsons' apple orchard remains, and efforts are underway to assure its survival.

These changes notwithstanding, the Olson House and its site remain a powerful document of the many ways in which the lives of Alvaro and Christina Olson and Andrew Wyeth intersected there. Through Wyeth's work, all three of them gained some measure of immortality. It is the Farnsworth Art Museum's commitment to preserve their shared legacy, and to continue to make that legacy accessible to all those who journey to the Olson House's quiet and starkly beautiful site on the Cushing peninsula.

ARCHIVAL PHOTOGRAPHS *of the* OLSON HOUSE

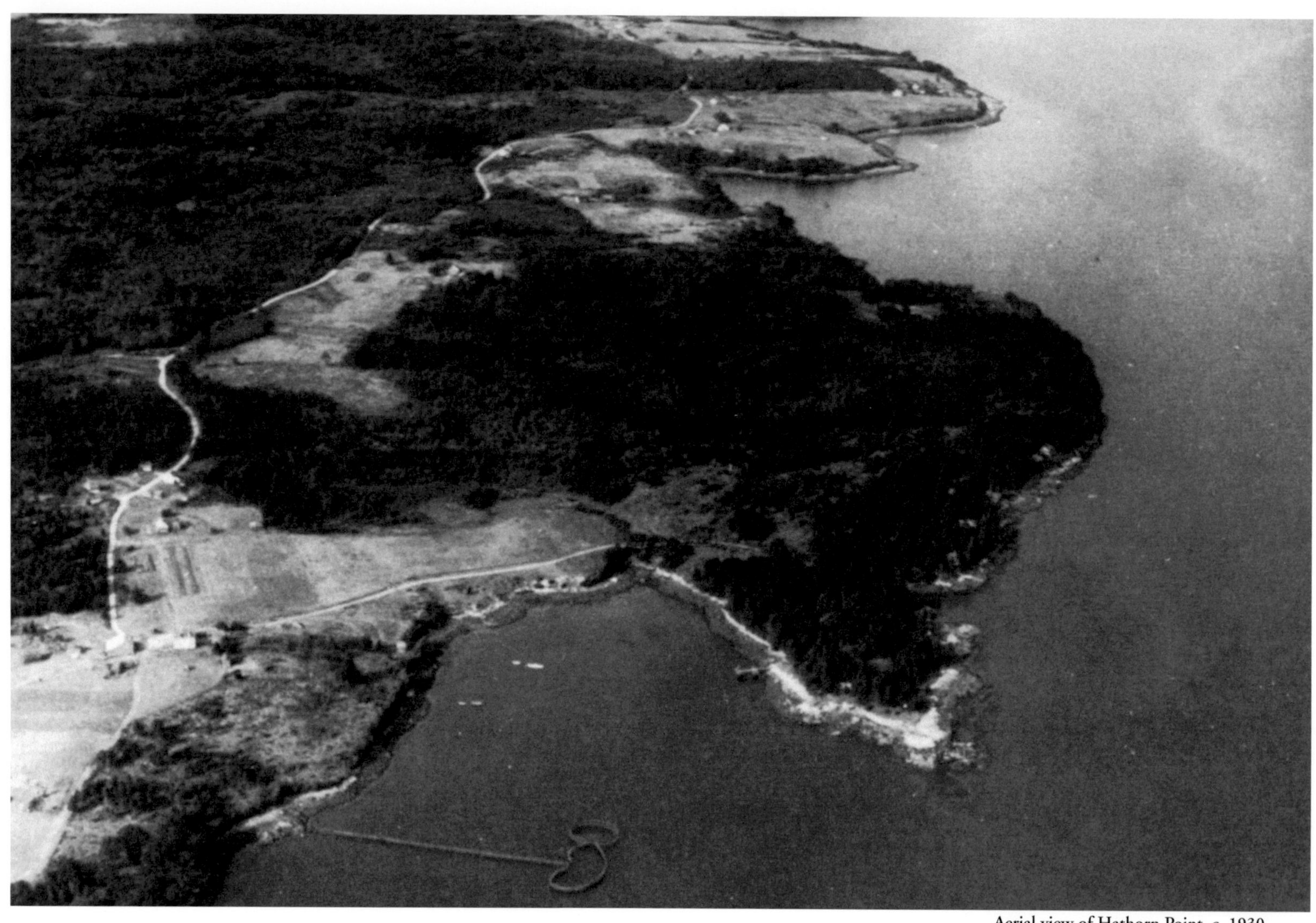

Aerial view of Hathorn Point, c. 1930

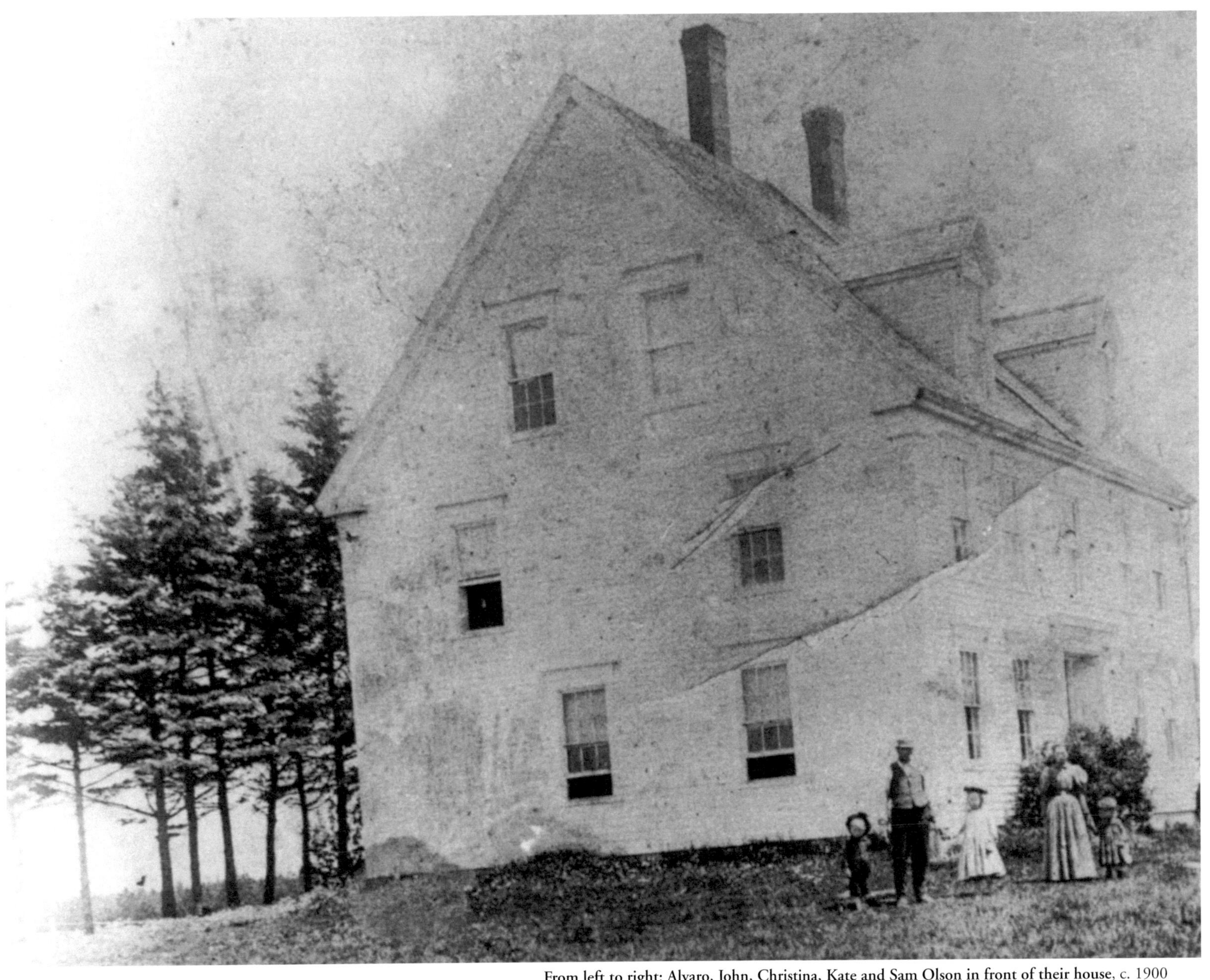

From left to right: Alvaro, John, Christina, Kate and Sam Olson in front of their house, c. 1900

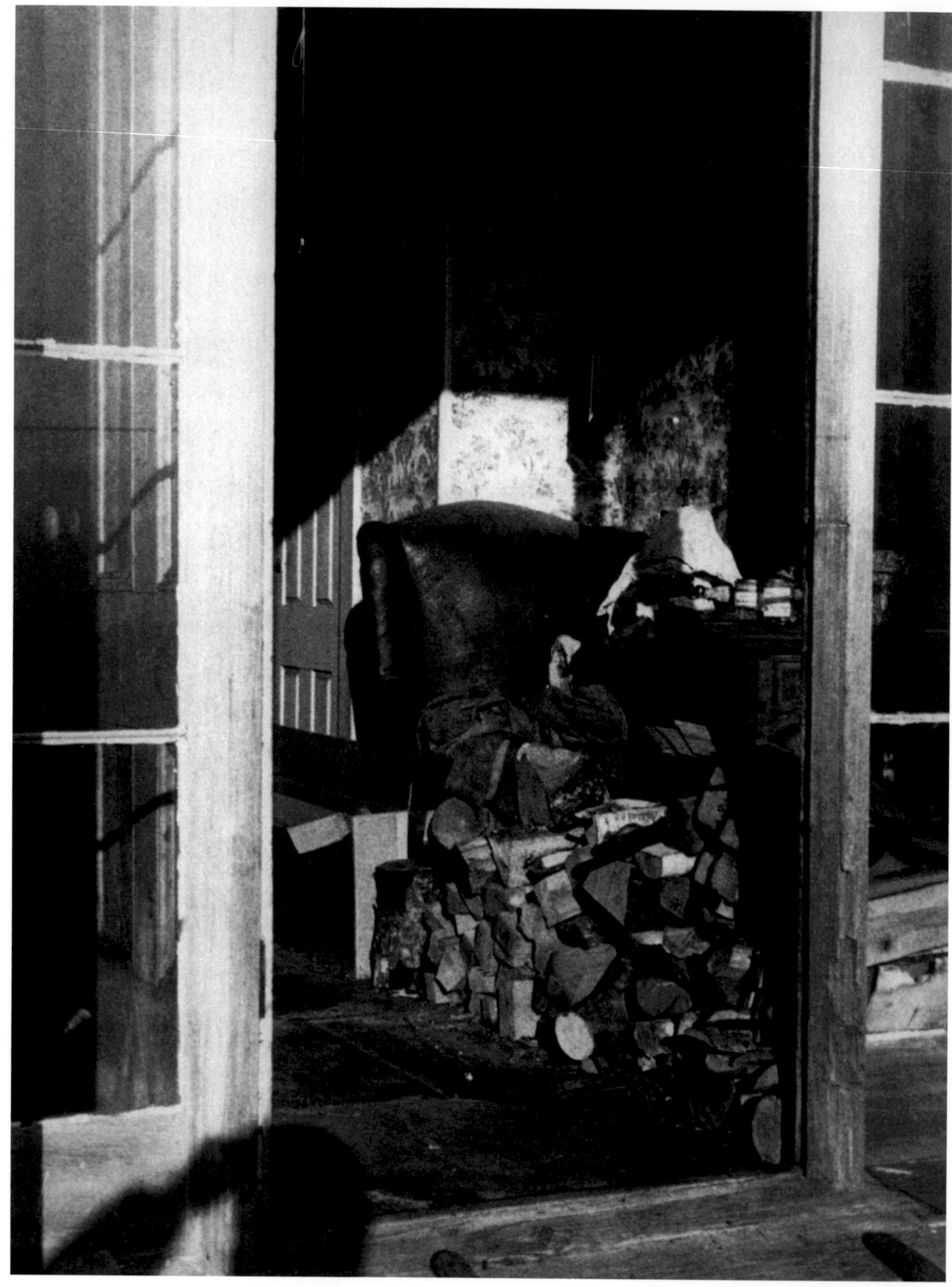

Entry hall of Olson House, c. 1950

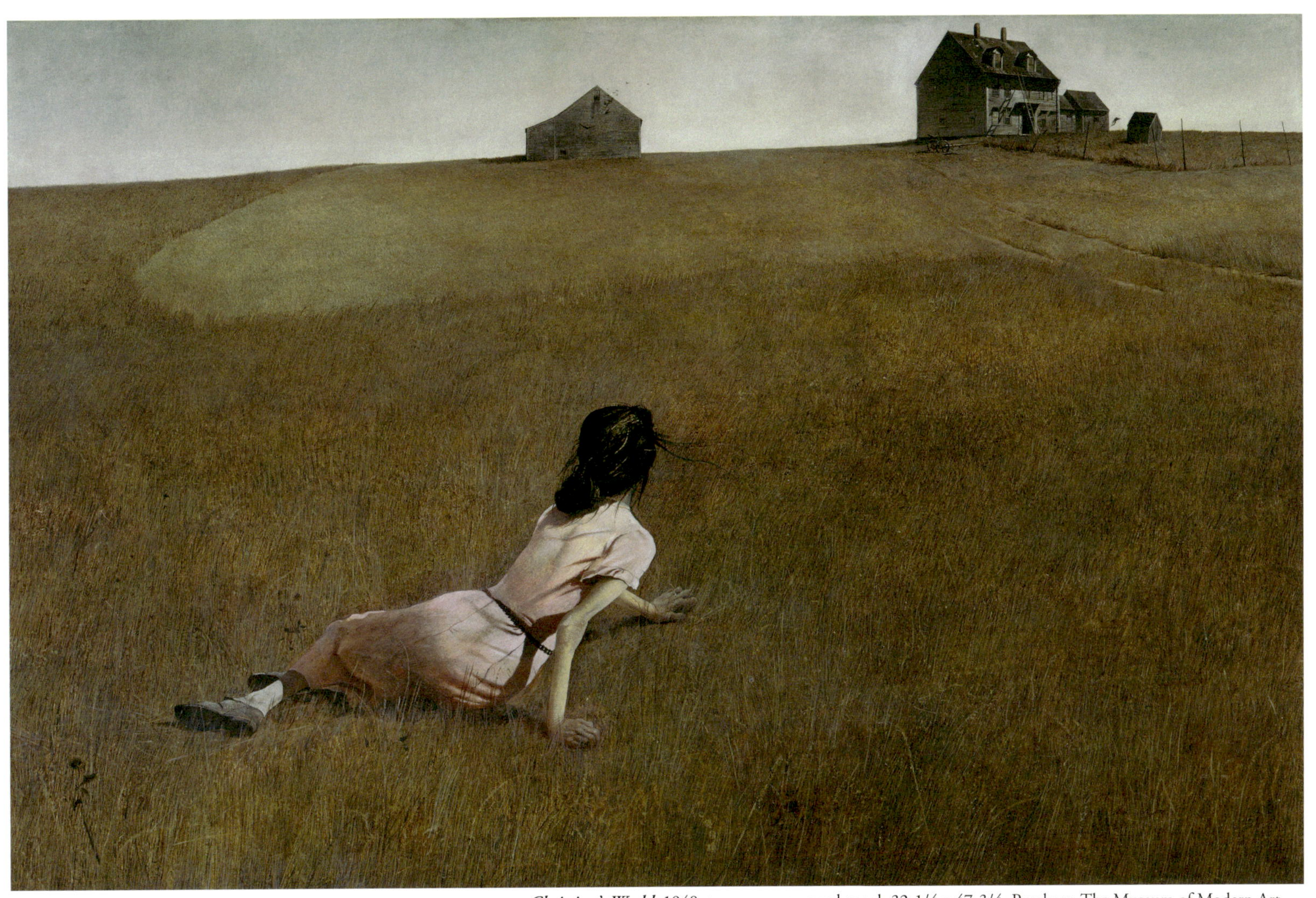

Christina's World, 1948, tempera on gessoed panel, 32-1/4 x 47-3/4, Purchase, The Museum of Modern Art, New York. Digital image © The Museum of Modern Art/Licensed by SCALA/Art Resource, New York

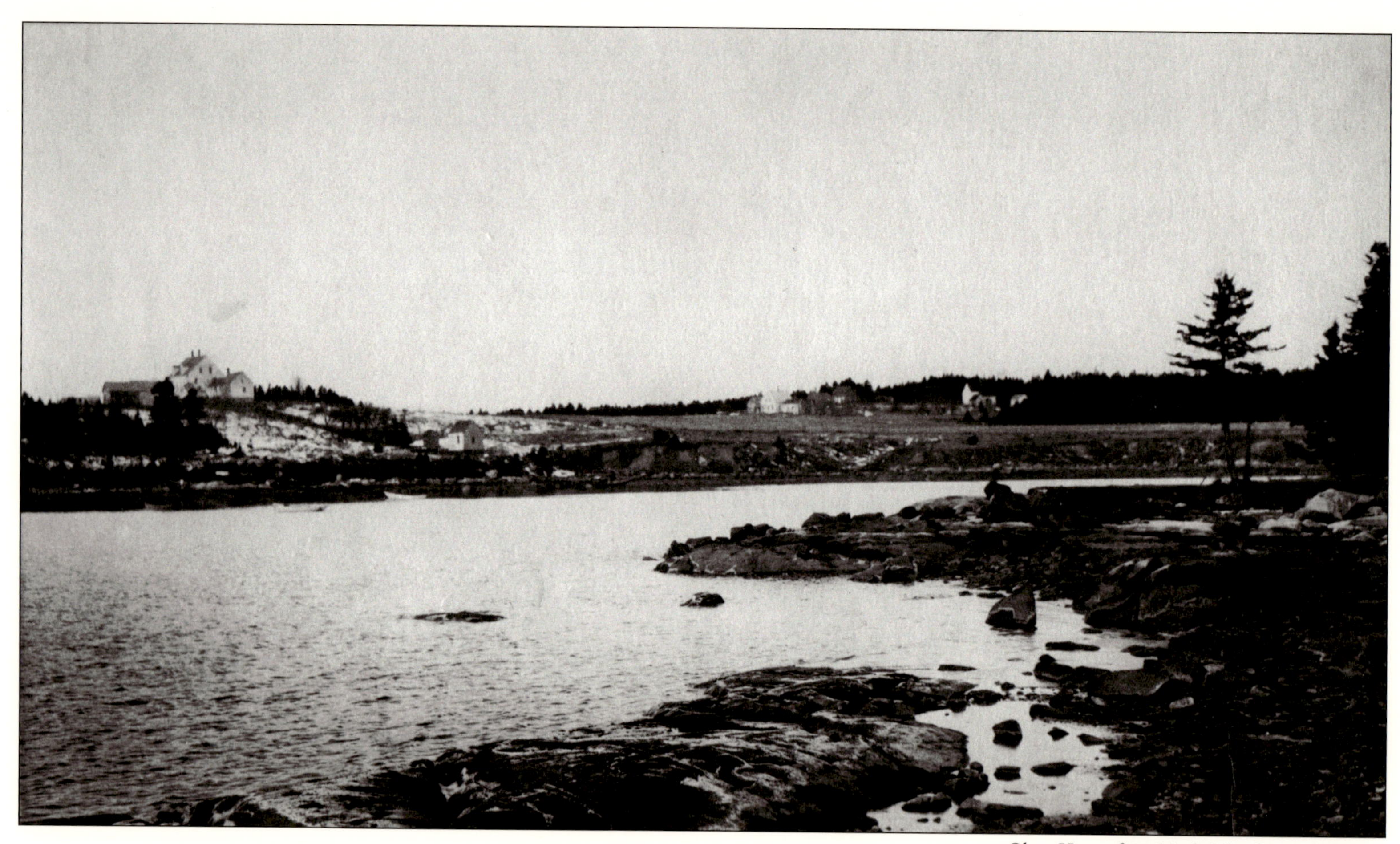

Olson House, from Maple Juice Cove, c.1930

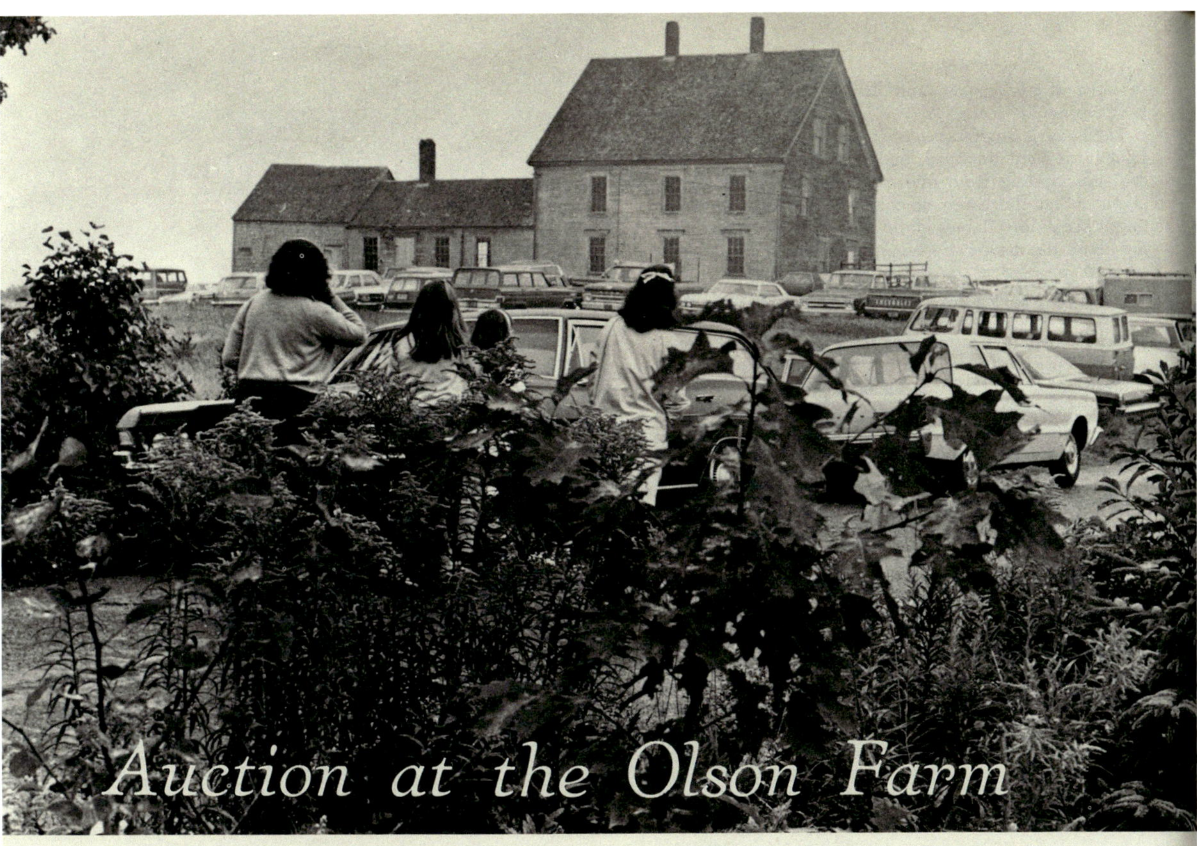

Auction at the Olson Farm

Text and photos by Leo L. Chabot

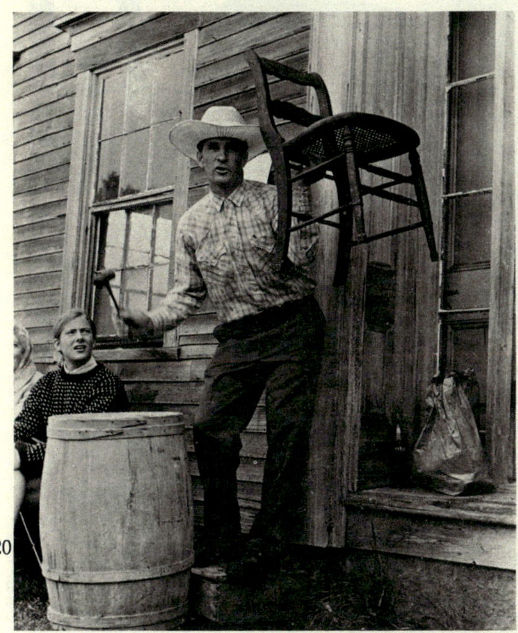

ONE auctioneer had refused to handle the sale because he hadn't seen enough of value inside the huge, unpainted three-story farmhouse to make it worth his while. And although relatives of the former tenants described the late elderly brother and his semi-invalid sister as "hardly poor," all that remained were the tools of a fisherman-farmer and household furnishings that had fallen into disrepair over years of everyday use.

Yet, clam hods, which can be built for less than 50 cents apiece, sold as high as $4.50 each – and there seemed to be dozens of them in the ell and back shed. A hayrack was purchased for a dollar by a local woman who found it too large to carry away in her small foreign-made car. The most expensive item was a 100-year-old wood stove, kept in storage for nearly as long, which brought $40. Priced somewhere between the stove and the hayrack were a variety of chairs, bedroom sets, firewood boxes, a pair of baby shoes, books and farm tools – things used at some point during the lives of Alvaro and Christina Olson. (DOWN EAST, June 1967).

What attracted some 200 persons and held them standing in a cold August fog rolling across Hathorne Point in Cushing was not the farm tools and old chairs in themselves, but the fact that they were mementos

20

Olson House Estate Auction, August 1968; courtesy of *DownEast Magazine*

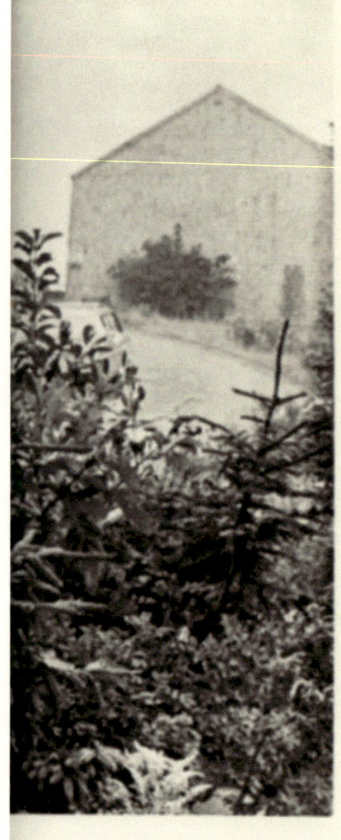

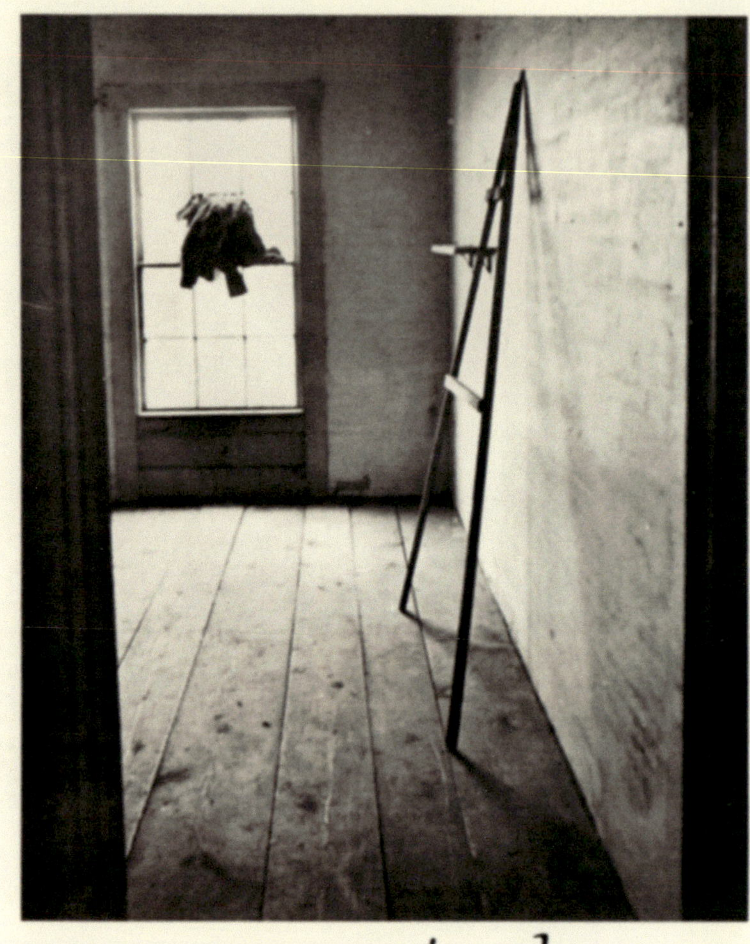

Above left – Fog shrouds the Farm at Hathorne Point on auction day.

...in the Wyeth Mood

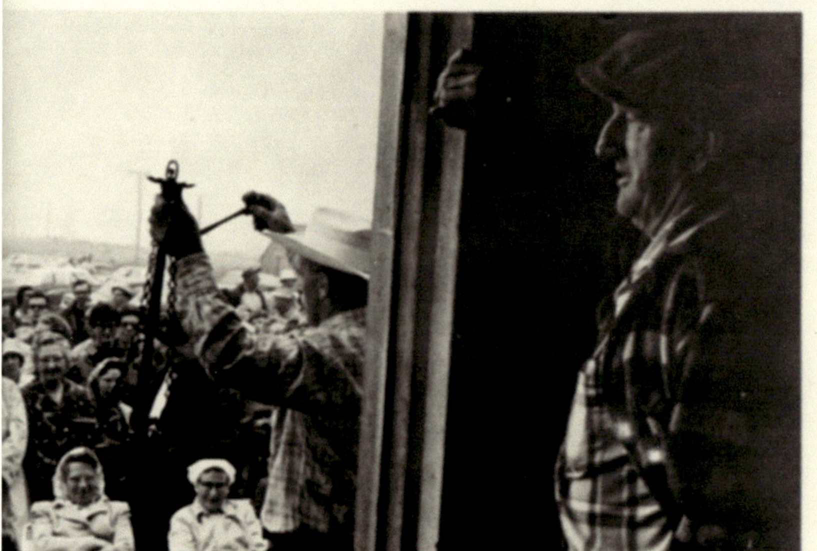

Above – Wyeth mementos in a bedroom. The artist painted the rag in the window in "Weather Side." Left – Sam Olson looks on from a darkened doorway.

Opposite page – Auctioneer Harvey Gurney asks for bids on an old chair.

21

Olson House Estate Auction, August 1968; courtesy of *DownEast Magazine*

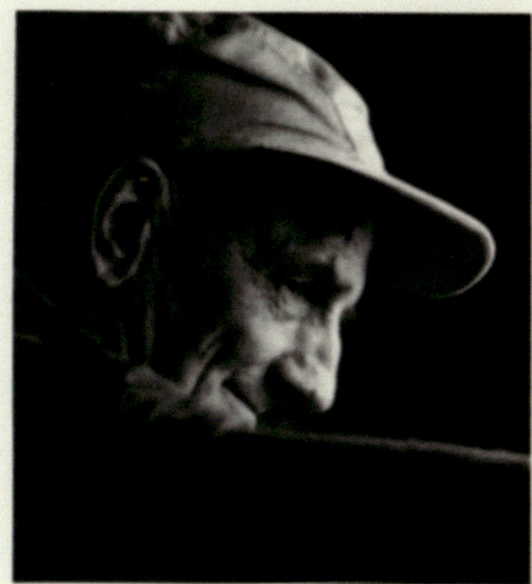

Above — Fred Olson, Christina's and Alvaro's other brother, watching the sale.

of one of the nation's best known contemporary artists. Andrew Wyeth first painted his coastal neighbor, Christina Olson, in 1947 and since had returned to execute more than fifty paintings of the Olson farm. Alvaro posed only once for Wyeth, early in the artist's career. The painting, entitled "Oil Lamp," is in Houston, Texas.

***Right** — Fred and Sam Olson select farm tools to sell from the woodshed.*

Among the more widely known Wyeth paintings of the Olson farm is the tempera, "Christina's World," created in 1948, showing the invalid woman looking back across a field toward the farmhouse. Residents in the mid-coastal area are particularly familiar with such paintings as "Wood Stove," a kitchen scene inside the Olson house, and "Alvaro's Hayrack," showing the vehicle purchased for one dollar at the auction. Both paintings are owned by the William A. Farnsworth Library and Art Museum in Rockland, which has several Wyeth paintings in its permanent collection.

Christina and Alvaro Olson spent their entire lives in the weathered farmhouse that was built in the early 1800s by their grandfather, Captain Samuel Hathorne. (DOWN EAST, June 1961). For the past twenty years, however, the upper two floors had not been occupied. Following the deaths of Christina and Alvaro last winter, the surviving brothers, Sam and Fred Olson, decided to auction off the contents of the building and sell the family homestead. The 14-room house and 70 acres of land, including 4000 feet of shore frontage on the tidal St. George River, are on the market for $180,000.

Andrew Wyeth did not attend the auction. It made one wonder if the reason for his absence may not have been stated by the artist himself only recently after completing a tempera of the Olson house entitled "Weather Side."

"I've had some sad experiences," he said. "Things disappear before I can get to them."

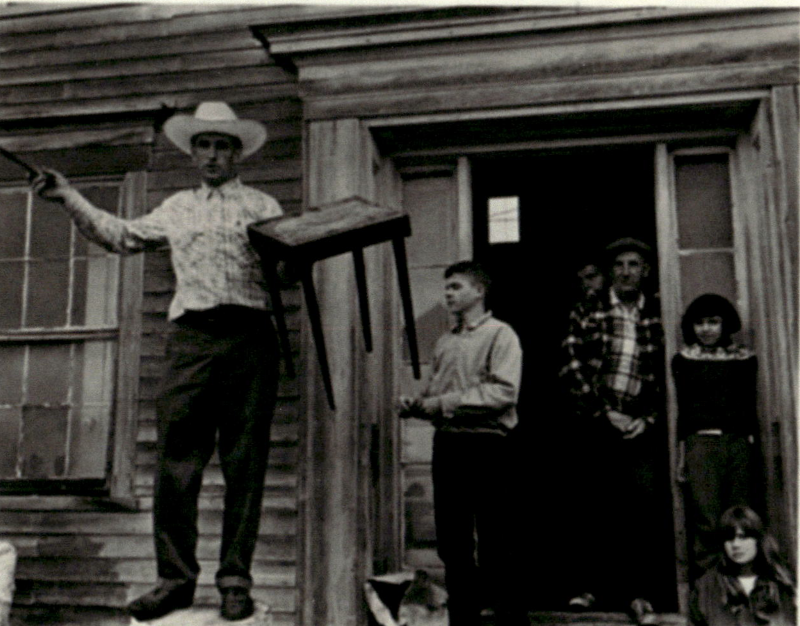

***Left** — Sam Olson watches as an old table is put up for bid.*

***Right** — Curious onlookers peer in the windows of the old farm made famous by Andrew Wyeth. Far right, top to bottom — Fred and Sam carry out a woodstove that brought $40; Christina's sewing machine, which was bought by a relative; and the cashier adds up a purchaser's bill.*

Olson House Estate Auction, August 1968; courtesy of *DownEast Magazine*

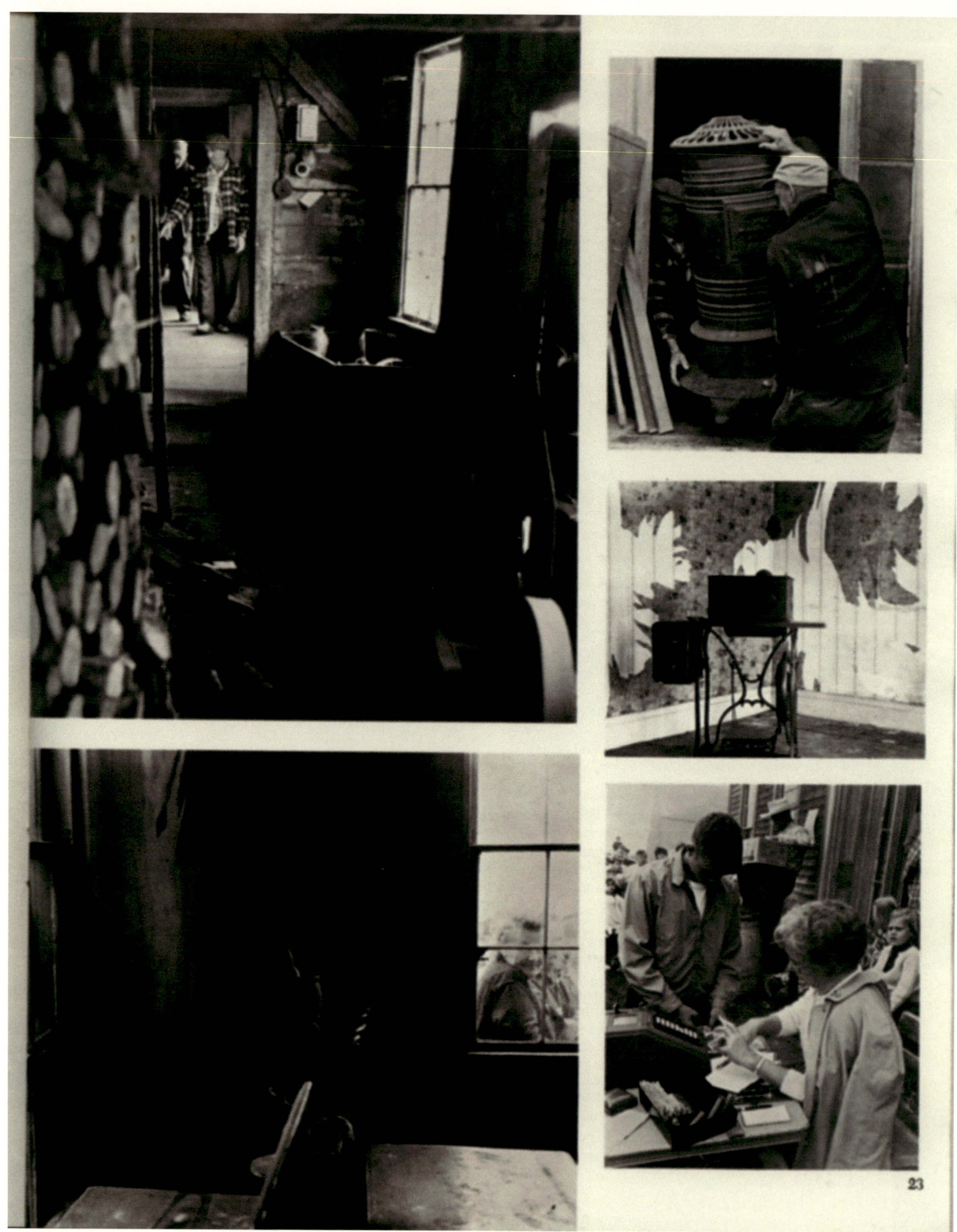

Olson House Estate Auction,
August 1968; courtesy of
DownEast Magazine

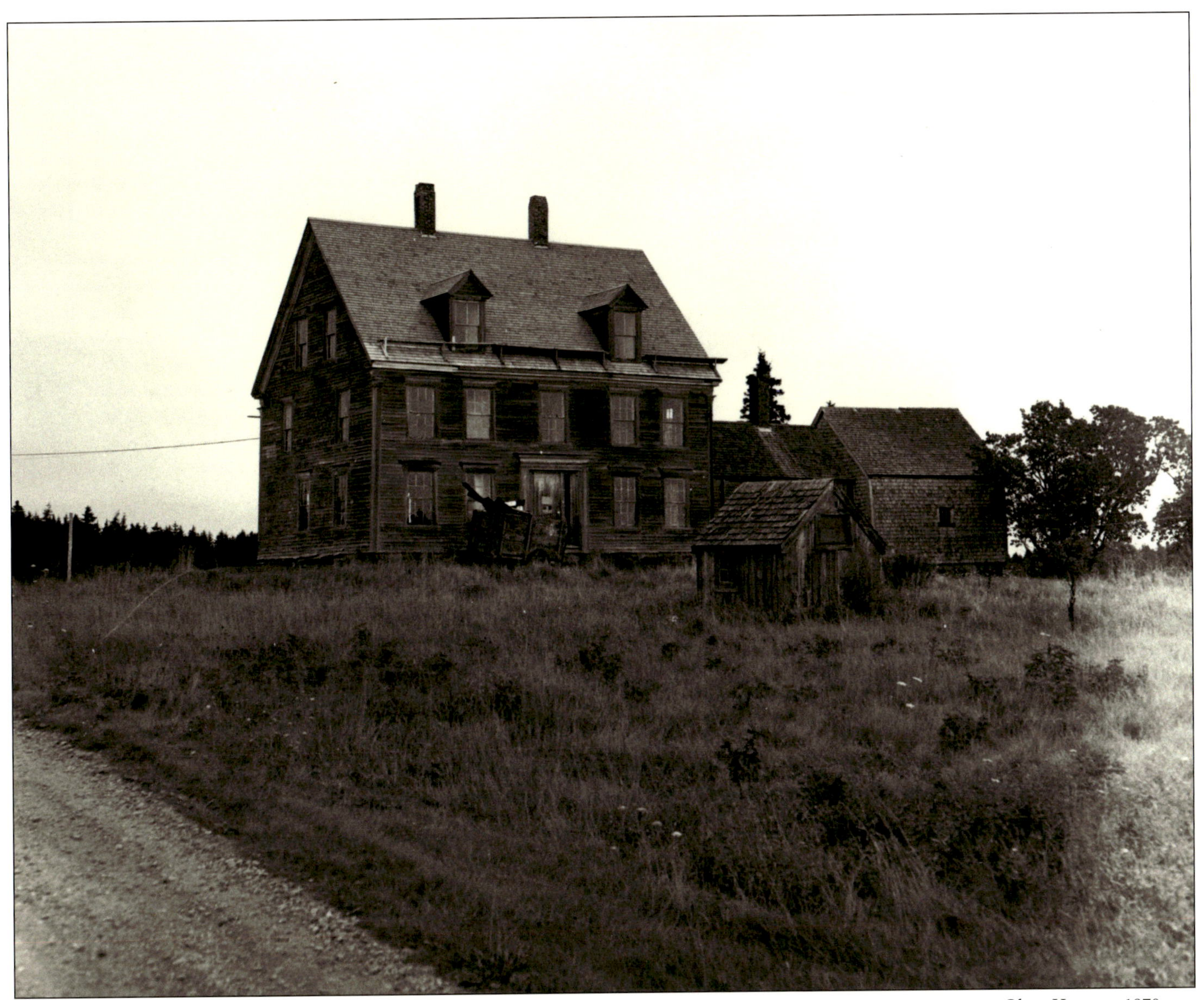

Olson House, c. 1970

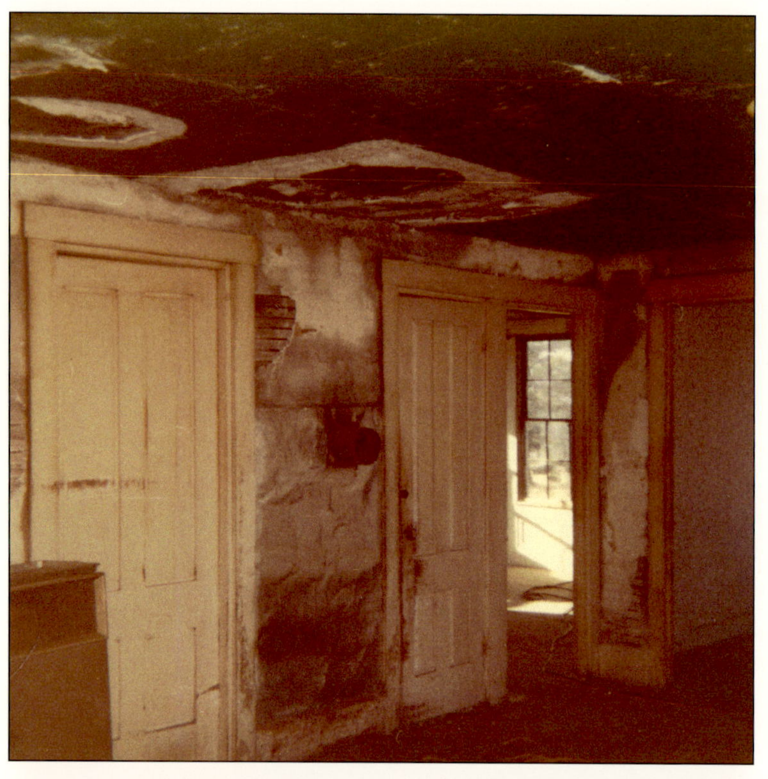

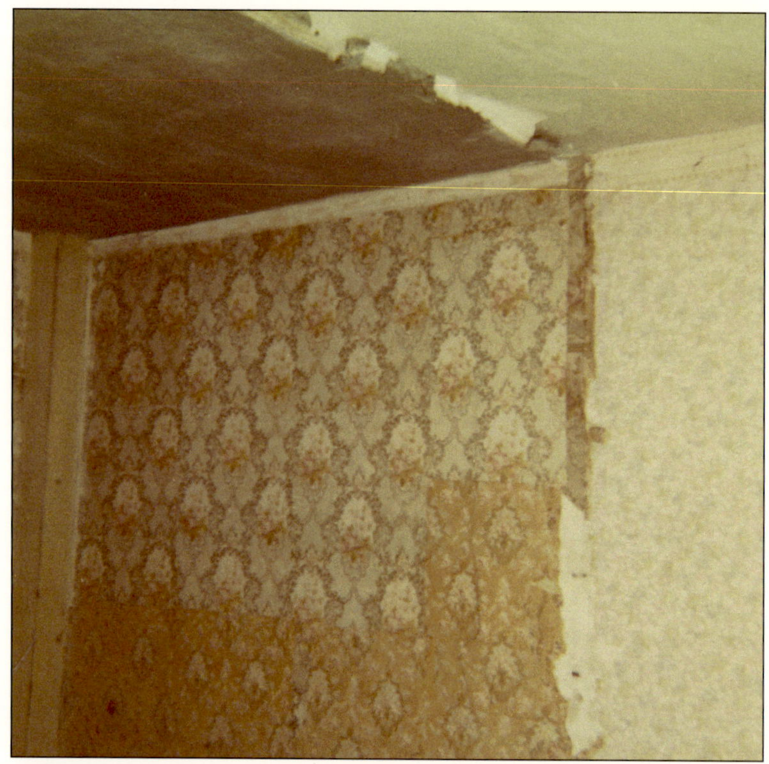

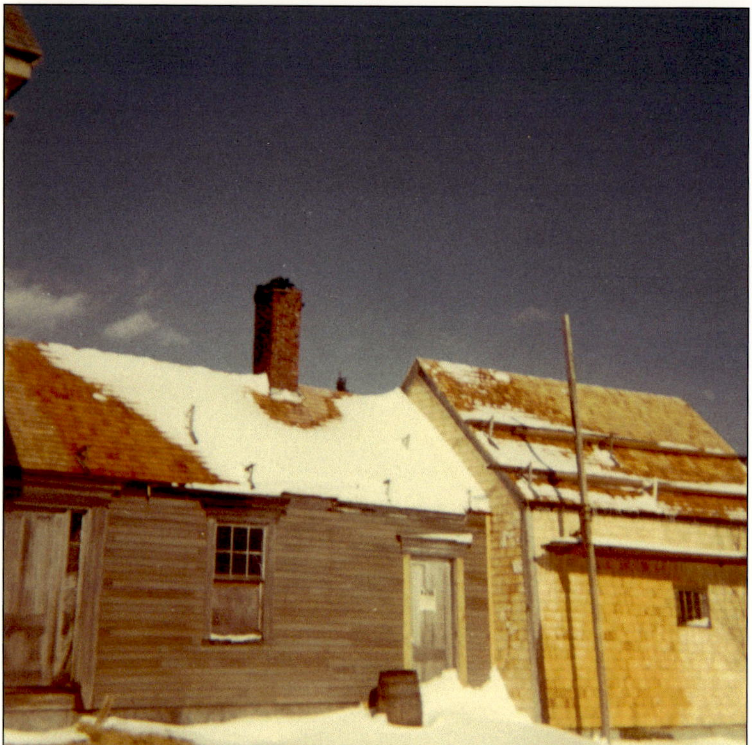

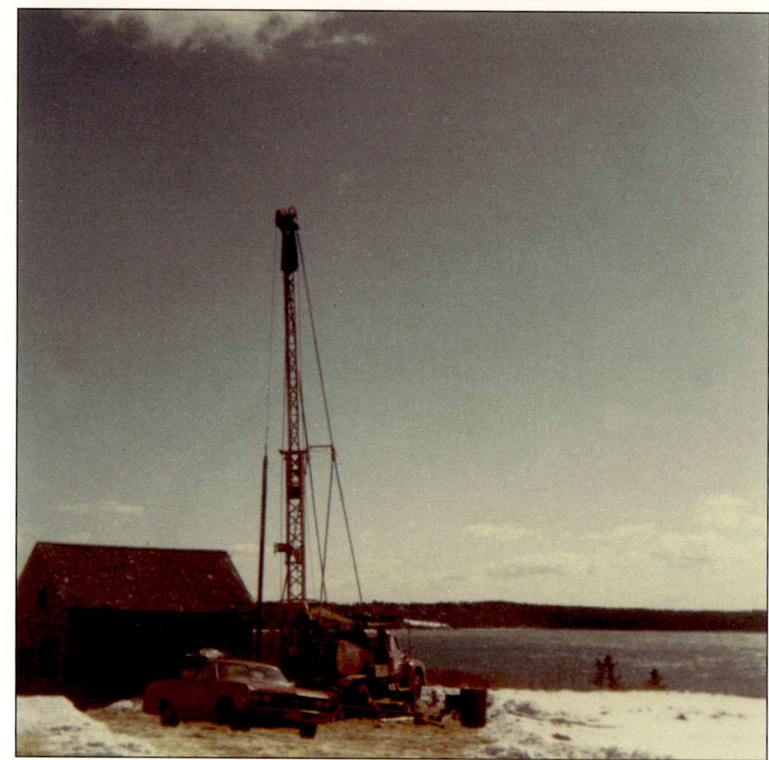

Clockwise, from upper left: **Interior of Olson House before renovation; original wallpaper; digging a new well; installation of new roof and shingles on shed;** all photographs 1970 by Wayne Starrett

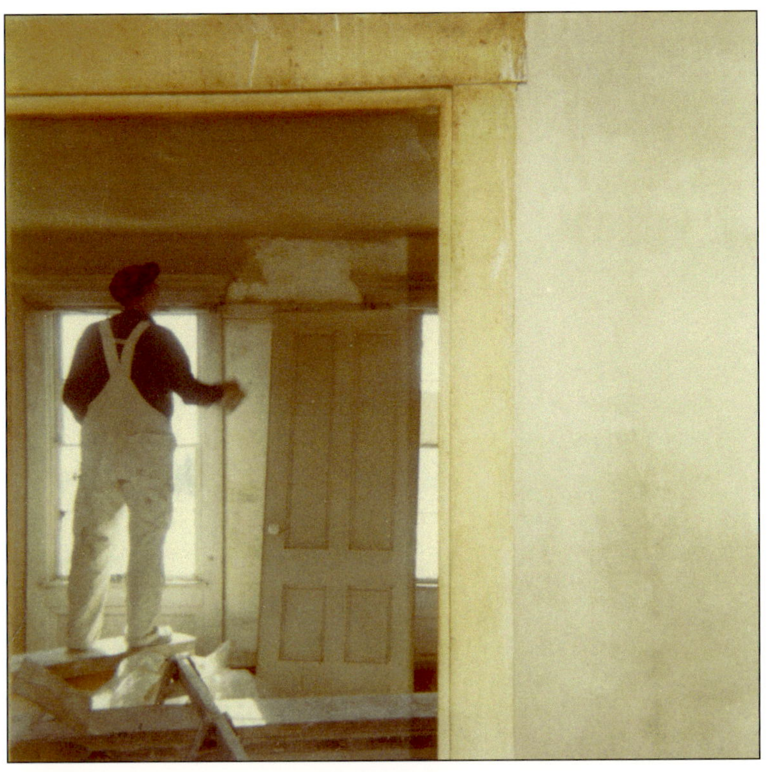

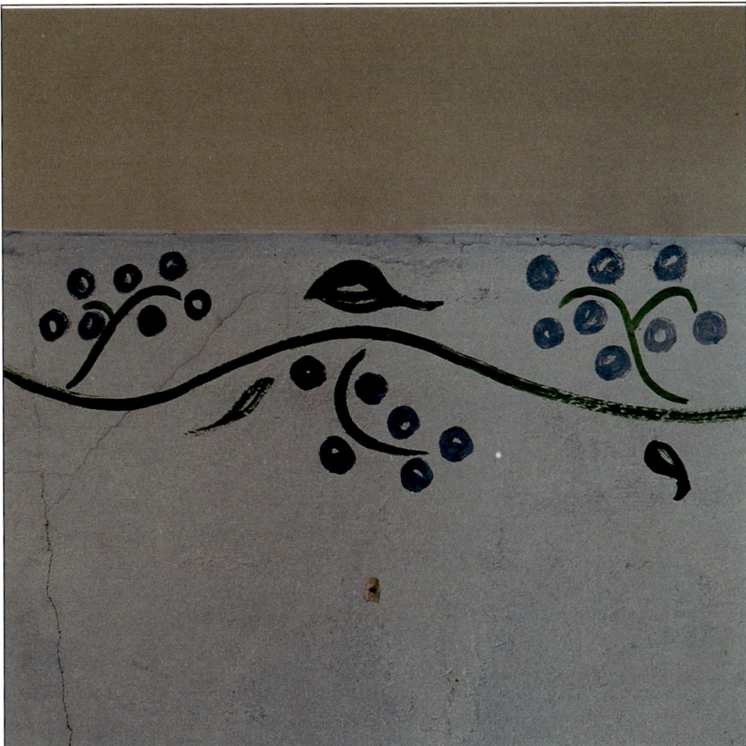

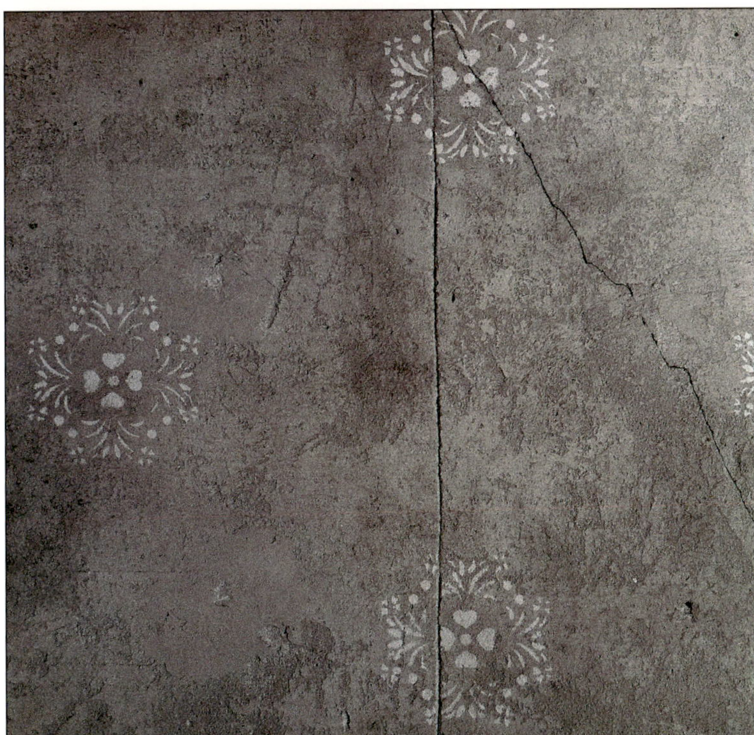

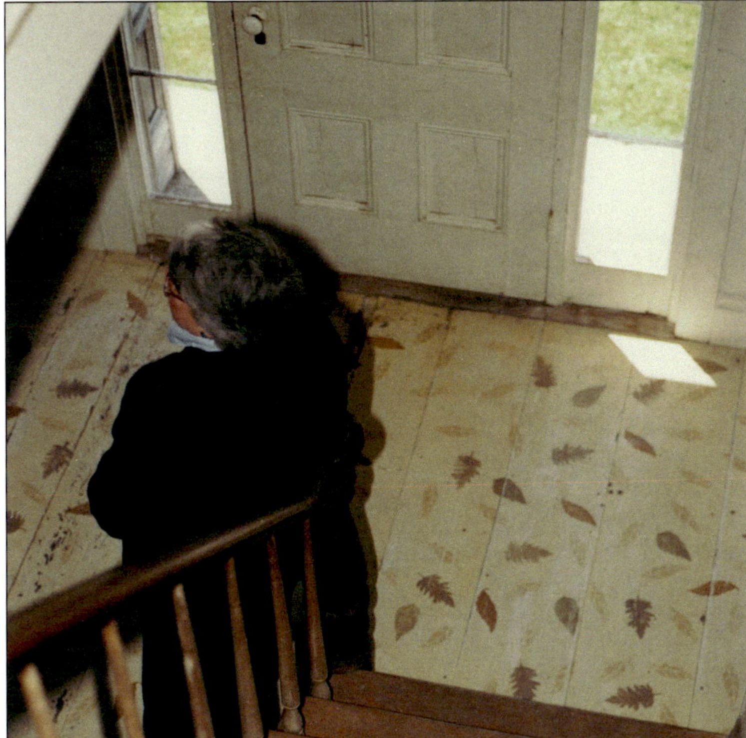

Clockwise, upper left: **Repairing ceilings and walls,** 1970, photograph by Wayne Starrett; **decorative border by Betsy Wyeth in second floor master bedroom,** 2011 photograph by Michael K. Komanecky; **Stenciled leaf pattern by Betsy Wyeth on entry hall floor;** c. 1990, **stenciled floral pattern by Betsy Wyeth in second floor room,** 2011 photograph by Michael K. Komanecky

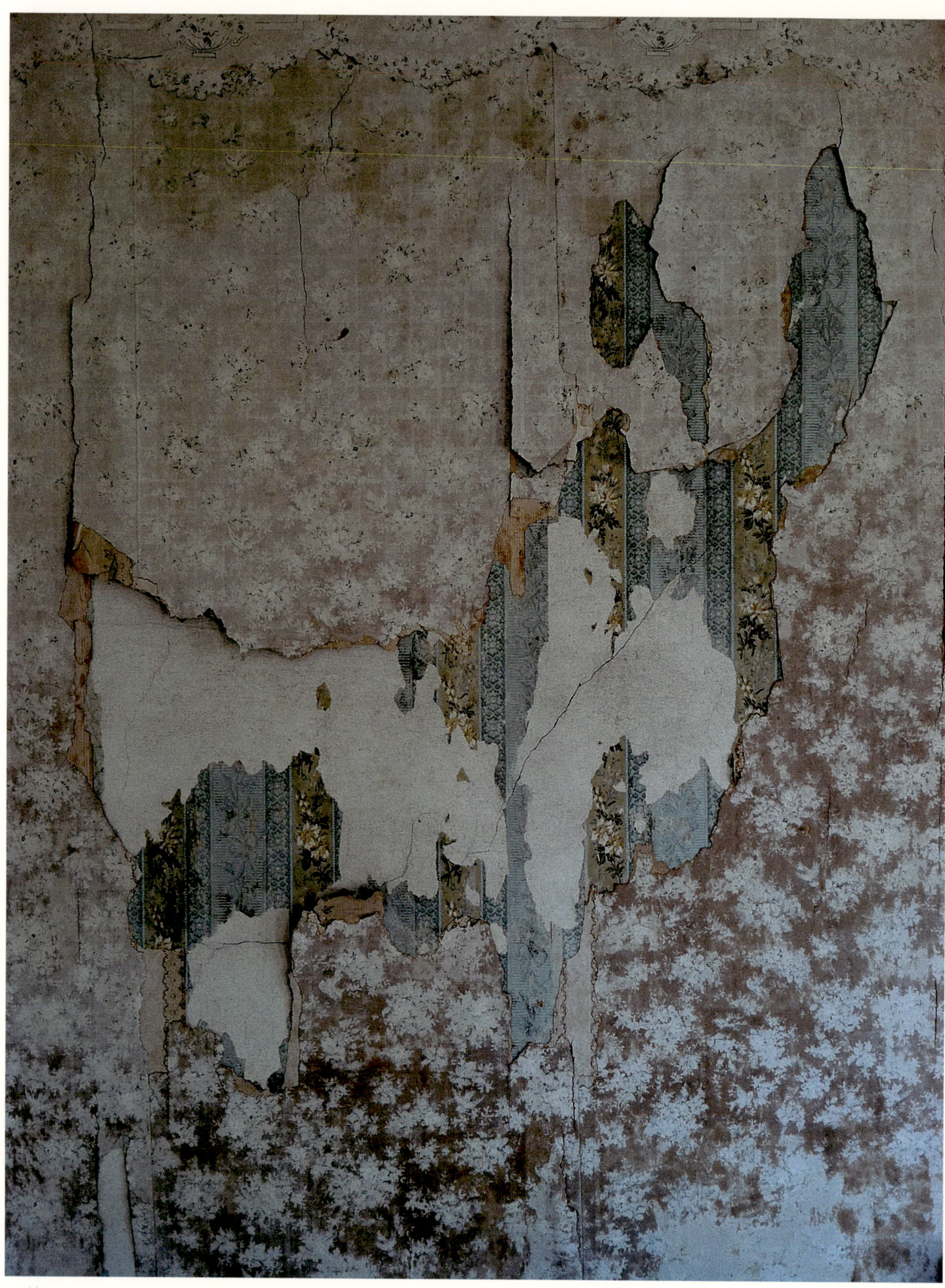

Original wallpaper in Christina's second floor childhood bedroom, 2011 photograph by Michael K. Komanecky

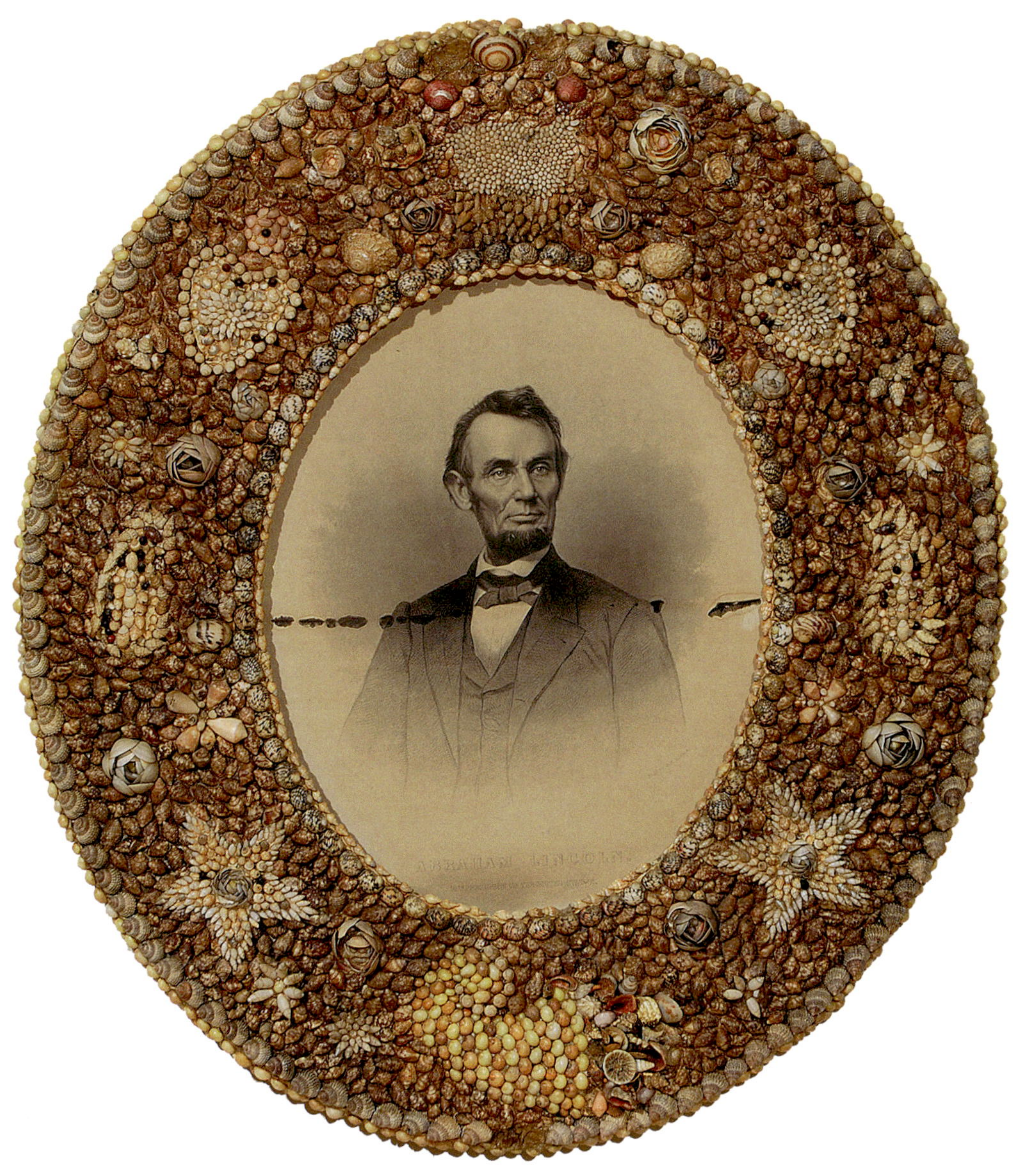

Unknown American maker,
Memorial to Abraham Lincoln,
c. 1865, lithograph on paper in
shell frame, 24 x 22 inches,
Farnsworth Art Museum: gift of
Mrs. Fred Olson

56 C THE NEW YORK TIMES, TH

Disputed Wyeth Museum May Move

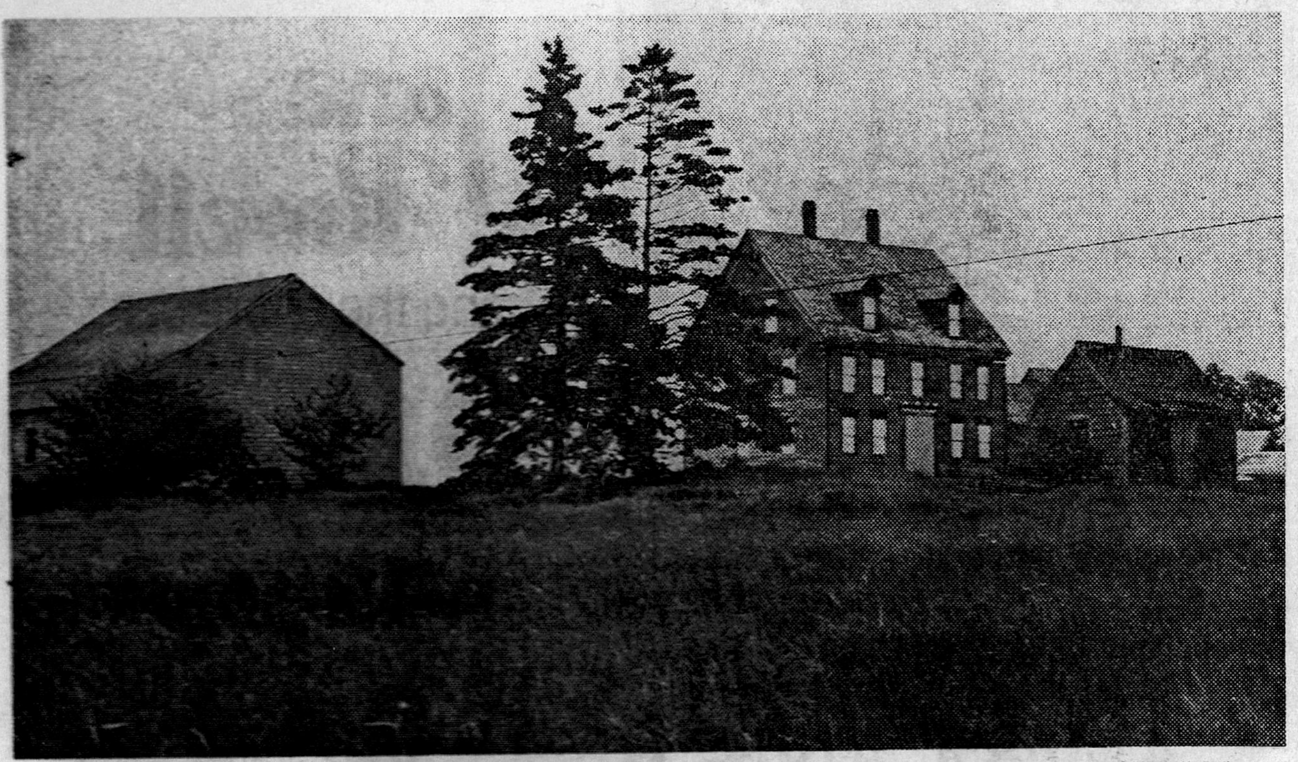

William H. Raftery

The Olson house, second from right, now a museum, may be moved from Cushing, Me., to Waterloo Village, N. J.

CUSHING, Maine, June 26 (AP)—Andrew Wyeth may leave this coastal village, which has been made famous by his paintings and sketches, because of a dispute with townspeople.

The Olson farmhouse, depicted in Mr. Wyeth's painting "Christina's World" and made into a public museum for the artist's work, may also be moved, possibly to New Jersey. The museum, which was opened in 1971, was closed last summer after two lawsuits and complaints from Cushing residents about the heavy tourist traffic.

"There was incredible bitterness in the community," Mr. Wyeth's wife said. "And the important thing is that no one here came forward and supported it."

Joseph E. Levine, movie producer and art collector, bought the farmhouse in 1969 from a developer whose plans for the property had included construction of 25 ranch houses. The weather-beaten building was restored and made into a museum.

"Moving the home is the only solution Mr. Levine, my husband and I can think of," Mrs. Wyeth said. "Not one person gave us a vote of confidence, not one. I had a hard time convincing Andrew to come back to Cushing this summer, and we're thinking of leaving permanently."

Mr. Levine said he has had an offer from Waterloo Village, a restored pre-Revolutionary town in New Jersey, to place the house there.

"Right now I feel like I just want to get rid of it. I feel betrayed, like they spit on my face," he said.

Opponents of the museum are reluctant to comment. One said, "Things have finally quieted down and we don't want to get this mess started up all over again."

Another resident said that the Wyeth's desire for vocal town support contradicted the family's long-standing request for anonymity.

"The thing they always appreciated," she said, "was that they could come in here and be just regular people in the town, with no one coming down their driveway and bothering them. I know that I and a lot of other people here have protected Andy by lying and telling tourists we didn't know where he lived."

"Disputed Wyeth Museum May Move," *New York Times,* June 24, 1974

Levine, Wyeth approached

State may buy Olson house

By Pat Sherlock
Associated Press Writer

AUGUSTA, Maine (AP) — The Olson farmhouse, where crippled Christina Olson was immortalized by painter Andrew Wyeth in "Christina's World," may be purchased by the state to keep the Olson home from being moved to New Jersey.

Gov. Kenneth M. Curtis said Monday that the state has contacted film director Jospeh Levine, current owner of the building, and has offered to either purchase or take over and maintain the property.

"Wyeth's association with Maine is one the state should be proud of," the governor said.

The old farmhouse, located in the coastal town of Cushing, has become a museum and showplace for Wyeth paintings. It has been attracting Wyeth followers from throughout the Eastern Seaboard since it opened several summers ago.

Many residents of that quiet little town have objected to the increase in traffic bringing visitors to the Olson house.

Levine, who owns a summer home in Maine, recently announced he is considering moving the old wooden-frame building to New Jersey because of adverse local pressure.

The house was the ancestral home of the Olson family, whose crippled daughter, Christina, was pictured crawling through the grass in the foreground of what has become Wyeth's most well known work.

"Maine is extremely proud of Andrew Wyeth and the time he has spent here," Curtis told a State House news conference. "It would be good for the state to take it over and maintain it."

The governor said Dr. Donaldson Koons, commissioner of the Department of Conservation, has already informed Levine and Wyeth of the state's desire to obtain the Olson farmstead.

"We told them the state is willing to either buy it or to take it over. They were very pleased that the state is interested," Curtis said.

Levine has not yet responded to the state's offer.

Discussing local resentment, Curtis noted that much of the opposition came from summer residents of Cushing.

"We hear much more from our summer visitors than we do from Maine people," he said.

Curtis said the controversy will eventually fade, but the Olson farm will remain.

"And we're talking about preserving something," he said.

"State may buy Olson House," *Bangor Daily News*, July 9, 1974

Portland Press Herald

Press Herald, Tuesday, July 2, 1974 17

In Maine Today

Wyeth, Levine Ponder Fate Of Olson Farm

By DAVE HIMMELSTEIN
District Correspondent

CUSHING — Andrew Wyeth will meet with film producer Joseph E. Levine today and probably decide the fate of the embattled Olson farmhouse.

Mrs. Betsy Wyeth, the artist's wife, told the Press Herald Monday that Levine will fly to their home here from New York, accompanied by their son Nicholas and his wife.

Wyeth and Levine have been embroiled in a five-year controversy with some Cushing residents over Levine's purchase and conversion of the Olson farmhouse into a museum for Wyeth's works. The farmhouse, according to Mrs. Wyeth, appears in many of her husband's works.

Charges were hurled that the museum attracted a horde of tourists who turned quiet Cushing roads into Hollywood-style freeways, scattering litter over adjoining property.

The feud came to a head last week with the simultaneous disclosures that the Wyeths were thinking of giving up their long-time summer residence here, and that Levine was "seriously considering" an offer to relocate the farmhouse in a restored pre-Colonial village in Stanhope, N.J.

Mrs. Wyeth said she has received a large volume of mail during the past week urging the family to remain in Maine.

"We got the nicest letter from Searsport which asked us to move there and take the Olson house with us," she said.

Mrs. Wyeth has stated on several occasions that she favors moving the house out of Cushing, but she emphasized Monday that final plans for the house and her family have not yet been made.

The director of Stanhope's Waterloo Village, Percy Leach, had been scheduled to travel here with Levine but will not be making the trip, she said.

While the Wyeths and Levine deliberate over the museum's future, a CBS television crew will be filming a news story at the Olson house on the latest episode in the nationally publicized brouhaha.

Cushing chief assessor June Champlin, an outspoken critic of the museum, said he will be interviewed by a CBS reporter. Mrs. Wyeth said she and her husband had not been asked by the network to give their view, but there is some indication that Levine will present the museum's position.

"Wyeth, Levine, Ponder Fate of Olson Farm,"
Portland Press Herald, July 2, 1974

IN OUR OPINION

The Olson House

Bangor Daily News

18 Sat.-Sun., July 13-14, 1974

Christina's world isn't likely ever to be the same.

If it is true that man creates as well as destroys, his dual-capacity is taking on an ugly shape in Cushing, a small Maine town that apparently just wants to be left alone.

"Christina's World," which was made famous by painter Andrew Wyeth, consisted simply of a sentinel-like house isolated by amber fields. Now, sadly, people — too many people, some seemingly handicapped worse than Christina — are pushing and tugging at the Olson home as if it were walled with gold, instead of weathered clapboards.

Joseph Levine, movie magnate and owner of the Olson House-Wyeth Shrine, threatens to move the house to New Jersey. He curses the "rednecks," and talks of lawsuits.

Andrew Wyeth ruminates: he "may leave Cushing" in search of solitude. His reflection is subtle — not the bold, naked bombshell of a Levine tirade — but, from a man whose private elbow room is already measured in acres, there is a disturbing petulance in his public regrets.

"Maine is proud . . . of the time he (Andrew Wyeth) has spent with us," says the governor.

And Maine is proud. Too proud, hopefully, to put up much longer with all of this intimidation, publicity stuntsmanship for profit, and prima donna attitudes.

From what we've heard, the people of Cushing have long-respected Mr. Wyeth's wish for privacy and anonymity. And, however well thought of by his neighbors, the controversy Mr Wyeth has been drawn into in his association with Mr. Levine, hardly indicates that the townspeople in Cushing are being treated with the same respect and deference they have accorded their famous painter.

In blunt terms, this trouble over the Olson House is, as one Cushing resident observed, "a Wyeth-Levine affair." By now, those who most appreciated Cushing's pleasant obscurity are probably ready to point out that the main drag there is a two-way street.

For all his gift, skill and sensitivity, Mr. Wyeth is still just a man who lives in Cushing. Perhaps he could do something elemental for his town, and his adopted state (which by the way is waiting eagerly

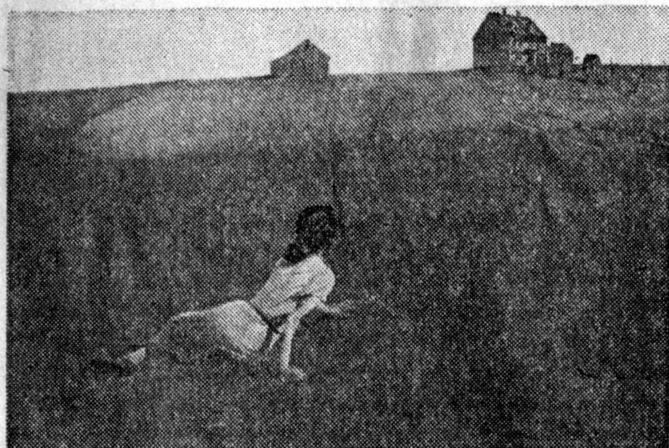

Reprinted courtesy Museum Modern Art, New York City

to fatten Mr. Levine's already bulging pockets by buying the Olson House with taxpayer's money).

For starters, perhaps Mr. Wyeth could persuade his outspoken associate, Mr. Levine, to dismiss the New Jersey idea, and move the old place six miles down the road to the 140-acre Wyeth homestead. With all the river frontage there, Mr. Levine ought to be able to find a site that would both accommodate the Olson museum, and provide a good view, to boot.

This move would leave the Wyeth shrine intact and in Maine, Mr. Levine could return to New Jersey, or wherever his vulgar flamboyance might be less obtrusive, and Maine would not be obliged to be taken in by scheme that has all the nuance of blackmail.

Best of all, the people of Cushing might get some peace and quiet.

"In Our Opinion: The Olson House," *Bangor Daily News,* July 13-14, 1974

Portland Press Herald

Second Class Postage Paid At Portland, Maine
PORTLAND, MAINE. WEDNESDAY MORNING, JULY 17, 1974

Gov. Curtis, Levine Talks Set For Olson Farmhouse

By MAUREEN CONNOLLY

AUGUSTA, Maine (AP) — The Olson farmhouse which has stirred controversy in the town of Cushing, will be the scene ot quiet negotiations Thursday between Gov. Kenneth M. Curtis and film producer Joseph E. Levine.

Curtis and Conservation Commissioner Dr. Donaldson Koons plan to outline the state's offer to take over or purchase the house which is depicted in a number of paintings by Maine artist Andrew Wyeth.

Levine purchased the house as a museum for Wyeth's work. However it was closed recently after Cushing residents complained that it attracted many tourists and heavy traffic to the coastal community.

As a result of the residents' complaints, Levine threatened to relocate the house in New Jersey.

Koons said the meeting will be informal and the state will make no price offer for the old wooden house, its outbuildings and some 23 acres of waterfront land. Koons said Levine may be willing to donate the house to the state.

A spokesman for the governor said Curtis wanted to attend the meeting because of his personal interest in saving the house.

Koons said he has been in contact with Levine, and said Levine has been receptive to the state's proposal. "He wants to talk about it."

Koons added that he feels Levine had not seriously planned to move the house. "I don't think that's on his mind. I don't think it ever really was. I think it was just something he said casually and someone picked up on it.

"He's been entirely friendly and open and responsive to suggestions," Koons said.

The Olson house was the home of Christina Olson, a crippled woman, who was portrayed in "Christina's World," one of Wyeth's best known works.

Koons said the state would use the house as a historical monument, and its grounds would be maintained as a state park. He said if the building is taken over, the state Museum Bureau would probably be responsible for the house. Koons said Levine, who owns a number of Wyeth works, might be willing to loan paintings to the museum for an indefinite period.

The state maintains other historic homes, Koons said, including the Gen. Knox house at Thomaston.

Olson House Donated To State As Museum

CUSHING — The mounting controversy over the embattled Olson House was dramatically stilled Thursday with the announcement by Joseph E. Levine that he will donate the property to the State of Maine.

Flanked by a beaming Gov. Kenneth M. Curtis and artist Andrew Wyeth, the movie producer told a horde of state and national newsmen that he would hand over the farmhouse "only on the condition that it be maintained as a museum to Andrew Wyeth, that it be run with simplicity and that no admission will ever be charged."

An adjoining 17 acres of land including the small cemetery containing the grave of Christina Olson, the subject of Wyeth's most acclaimed work, "Christina's World," will be leased to the state for one dollar a year, Levine said.

For his part, Curtis pledged "not to move a blade of grass (on the site) until we contact Mr. and Mrs. Wyeth to review whatever plans we come up with."

CURTIS THANKED Levine for his gift, joking that "I had brought my check book along," and assured Cushing residents the museum will be operated "quietly and with great taste."

The last remark was a not-so-veiled reference to the nationally publicized flap over Levine's purchase and conversion of the house into a showcase for Wyeth's works.

Several local citizens have charged the museum was an unwelcome magnet attracting throngs of ill-mannered tourists who choked local traffic and littered neighboring property.

Curtis offered no specific solutions to the alleged tourist problem, but said the state had the resources and experience in operating other historical monuments such as the Gen. Knox House in nearby Thomaston.

"THE MOST IMPORTANT thing that we've accomplished today is that we've made sure that this house will be here long after we've gone, to show future generations the place where Andrew Wyeth lived and worked," Curtis said.

Wyeth called the transfer "a happy ending . . . I had always felt the building should stay in Cushing. I have very strong feelings about the area. Betsy (his wife) took me out here 20 minutes after we first met."

Levine heatedly rejected reporters' requests to place a dollar value on the property, retorting that "this isn't a money question" but adding he had received offers from four other states to purchase and transport the building.

LEVINE PAID $30,000 for the house in 1969 and has claimed

Turn to Page 17

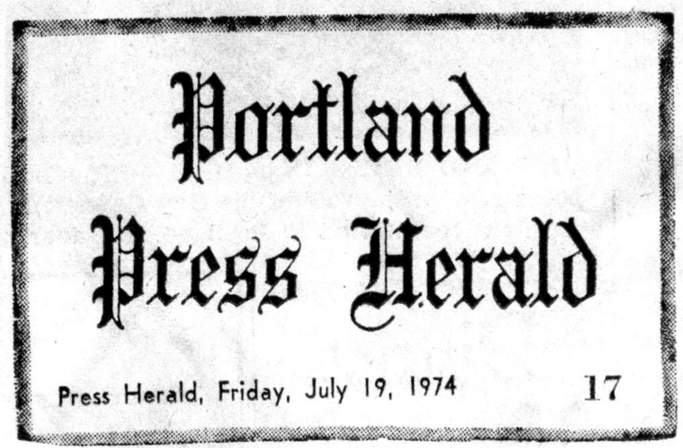
Portland Press Herald

Press Herald, Friday, July 19, 1974 17

Left: "Gov. Curtis, Levine Talks Set for Olson Farmhouse," *Portland Press Herald,* July 17, 1974
Above: "Olson House Donated to State as Museum," *Portland Press Herald,* July 19, 1974

Olson House Donated As Museum

(Continued from Page One)

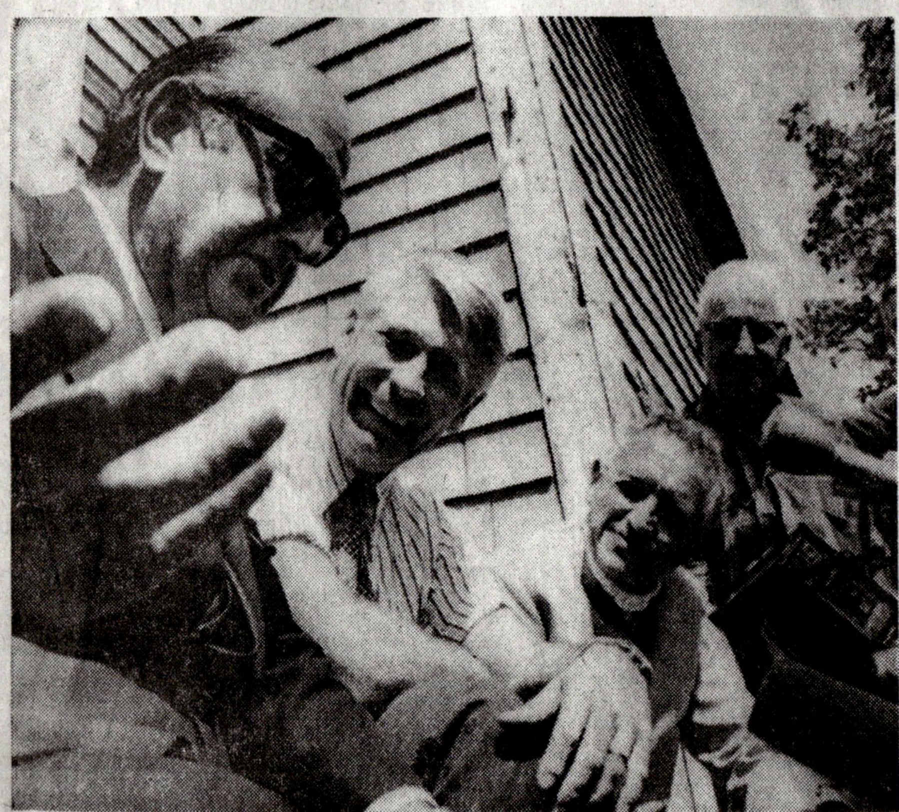

MAINE TAKES OVER — Sitting on the steps of the Cushing, Maine, Olson farmhouse made famous in many paintings by Andrew Wyeth, three of the central figures in a discussion that saw the farm become Maine property explain what happened. Movie producer Joseph E. Levine, left, Thursday donated the farm and its property to the State of Maine, represented by Gov. Kenneth M. Curtis, center. Artists Wyeth, beside Curtis, looks on. (UPI)

to have spent more than $100,000 in restoring it. The other 17 acres of land was reported to have sold in the neighborhood of $200,000.

Announcement of the gift came after Levine, Wyeth, Curtis and a pack of his aides, including conservation commissioner Donaldson Koons, huddled for 30 minutes inside the house.

The decision was preceded by a media spectacle that threatened to engulf the tranquil tip of Hawthorne Point.

More than 40 reporters and cameramen — including ABC and NBC News — trailed after Wyeth and Levine, jostling for camera angles competing for questions and barking at startled tourists who kept getting emeshed in yards of trailing wires and audio cables.

WHILE WAITING for Curtis to appear — who was a half hour late because his driver got lost on the Cushing backroads — Levine leveled his familiar harrangue at several local residents, particularly the J. S. Coolidge's who own abutting property.

Levine repeated his threat to hire lawyer Louis Nizer to sue the Coolidges to remove a mound of earth they erected on their property, and which Levine claims deprives the museum of a view of the St. George's River.

"It's unconstitutional . . . I'll sue him for half a million bucks," Levine rasped.

His anger appeared to dissipate with the belated appearance of the Governor, but after he took Curtis on a tour of the property, he suddenly grabbed Curtis's arm and pointed him in the direction of the offending earthern pile.

"Now it's your problem. Why don't you take one of your bulldozers and knock the damn thing down?"

"Olson House Donated to State as Museum," *Portland Press Herald*, July 19, 1974

8A Maine Sunday Telegram, August 25, 1974

Maine Politics

Executive Council Unsure About Christina's World

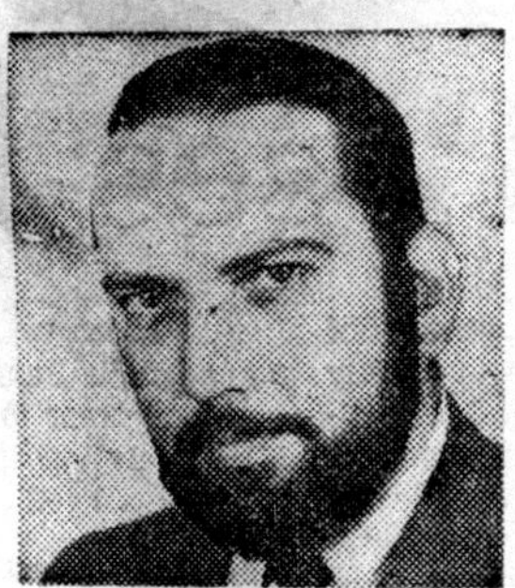

By JIM BRUNELLE

"Christina's World" continues to be a troubled place.

Everybody thought the controversy over the Olson farmstead at Cushing where Andrew Wyeth's famous painting was conceived had been settled last month when movie producer Joseph E. Levine announced that he would donate the property to the State of Maine.

Not so. It seems that some members of the Executive Council are now balking at accepting the gift from Levine. Council acceptance is required to complete the transfer of ownership.

THOSE COUNCILORS who are reportedly cool toward the Levine offer question the worth of the gift, and express concern over the cost to the state of maintaining the property as a tourist attraction.

"I'm leaning against it," admits Councillor Howard W. Mayo of Bath. "I don't feel it warrants the expense to the taxpayers to set up the facilities it would require."

Mayo says it would cost the state $25,000 or more in capital improvements to prepare the site for visitors.

"The building is not a historical monument as such," he says. "I think we may be opening a Pandora's box in which they'd be trying to save every little landmark in the state."

Councillor Hattie Bickmore of Cumberland also has reservations about accepting the Olson House, although she says she has made no firm decision yet.

"I JUST HONESTLY don't know at this point," she says. "My prime concern is the precedent we'd be setting. But by the same token I want what's good for the state. I'm trying to keep an open mind."

The Olson place has been the object of controversy almost from the time Levine bought it five years ago and turned it into a museum displaying a number of Wyeth's works.

Local residents of Cushing complained about the tourist traffic the museum generated. The complaints eventually reached such a pitch that Levine threatened to have the house carted away and relocated on a site in New Jersey.

By last month everybody had cooled off a bit and Levine, following a meeting in the Olson House with Gov. Curtis and conservation commissioner Donaldson Koons, announced that the property would be donated to the state "only on the condition that it be maintained as a museum to Andrew Wyeth, that it be run with simplicity and that no admission will ever be charged."

ARTIST WYETH pronounced the gift proposal "a happy ending" to an unhappy episode, and Gov. Curtis thanked Levine, promising that the museum would be operated "quietly and with great taste."

But unless the all - Republican Executive Council acts formally to accept the gift, the museum may not be operated at all.

"There seems to be some resistance on the part of the council to accepting this," admits Commissioner Koons. "Quite frankly, I'm surprised and kind of disappointed. I think this property is enormously valuable to the state of Maine."

Council chairman Harvey Johnson of Smithfield, who made a complete inspection of the Olson House recently along with other members of the panel, expresses confidence that a majority of the seven - member council will accept the gift.

"As far as I'm concerned, it would be a good thing for the state to accept," says Johnson. "I think we have the votes to approve it."

Actually, the matter is not yet before the council. Although the state has a "clear verbal agreement" with Levine, according to Koons, it must be put into writing before final action can be taken.

"Executive Council Unsure About Christina's World," *Maine Sunday Telegram*, August 25, 1974

Bangor Daily News

★ ★ ★

BANGOR, MAINE, THURSDAY, SEPT. 19, 1974

State accepts Olson house

By John S. Day
NEWS State House Bureau

AUGUSTA — The Olson home in Cushing, depicted in many paintings by artist Andrew Wyeth, now belongs to the people of Maine.

Members of the Governor's Executive Council, meeting here Wednesday, agreed to accept the weather-worn farm house as a gift from movie producer Joseph E. Levine, whose only stipulation on the bequest is that the dwelling be maintained "in its simple state" as a museum during the summer months, with no admission price for tourists, and that "the hay and grass be cut periodically."

There was no debate on the museum proposal before the executive council approved acceptance of Levine's bequest despite earlier indications that two members of the seven-member council opposed the plan because it might cost upwards of $25,000 a year to maintain the farmhouse as a summer museum. State officials claim the actual cost will be more in the neighborhood of $10,000 a year.

Councilor Howard Mayo of Bath was the only member who voted against the museum plan. Mrs. Hattie Bickemore of Cumberland, another member who had expressed reservations about the acquisition, was not present at Wednesday's meeting.

(Cont'd. on Page 3, Col. 3)

Council accepts Olson house

(Cont'd. from Page 1)

Levine purchased the farmhouse for $30,000 and says he spent another $100,000 to restore the home as a historical landmark.

Tourist traffic to the farmhouse angered summer residents in Cushing; and their opposition to Levine's operation of the Olson property prompted the movie producer to threaten to move the farmhouse by barge to a New Jersey amusement park.

The movie producer, in a histily arranged meeting with Gov. Kenneth M. Curtis last July, agreed to sell the Olson farmhouse to the state for "one dollar . . . and if that's too much, how about 50 cents?"

Wednesday's action by the executive council places the farmhouse under the juristiction of Maine's Bureau of Parks and Recreation.

State officials are still negotiating with Levine to lease an additional 17 acres adjacent to the Olson farmhouse. Levine's gift to the state included only the three-acre plot on which the house sits.

Levine's deed transferring title to the property to the state will stipulate that his gift be maintained in a way that will "perpetuate the dwelling in the simplistic form depicted in many of the paintings of Mr. Wyeth."

The 2½-story farmhouse forms the backdrop for Wyeth's most famous painting, "Christina's World."

"State Accepts Olson House," *Bangor Daily News,* September 19, 1974

Olson House, Cushing, Maine

SOTHEBY'S
INTERNATIONAL REALTY

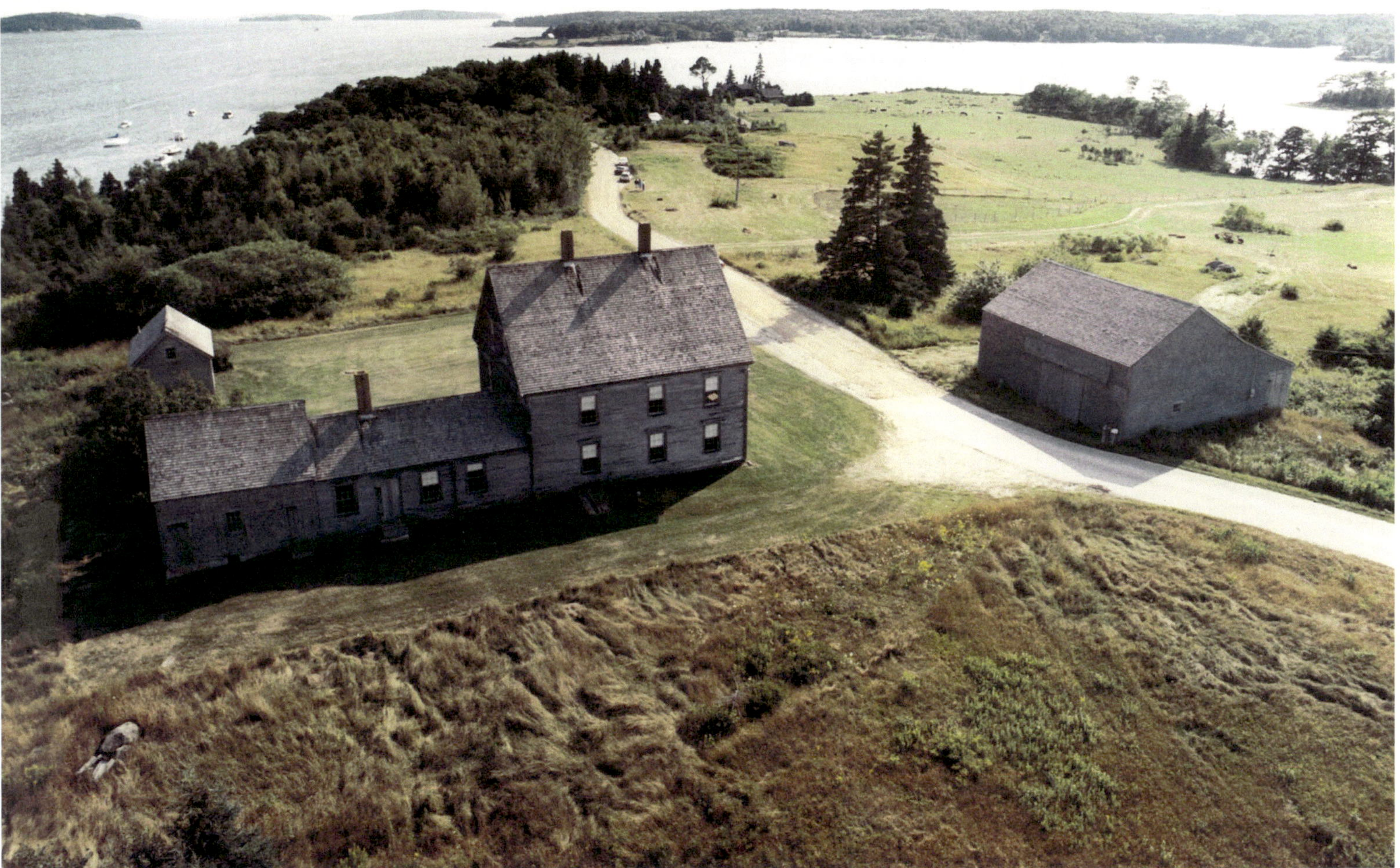

Sotheby's International Realty Brochure, 1990; courtesy of Sotheby's New York

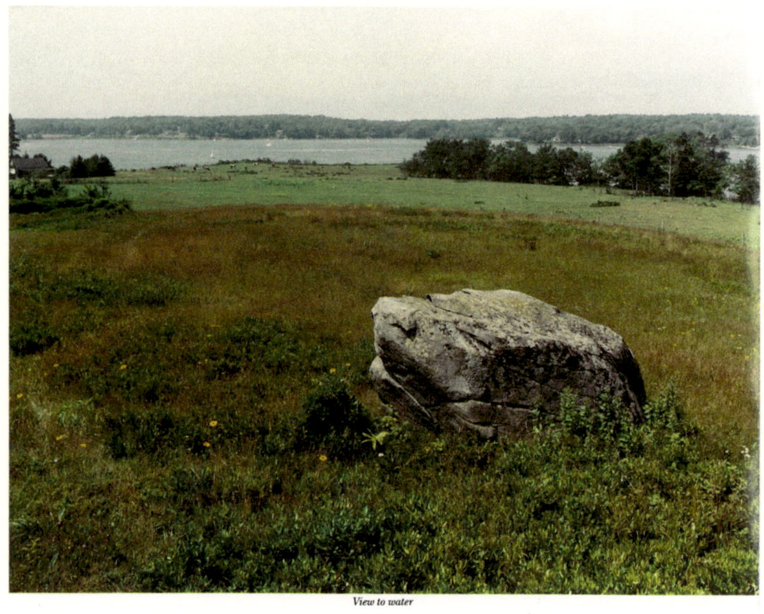

View to water

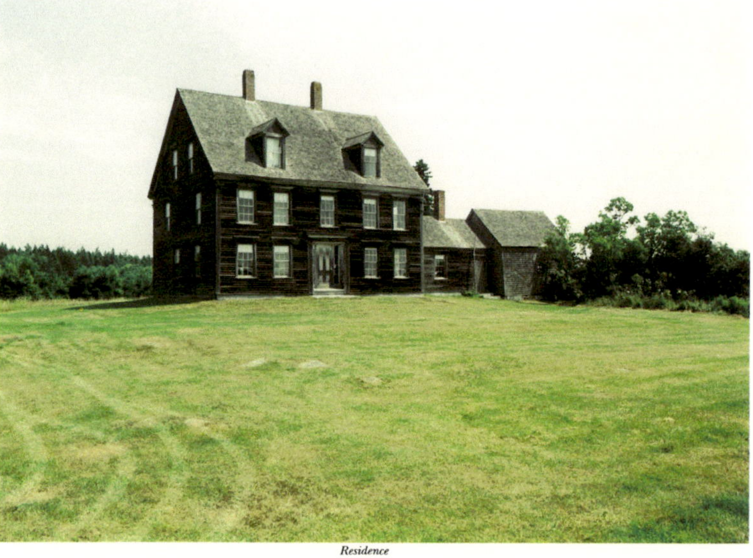

Residence

A classic example of rural American architecture, immortalized in Andrew Wyeth's painting "Christina's World"

"Each detail, each window has a life of its own. The weathered clapboards in the sunlight are bathed in bright light; yet the house had to appear both solid and hollow…" Thus the artist, Andrew Wyeth, described the Olson House as he captured it in his famous painting "Weather Side"; the house was also immortalized most notably in Wyeth's renowned painting "Christina's World."

Built in the mid nineteenth century, this fourteen-room American classic is sited on over twenty acres of lovely coastal meadowland with approximately 1,800 feet of picturesque, rocky shore frontage on Maple Juice Cove, which is known for its fine anchorage. The property enjoys commanding views overlooking the cove to the St. George River and Atlantic Ocean beyond. Originally the homestead of Captain Samuel Hathorn and subsequently that of his daughter, Katie Olson, the residence was used as an inn during the mid nineteenth century by sailors and lobster fishermen. From 1929 until 1968, the clapboard structure was the home of Christina and Alvaro Olson. The property is currently owned by Apple Computer Chairman, John Sculley, a long-time summer resident of Maine.

The rough hand-hewn framing and low seven-foot ceilings of the first floor reinforce the feelings of both solidity and tenuousness which Wyeth described. The front entry hall features period plaster walls and ceiling. The living room is adjacent to the dining room as well as to a southwest corner library. A storage pantry is located off of the kitchen. On the second and third floors are five and four rooms respectively, arranged around a center hall. Christina's bedroom is located in the southeast corner.

Conveniently located just three and one-half hours from Boston, the picturesque town of Cushing supports a lobstering operation on the Point as well as a boat builder, and has long been a haven for artists. This section of Maine's coastline has become an increasingly popular area for weekend and summer vacationing.

Sotheby's International Realty Brochure, 1990; courtesy of Sotheby's New York

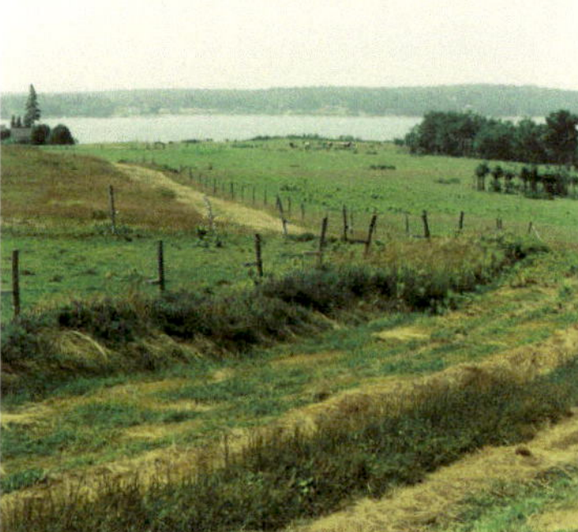

View to water

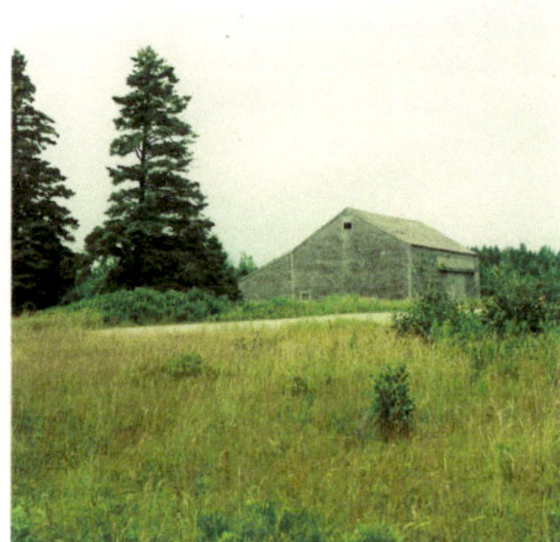

Barn

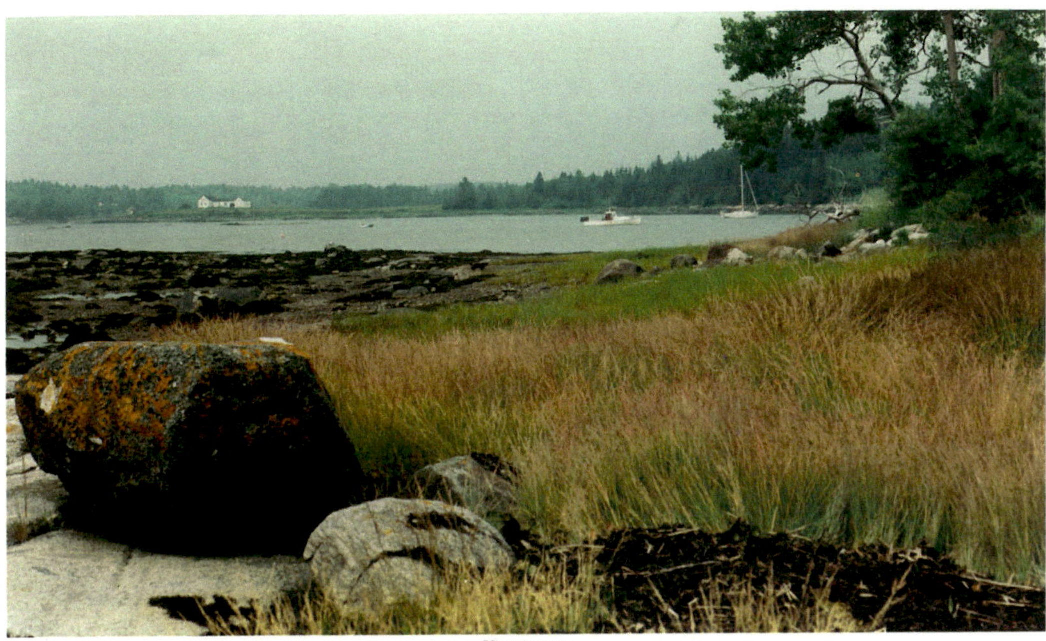

View to cove

Location

Hathorn Point, Cushing, Knox County, Maine. Approximately 8 miles from Thomaston; 12 miles from Rockland; 20 miles from Camden; 3½ hours from Boston by car. Shopping and dining in Rockland, Thomaston, and Camden. Served by public schools in Cushing and Thomaston. Among the area's recreational offerings are freshwater and saltwater beaches; golf and tennis facilities are within 30 minutes. Nearby cultural offerings and points of interest include Cushing Historical Society, Farnsworth Museum, Owls Head Transportation Museum, and the Shore Village Museum in Rockland.

Property

Over 20 acres comprised primarily of meadows and fields with natural landscaping. Approximately 1,800′ of rocky shore frontage on Maple Juice Cove in the St. George River offers picturesque vistas to the Atlantic Ocean beyond; the Cove is known for its fine anchorage. Gravel driveway. Real estate taxes for 1988 were approximately $2,226.

Residence

3-story Colonial residence built in the mid 19th century. Andrew Wyeth captured the Olson House in his famous painting "Weather Side"; the house was also immortalized most notably in Wyeth's renowned painting "Christina's World." 14 rooms (9 bedrooms), offering approximately 3,000 sq. ft. of living space. Hand-hewn wood frame construction with clapboard exterior; cedar shingle roof; double-hung 6-over-6 windows. Pine floors throughout.

First Floor: Living Room (13′ x 14′). Parlor (12′ x 14′). Library (9′ x 14′). Dining Room (14′ x 19′). Kitchen (13′ x 13′) has wood shelves and adjoining Pantry.

Second Floor: 5 bedrooms (3 at 12′ x 14, 10′ x 11′, 11′ x 13′).

Third Floor: 4 bedrooms (13′ x 13′, 10′ x 12′, 10′ x 13′, 9′ x 13′).

Basement Level: Partial.

Outbuildings: Attached Woodshed (17′ x 21′). Barn (41′ x 46′). Equipment Shed (15′ x 21′).

Inspection by appointment only. *0595035/9*

Aerial photography by Benjamin Magro
Additional photography by Thomas Ballantyne

Offered at $1,250,000

SOTHEBY'S
INTERNATIONAL REALTY

Regional Office
101 Newbury Street, Boston, MA 02116
Telephone: 617 536 6632

Exclusive Affiliate

C.R. de ROCHEMONT
104 Pleasant Street, Rockland, ME 04841
Telephone: 207 594 8124
Please contact C.R. de Rochemont

Sotheby's International Realty Brochure, 1990Courtesy of Sotheby's New York

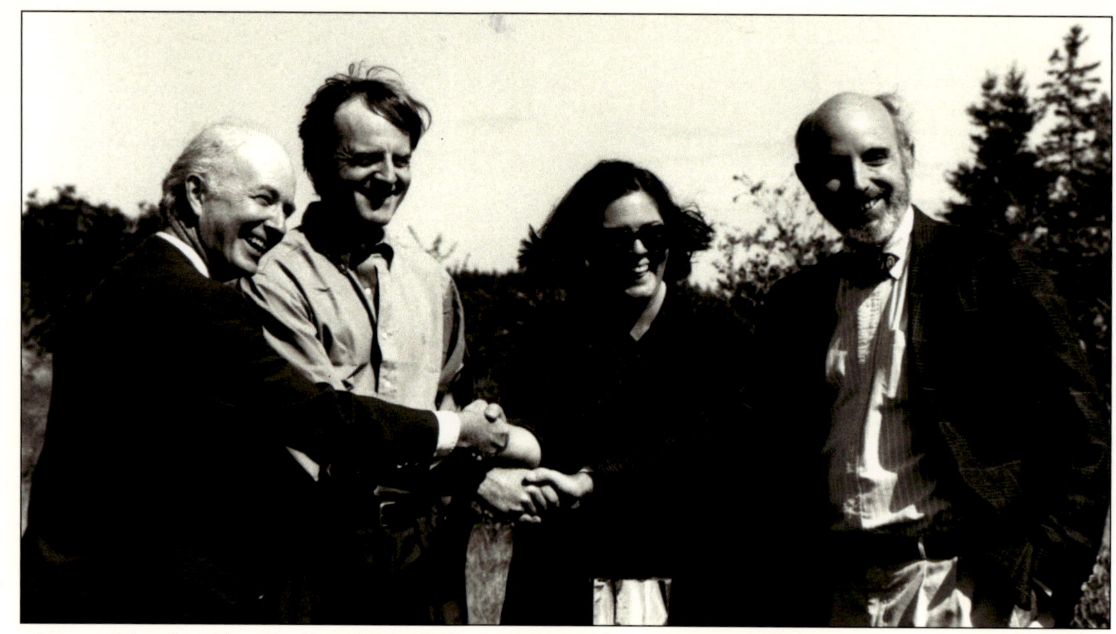

Farnsworth board president Alan Fernald, John Sculley, Lee Adams Sculley and Farnsworth director Christopher B. Crosman, 1991

List of illustrations

Unless otherwise indicated all illustrations are from works in the Farnsworth Art Museum, and the photographer, when known, is identified. The number in brackets [ ] refers to the page number on which the illustration appears.

[4] Olson House, c. 1968

[8] Olson House, 1940s

[10] Marunuma Art Park, Asaka, Japan

[12] Olson House, c. 1970

[14] Lectures and classes at Marunuma Art Park, with curator Otoyo Nakamura lecturing (top) and director Katsushige Susaki (seated in dark jacket, bottom)

[17] Andrew Wyeth and Alvaro Olson, 1951; photograph by Kosti Ruohomaa, courtesy Black Star Publishing Co., Inc.

[18-19] Olson House, 1995; photograph by Brian vanden Brink

[20] Alvaro and Christina Olson with Andrew Wyeth, c. 1950; photograph by Kosti Ruohomaa, courtesy Black Star Publishing Co., Inc.

[00] Aerial view of Hathorn Point, c. 1930

[00 From left to right: Alvaro, John, Christina, Kate and Sam Olson in front of their house, c. 1900

[00 Entry hall of Olson House, c. 1950

[32] *Christina's World*, 1948, tempera on gessoed panel, 32-1/4 x 47-3/4, Purchase, The Museum of Modern Art, New York. Digital image © The Museum of Modern Art / Licensed by SCALA/Art Resource, New York

[35] Olson House, from Maple Juice Cove, c. 1930

[36-39] Olson House estate auction, August 1968; courtesy of DownEast Magazine

[40] Olson House, c. 1970

[42] Clockwise, from upper left; all photographs 1970 by Wayne Starrett:
Interior of Olson House before renovation
Original wallpaper
Digging a new well
Installation of new roof and shingles on shed

[43] Clockwise, from upper left:
Repairing ceilings and walls, 1970, photograph by Wayne Starrett
Decorative border by Betsy Wyeth in second floor master bedroom, 2011 photograph by Michael K. Komanecky
Stenciled leaf pattern by Betsy Wyeth on entry hall floor, c. 1990
Stenciled floral pattern by Betsy Wyeth in second floor room, 2011 photograph by Michael K. Komanecky

[44] Original wallpaper in Christina's second floor childhood bedroom; 2011 photograph by Michael K. Komanecky

[45] Unknown American maker, *Memorial to Abraham Lincoln*, c. 1865, lithograph on paper in shell frame, 24 x 22 inches, Farnsworth Art Museum: gift of Mrs. Fred Olson

[46] Sotheby's International Realty brochure, 1990. Courtesy of Sotheby's New York

[47] Farnsworth board president Alan Fernald, John Sculley, Lee Adams Sculley and Farnsworth director Christopher B. Crosman, 1991

[48] "Disputed Wyeth Museum May Move," *New York Times*, June 24, 1974

[00] "State may buy Olson House," Bangor Daily News, July 9, 1974

[49] "Wyeth, Levine, Ponder Fate of Olson Farm," *Portland Press Herald*, July 2, 1974

[50] "In Our Opinion: The Olson House," *Bangor Daily News*, July 13-14, 1974

[51] "Gov. Curtis, Levine Talks Set for Olson Farmhouse," *Portland Press Herald*, July 17, 1974

[52-53] "Olson House Donated to State as Museum," *Portland Press Herald*, July 19, 1974]

[54] "Executive Council Unsure About Christina's World," *Maine Sunday Telegram*, August 25, 1974

[55] "State Accepts Olson House," *Bangor Daily News*, September 19, 1974

[114] Andrew Wyeth at the Olson House, c. 1980

[116] Alvaro Olson in the kitchen at the Olson House, 1963; photograph by Jim Moore

[119] Christina Olson in the kitchen at the Olson House, 1963; photograph by Jim Moore

Select bibliography

Jean Olson Brooks and Deborah A. Dalfonso, Christina Olson: Her World beyond the Canvas (Camden: Down East Books, 1998)

Laura W. Cliff, Warren F. Clark, and Wayne A. Hathorn, *Hathorn/Harthorn: The Ancestors and Descendants of William Hathorn of Cushing, Maine* (unpublished manuscript, 1986, Farnsworth Art Museum Archive)

Christopher Crosman, *Andrew Wyeth at the Olson House: Spirit of a Place* (Rockland: Farnsworth Art Museum, 1995)

James H. Duff, *Working at Olsons: Watercolors and Drawings from the Holly and Arthur Magill Collection* (Chadds Ford: Brandywine River Museum, 1981)

Thomas Hoving, (Boston: Bullfinch Press Book, Little, Brown and Company, 1995)

Thomas Hoving, *Two Worlds of Andrew Wyeth: Kuerners and Olsons* (New York: Metropolitan Museum of Art, 1976)

Janice Kasper, *Christina Olson: Her World* (Rockland: Farnsworth Art Museum, 2000)

Gene Logsdon, *Wyeth People: A Portrait of Andrew Wyeth As Seen by His Friends and Neighbors* (Dallas: Taylor Publishing Company, 1969)

Richard Merryman, *Andrew Wyeth: A Secret Life* (New York: Harper-Collins Publishers, 1996)

Martha R. Severens, *Andrew Wyeth in Maine: Selections from the Holly and Arthur Magill Collections* (Portland: Portland Museum of Art, 1989)

Joyce Hill Stoner, *Guests, Ghosts, and Magical Moments: Comments from the Visitors to the Olson House* (unpublished manuscript, 2001, Farnsworth Art Museum Archive)

Shuji Takahashi, *Andrew Wyeth: Emotion and Creation* (Aichi Prefectural Museum of Art/The Chunichi Shimbun, 2008)

Betsy James Wyeth, *Christina's World: Paintings and Pre-studies of Andrew Wyeth* (Boston: Houghton Mifflin Company, 1982)

Collection of Marunuma Art Park. *Andrew Wyeth: Watercolors and Drawings* (Asaka: Marunuma Art Park, 2000)

Footnotes

[1] Documented in the exhibition catalogue, *Collection of Marunuma Art Park. Andrew Wyeth: Watercolors and Drawings* (Asaka: Marunuma Art Park, 2000).

[2] Laura W. Cliff et al., *Hathorn/Harthorn: The Ancestors and Descendants of William Hathorn of Cushing, Maine* (unpublished manuscript, 1986, Farnsworth Art Museum Archive, i).

[3] Austin J. Coolidge and John B. Mansfield, *A History and Description of New England, general and local. Vol 1, Maine, New Hampshire and Vermont* (Boston: A.J. Coolidge, 1859), 338–339.

[4] Cliff, viii-x.

[5] Cliff, iii.

[6] According to Wayne Starrett, who worked on the 1970 renovation of the Olson House, it was thought that the ell and shed of the Olson House may have been built on the foundation of the original log cabin, but no supporting archaeological evidence was found during the renovations. June 27, 1995 Interview conducted by Allison McLean with Wayne and June Starrett, in the Farnsworth Art Museum Archives.

[7] Cliff, Chapter IV-1, "Capt. Samuel Hathorn II," note 5. According to Betsy James Wyeth in *Christina's World: Paintings and Pre-studies of Andrew Wyeth* (Boston: Houghton Mifflin Company, 1982), 20, Christina Olson recounted that this house was erected in 1801. Cliff reports that it had a hipped roof, though Fred Olson is recorded as having said that the house "originally had a flat top on it, a widows', walk." See Gene Logsdon, *Wyeth People: A Portrait of Andrew Wyeth As Seen by His Friends and Neighbors* (Dallas: Taylor Publishing Company, 1969), 76.

[8] Cliff, Chapter IV-4, "Capt. Aaron Hathorn," note 8.

[9] Cliff, Chapters IV-12, "Capt. Samuel Hathorn IV," and IV-18, "Kate S. (Hathorn) Olson."

[10] Richard Merryman, *Andrew Wyeth: A Secret Life* (New York: Harper Collins Publishers, Inc., 1996), 11. The inn's name apparently derived from its first roof, described as "umbrella shaped." See Judge F.B. Millen and R. Filmore, *Chronicles of Cushing and Friendship* (Rockland: Maine Home Journal, 1892), 11. My thanks to Shirley Stenberg for this reference.

[11] The story of John Olson's arrival in Cushing is told in greatest detail in Jean Olson Brooks and Deborah Dalfonso, *Christina Olson: Her World Beyond the Canvas* (Camden: Down East Books, 1998), 5-6.

[12] John Olson, *My Story as told to his daughter Virginia Olson* (Topsham: Just Write Books, 2008).

[13] Cliff, Chapter IV–18, note 2.

[14] Betsy James Wyeth, *Christina's World*, 8.

[15] Betsy James Wyeth, *Christina's World*, 12.

[16] Though it has been reported repeatedly in the press and elsewhere, Christina Olson did not have polio. In a 2000 article, Dr. Robert M. Pascuzzi of the Department of Neurology at Indiana University School of Medicine published an article (with Jean Olson Brooks, Christina's niece) that recognized the diagnosis was not consistent with Christina's condition, but was unable to identify the likely progressive neuromuscular disorder that caused her paralysis. See Pascuzzi and Olson, "Neurology in the Art Museum: Andrew Wyeth's *Christina's World*," *Seminars in Neurology*, Vol. 20, No. 2 (2000). A subsequent visitor to the house that year, however, wrote to the Farnsworth indicating that her daughter suffered from the same condition as Christina, described as a "rare case of fibrous bone dysplasia." Letter in Farnsworth Art Museum Archives.

[17] Jean Olson Brooks and Deborah A. Dalfonso, *Christina Olson: Her World beyond the Canvas* (Camden: Down East Books, 1998), 10.

[18] Brooks, 38.

[19] Merryman, 79ff.

[20] Merryman, 133–147. For Betsy's relationship with the Olsons, see also Brooks, 73–74.

[21] Merryman, 144.

[22] *115 of Wyeth's works at the Olson House are reproduced in Collection of Marunuma Art Park. Andrew Wyeth: Watercolors and Drawings* (Asaka: Marunuma Art Park, 2000)

[23] This condensed account is taken from Merryman, Chapter One, "Prologue."

[24] Brooks, 82.

[25] January 29, 1968 edition of *The New York Times*, page 31.

[26] Logsdon, 76.

[27] See Leo L. Chabot, "Auction at the Olson Farm," *DownEast Magazine*, September 1968, 20–22. Alvaro's and Christina's niece, Jean Olson Brooks, inherited much of the furniture, which she later sold at auction at Thomaston Place Auction Gallery on October 31, 1999. See "Items of Wyeth's Christina bring in $7,755 at auction," *Portland Press Herald*, November 2, 1999, 3B.

[28] Logsdon, 74-75. Fred Olson's estimate of how many people attended the auction is at odds with that of Chabot's report in the 1968 *DownEast Magazine* article, which reported that "some 200 persons" were there. Based on the photographs in the *DownEast* article, the lower number seems the more accurate one.

[29] "Auction at the Olson Farm," 22.

[30] According to Brooks, the Olson farm originally was some seventy-five acres; see Brooks, 48.

[31] Marge Cook, "Christina Olson's World," *DownEast Magazine* (March 1971): 41.

[32] "Wyeths threaten to move, take that house," *Boston Globe*, June 27, 1974, page 24.

[33] David Himmelstein, "State May Offer To Buy Home in Wyeth Painting," *Portland Press Herald*, July 3, 1974, 1.

[34] Reported in "Scene of Wyeth Painting Comes to Life in Suits," *The Evening Gazette*, Worcester, Massachusetts, August 18, 1972, 9. The price of the house was reported in "Olson House Donated to State as Museum," *Portland Press Herald*, July 19, 1974, 1. A deed filed on July 25, 1969 in Knox Country registers the sale for $1 of the Olson House from Fred G. Olson and his wife Lora, Samuel H. Olson and his wife May I. Olson to Joseph E. Levine of New York City. In a deed filed on December 29, 1969 in the state of New York, Levine conveyed the house to The Joseph E. Levine Foundation, Inc. for $1. The Foundation's ownership of the house was officially recognized by a deed filed January 12, 1970 in Knox County, Maine.

[35] This account is taken from Cook, 41-42; the $100,000 figure was cited in an article in the Rockland newspaper, "Levine Donates Olson House As Maine Historical Site," *The Courier-Gazette*, July 20, 1974.

[36] Cook, 42.

[37] McLean-Starrett interview.

[38] In 1903, John Olson began an ice business, cutting ice from nearby ponds and storing them in an icehouse he built behind the barn (see Brooks, 12 and 71). This icehouse may be the structure seen at the back of the barn. These outbuildings are also documented in photographs taken in 1968 and 1969 of the renovations, in the Farnsworth Art Museum Archives.

[39] Merryman, 144-146, and 10.

[40] Merryman, 10.

[41] Merryman, 9.

[42] Merryman, 11; and Brooks, 53 and 70.

[43] McLean-Starrett interview.

[44] McLean-Starrett interview and Cook, 42.

[45] McLean-Starrett interview.

[46] Cook, 42.

[47] McLean-Starrett interview.

[48] McLean-Starrett interview.

[49] Cook, 43.

[50] These descriptions of the house can be found in Cook, 43.

[51] Reported in "Wyeth to Leave Maine 'Forever'," *The Miami Herald*, June 28, 1974, 2-A. There are no known records to verify this level of visitation; since the Farnsworth acquired the Olson House in 1991, it has attracted between 5,000 and 10,000 visitors annually on its Memorial Day to Columbus Day schedule.

[52] "Wyeths consider leaving Cushing," *Bangor Daily News*, June 27, 1974, 1.

[53] "Wyeths consider leaving Cushing," 1.

[54] The mound issue was reported in "Olson House Donated To State As Museum," *Portland Press Herald*, July 19, 1974, 17.

[55] "Scene of Wyeth Painting Comes to Life in Suits," 9.

[56] "Disputed Wyeth Museum May Move," *The New York Times*, June 24, 1974, 56.

[57] "Disputed Wyeth Museum May Move," *The New York Times*, June 24, 1974, 56.

[58] "Wyeth, Levine Ponder Fate Of Olson Farm," *Portland Press Herald*, July 2, 1974, 17; and "State Might Buy Olson House For Park If Levine Pulls Out," *The Courier Gazette*, July 4, 1974. The latter reports that Osgood's story was to appear on CBS's morning news program.

[59] "Wyeths consider leaving Cushing," 3.

[60] Dave Himmelstein, "Wyeth, Levine Ponder Fate of Olson Farm," *Portland Press Herald*, July 2, 1974. 17.

[61] "State may buy Olson House," *Bangor Daily News*, July 9, 1974, 12.

[62] "State Still Considering Olson Buy," *Portland Press Herald*, July 9, 1974, 1.

[63] "In Our Opinion: The Olson House," *Bangor Daily News*, July 13-14, 1974, 18.

[64] "Gov. Curtis, Levine Talks Set For Olson Farmhouse," *Portland Press Herald*, July 17, 1974, 1.

[65] "Levine Donates Olson House As Maine Historical Site," 1.

[66] "Olson House Donated To State as Museum," 17.

[67] "Levine Donates Olson House As Maine Historical Site," 1.

[68] "Points of View: Changing Owners Is No Solution," *The Courier-Gazette*, July 21, 1974.

[69] "Olson House Donated To State as Museum," 17.

[70] "State to get Olson House," *Bangor Daily News*, July 19, 1974, 3.

[71] Jim Brunelle, "Executive Council Unsure About Christina's World," *Maine Sunday Telegram*, August 25, 1974, 8A.

[72] "Maine is taking over the Wyeth museum … but on the other hand maybe it isn't," *Boston Globe*, August 26, 1974, 1. The story was carried by UPI and appeared in numerous other newspapers.

[73] Emmet Meara, "Olson house decision rests with council," *Bangor Daily News*, September 2, 1974, 13.

[74] John S. Day, "State accepts Olson house," *Bangor Daily News*, September 19, 1974, 1 and 3.

[75] "Levine withdraws Olson house offer," *Bangor Daily News*, July 22, 1975, 1–2.

[76] Emmett Meara, "Olson house goes on market," *Bangor Daily News*, April 13, 1977, 1-2.

[77] Deed registered in Knox County, filed September 22, 1986.

[78] "John Sculley Gives Away the Farm," *Fortune*, October 21, 1991.

[79] 1989 Sotheby's International Realty brochure, Farnsworth Art Museum Archives.

[80] In 1997 architectural preservation consultant John Leeke prepared a condition survey report at the Olson House, documenting even more thoroughly the condition of the house and further work needed on the exterior. Clapboards, trim, and window and door frames continue to be repaired and replaced.

PLATES

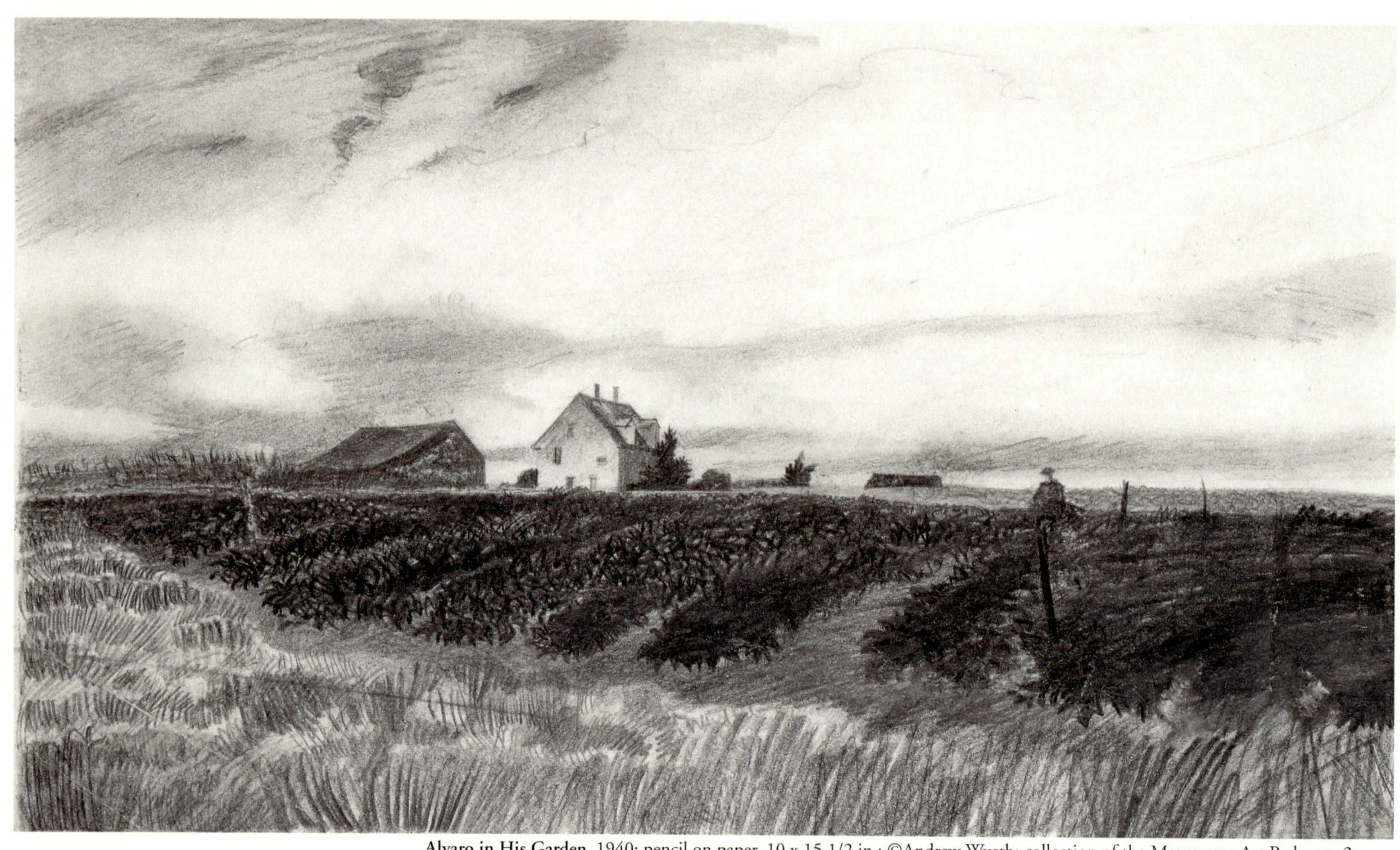

Alvaro in His Garden, 1940; pencil on paper, 10 x 15 1/2 in.; ©Andrew Wyeth; collection of the Marunuma Art Park, cat. 2

ALVARO *and* CHRISTINA

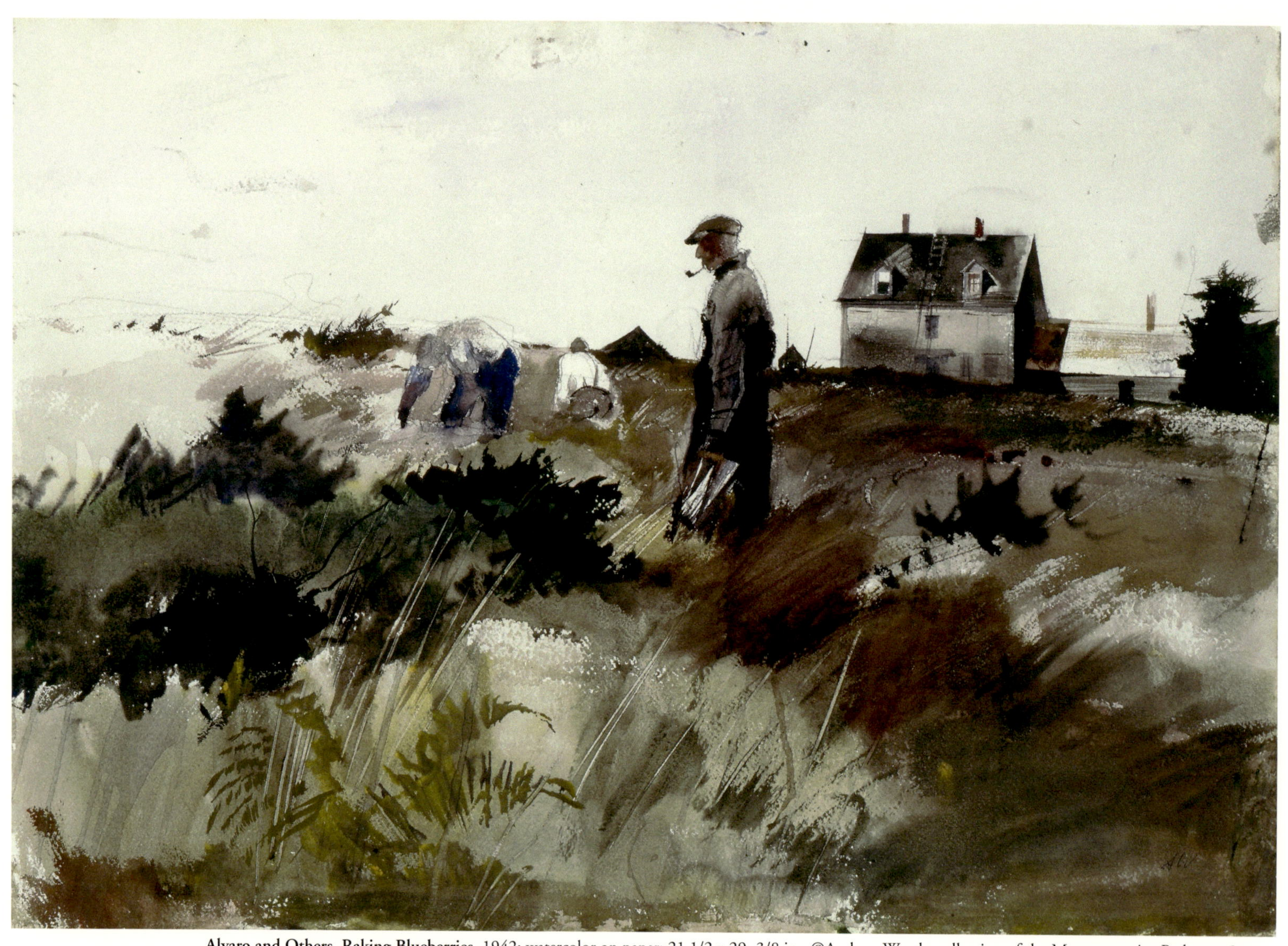

Alvaro and Others, Raking Blueberries, 1942; watercolor on paper; 21 1/2 x 29. 3/8 in.; ©Andrew Wyeth; collection of the Marunuma Art Park, cat. 3

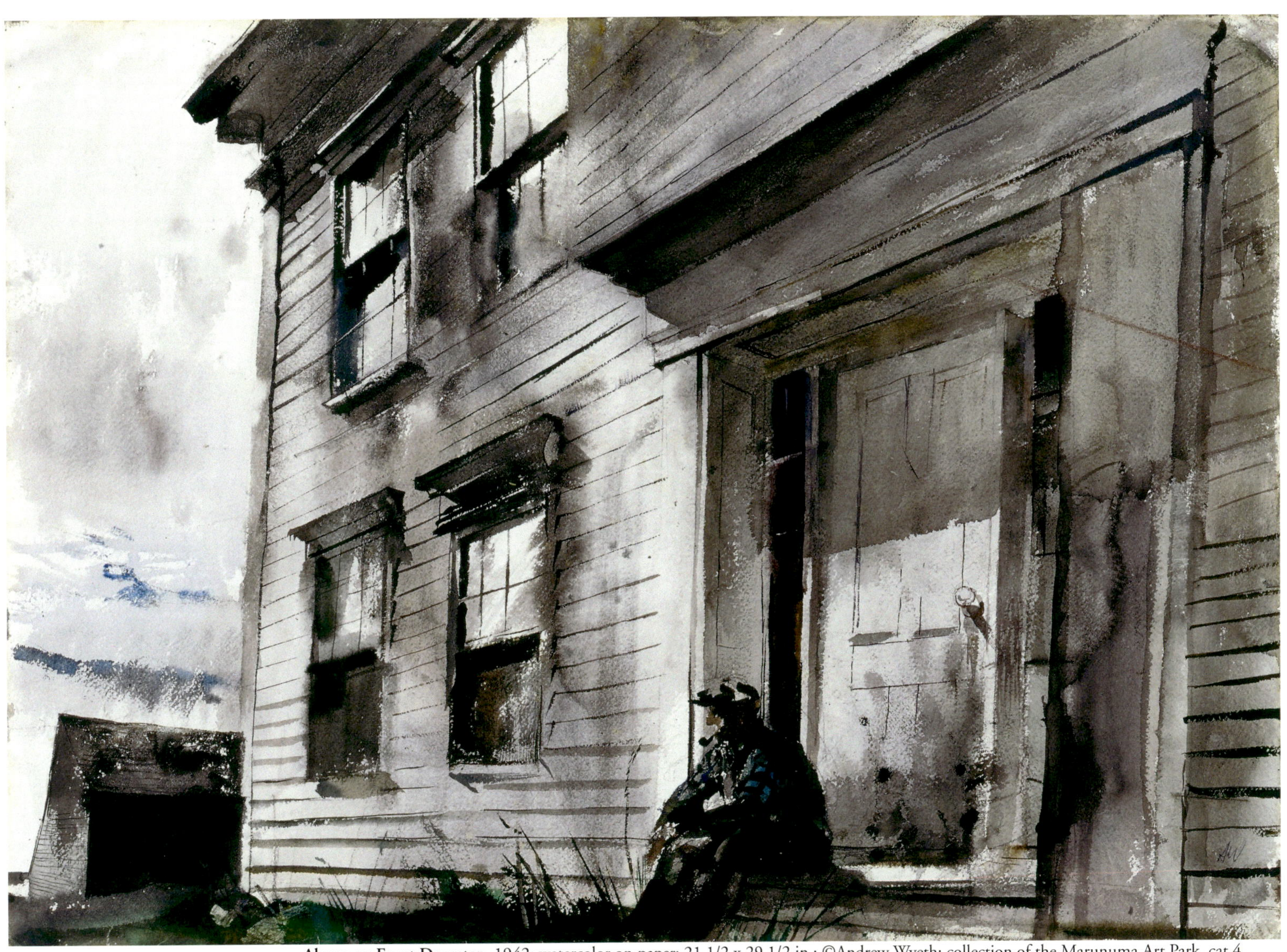

Alvaro on Front Doorstep, 1942; watercolor on paper; 21 1/2 x 29 1/2 in.; ©Andrew Wyeth; collection of the Marunuma Art Park, cat.4

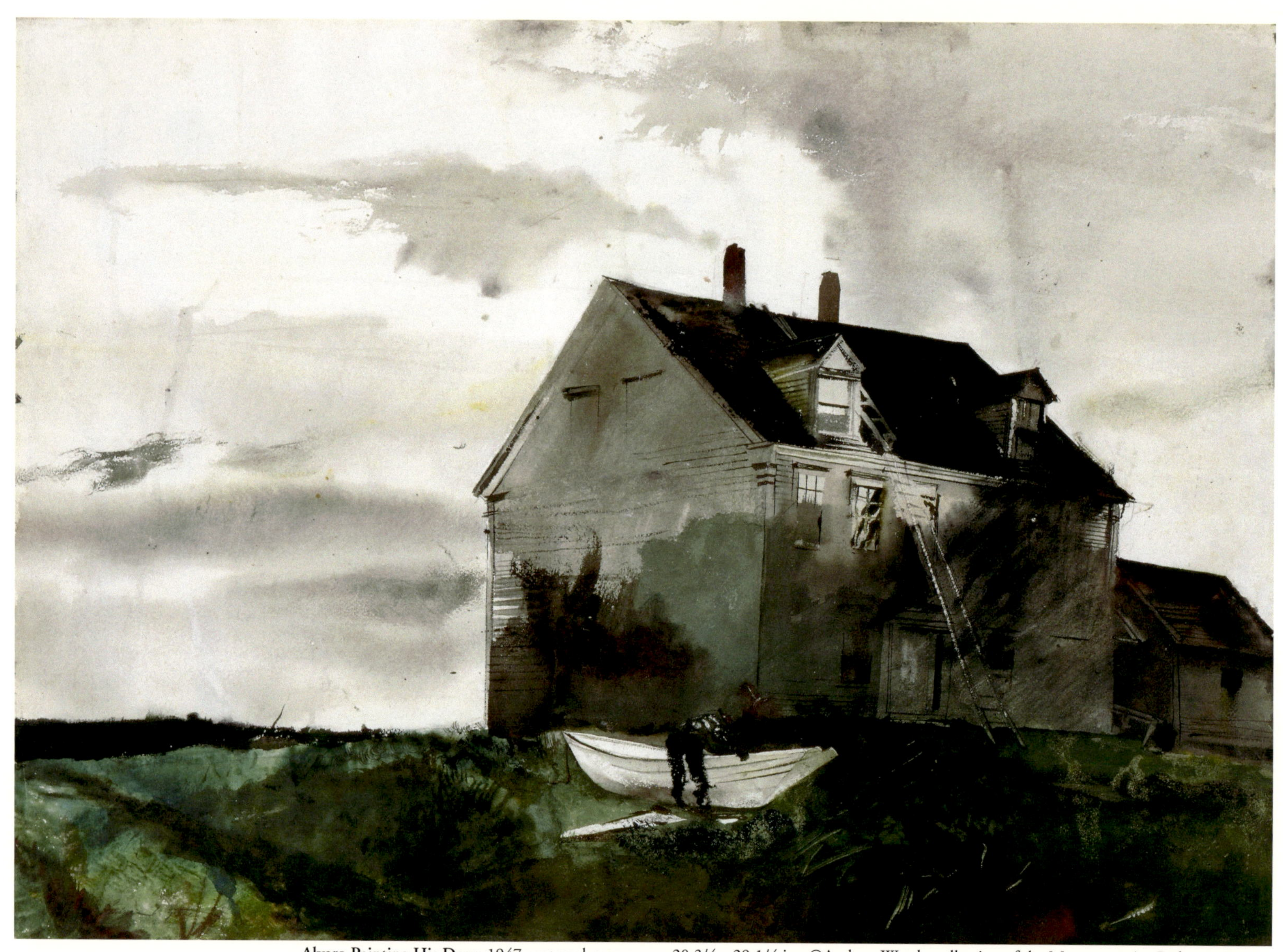

Alvaro Painting His Dory, 1947; watercolor on paper; 20 3/4 x 29 1/4 in.; ©Andrew Wyeth; collection of the Marunuma Art Park, cat. 7

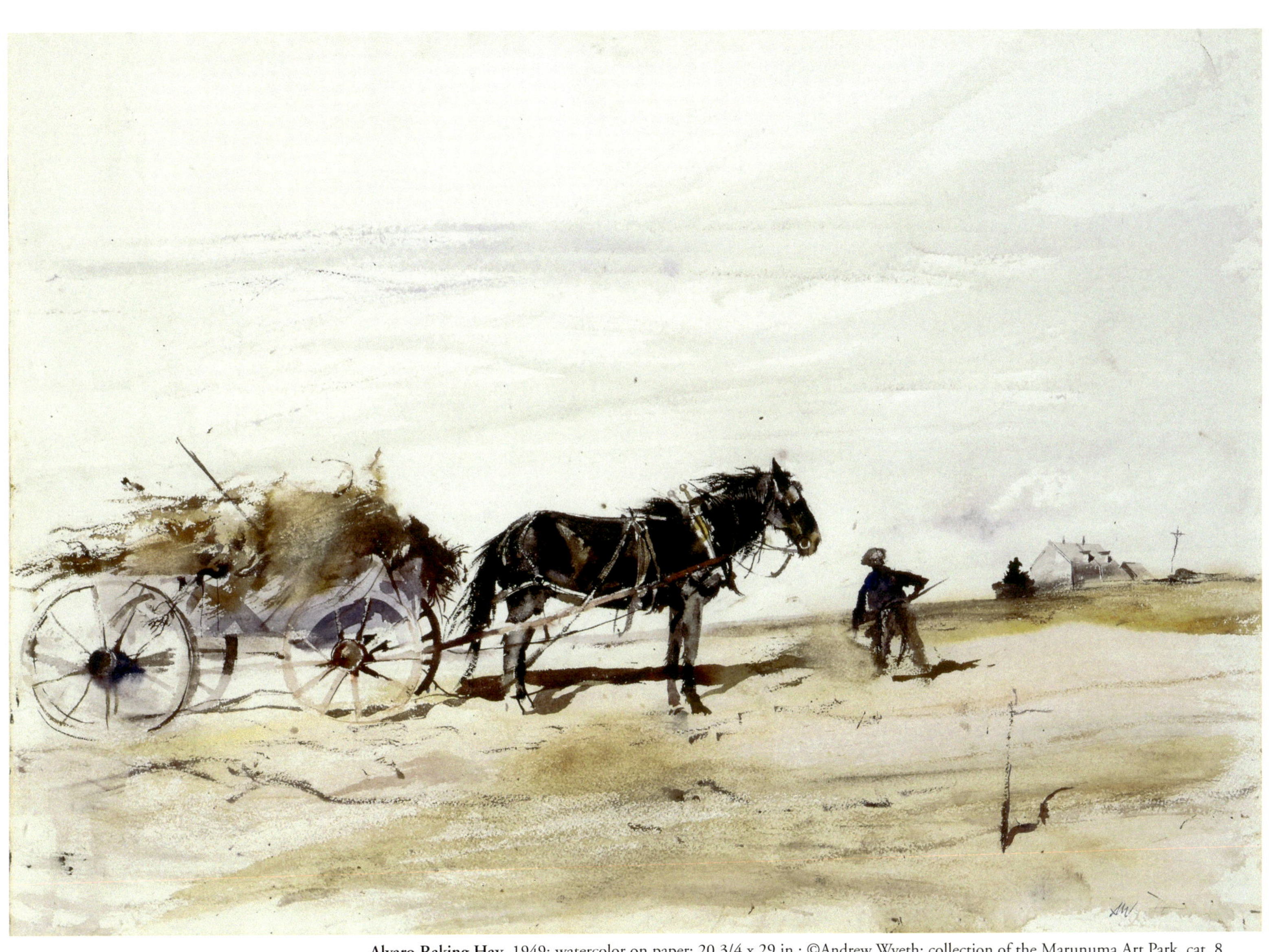

Alvaro Raking Hay, 1949; watercolor on paper; 20 3/4 x 29 in.; ©Andrew Wyeth; collection of the Marunuma Art Park, cat. 8

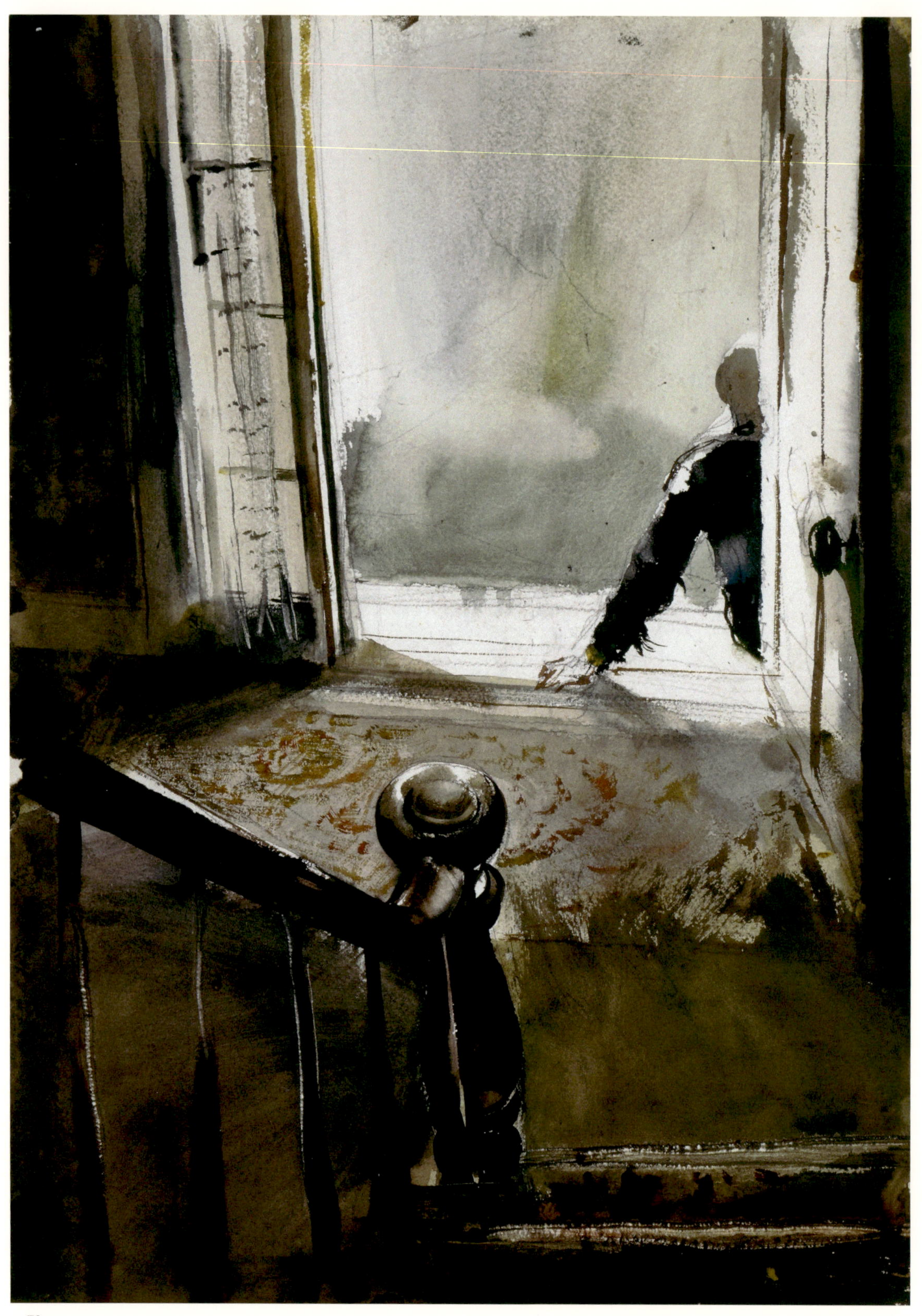

Stairway and Front Door, 1948;
watercolor on paper; 19 1/2 x 13 1/2 in.;
©Andrew Wyeth; collection of
Marunuma Art Park, cat. 9

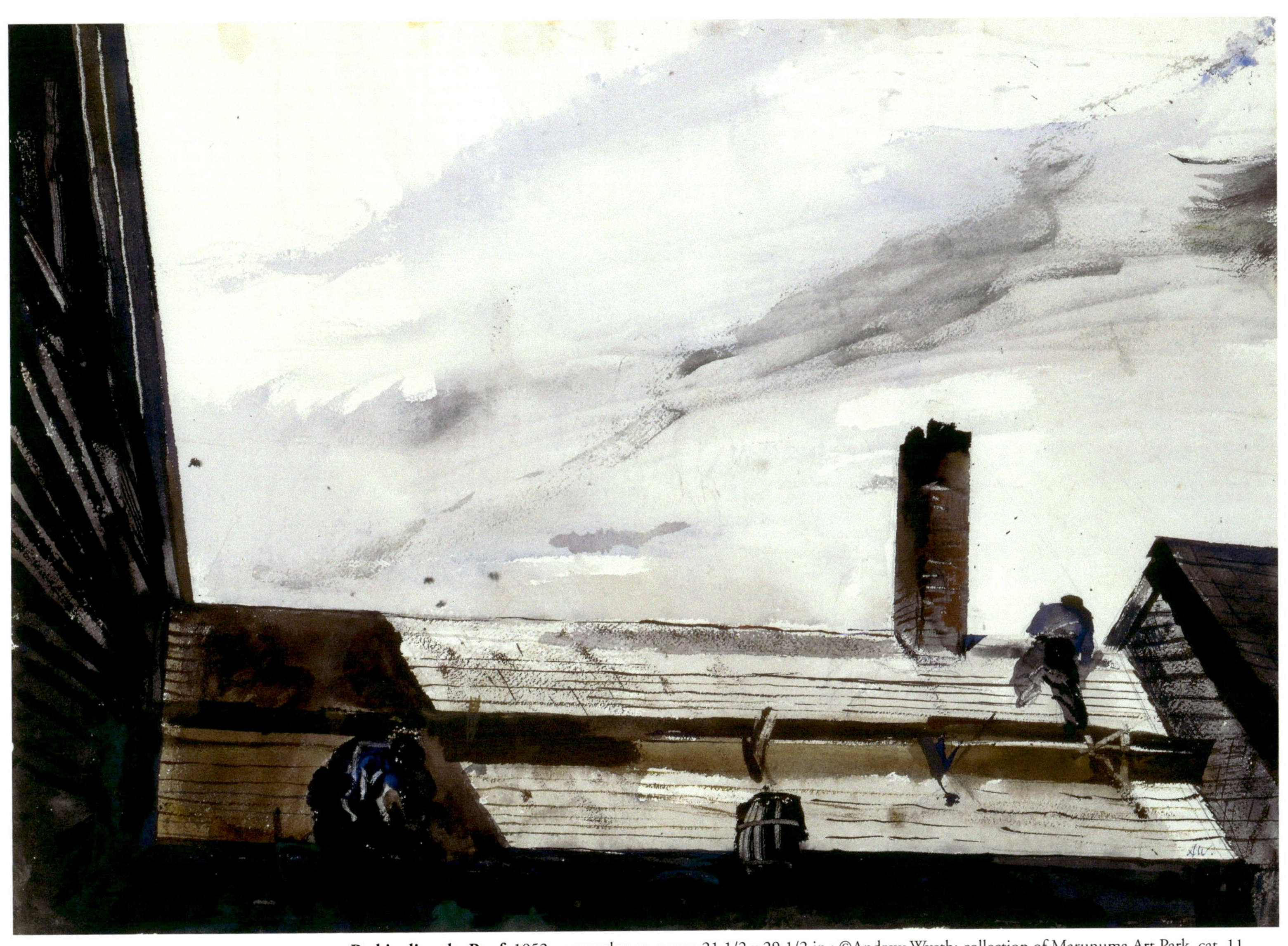

Reshingling the Roof, 1952; watercolor on paper; 21 1/2 x 29 1/2 in.; ©Andrew Wyeth; collection of Marunuma Art Park, cat. 11

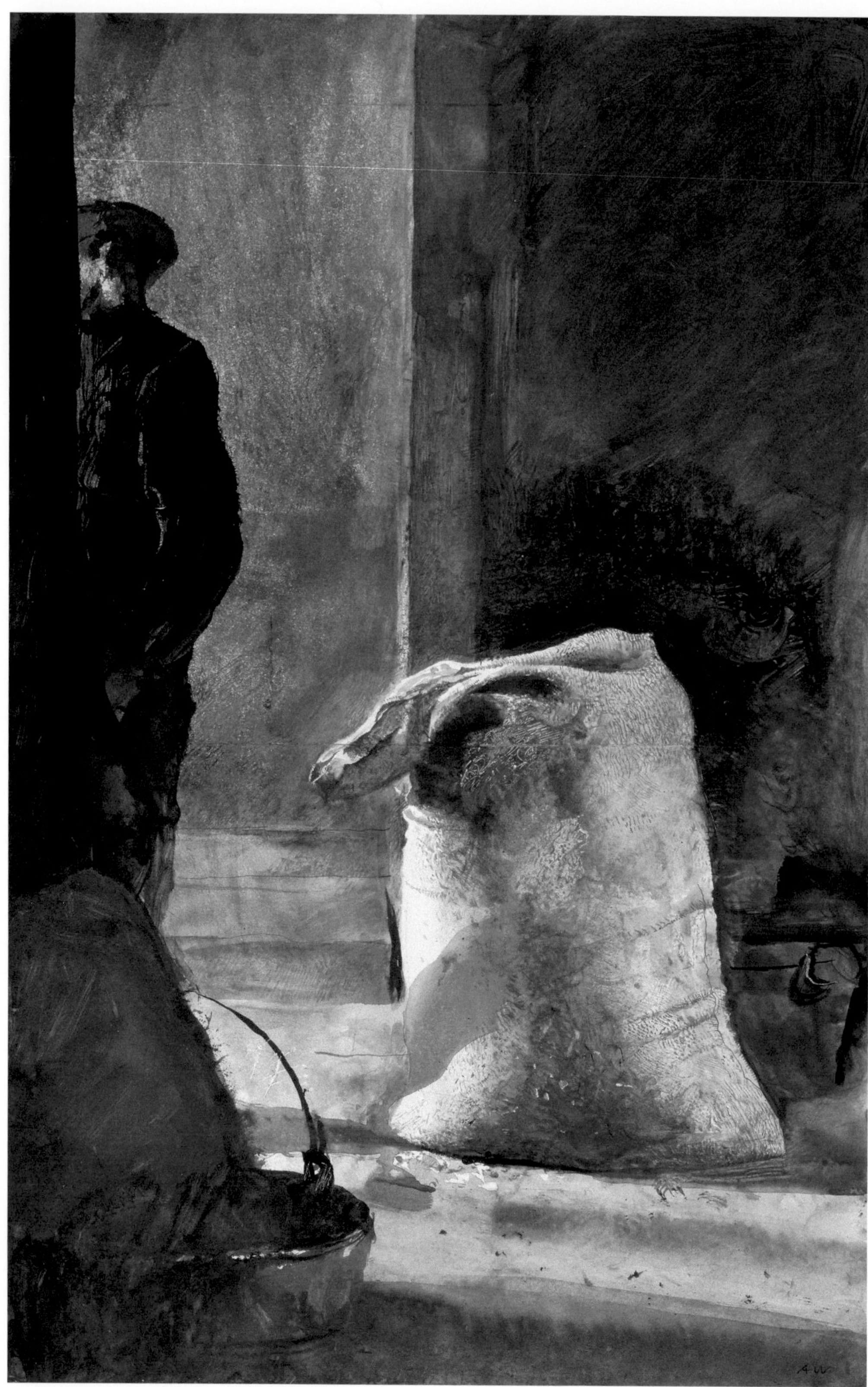

Grain Bag, 1959; watercolor on paper; 22 1/2 x 14 in.; ©Andrew Wyeth; collection of Marunuma Art Park, cat. 17

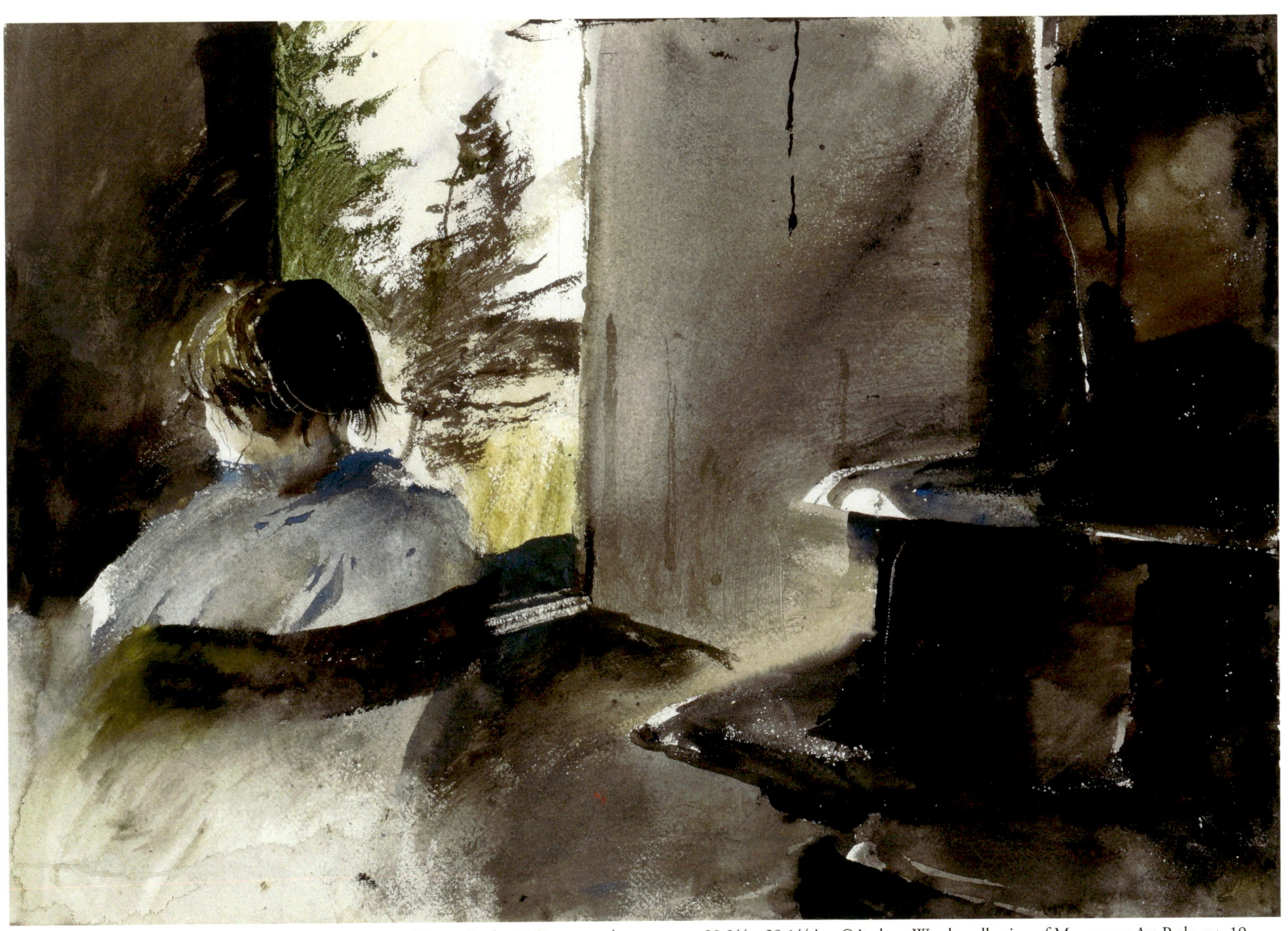

Wood Stove Study, 1962; watercolor on paper; 20 3/4 x 29 1/4 in.; ©Andrew Wyeth; collection of Marunuma Art Park, cat. 19

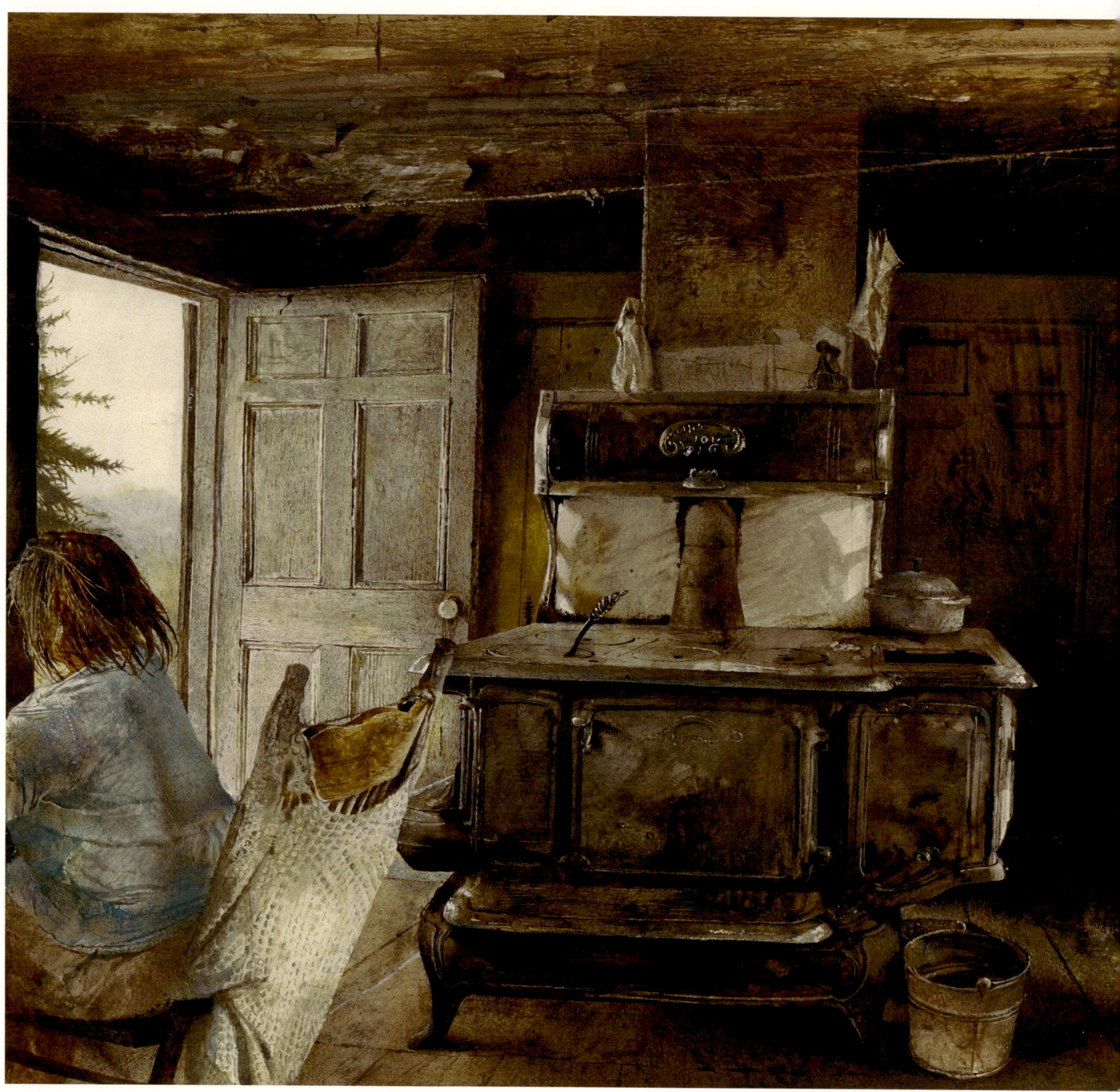

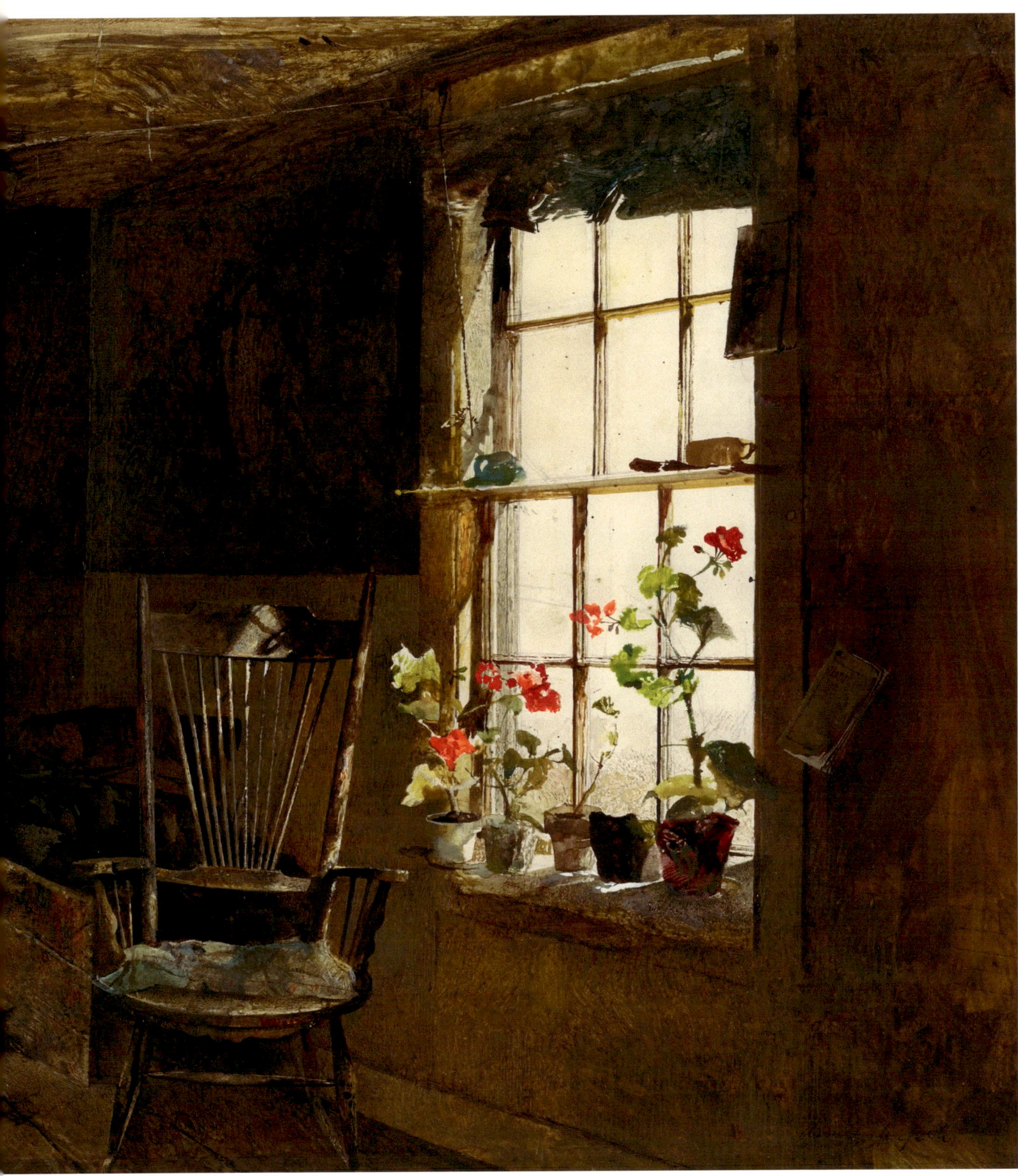

Wood Stove, 1962; drybrush watercolor on paper; 13 3/8 x 26 ¼ in.; ©Andrew Wyeth; Farnsworth Art Museum: museum purchase, 1962 , cat. 44

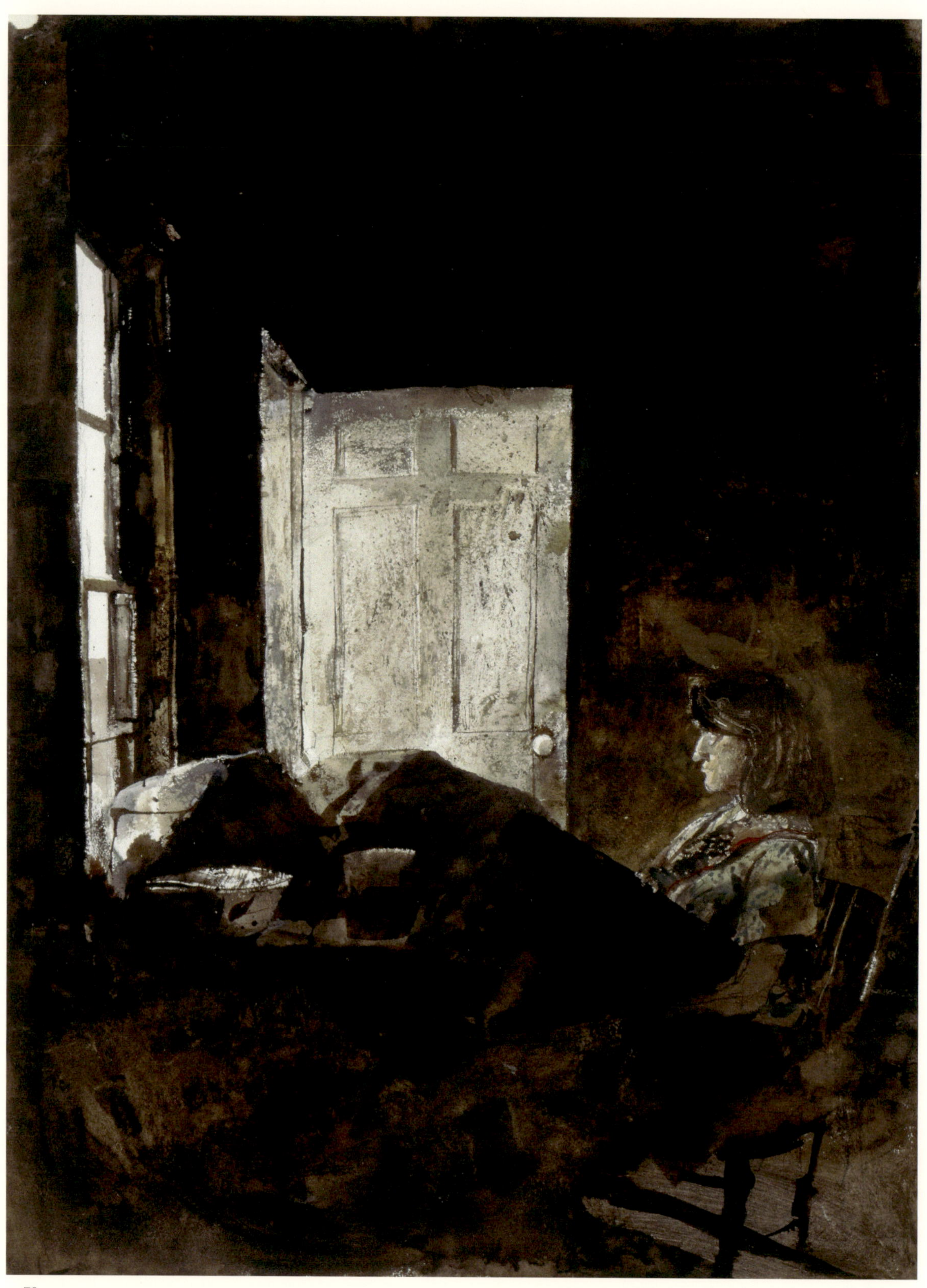

Anna Christina Study, 1967; watercolor on paper; 29 x 21 1/4 in.; ©Andrew Wyeth; collection of Marunuma Art Park, cat. 25

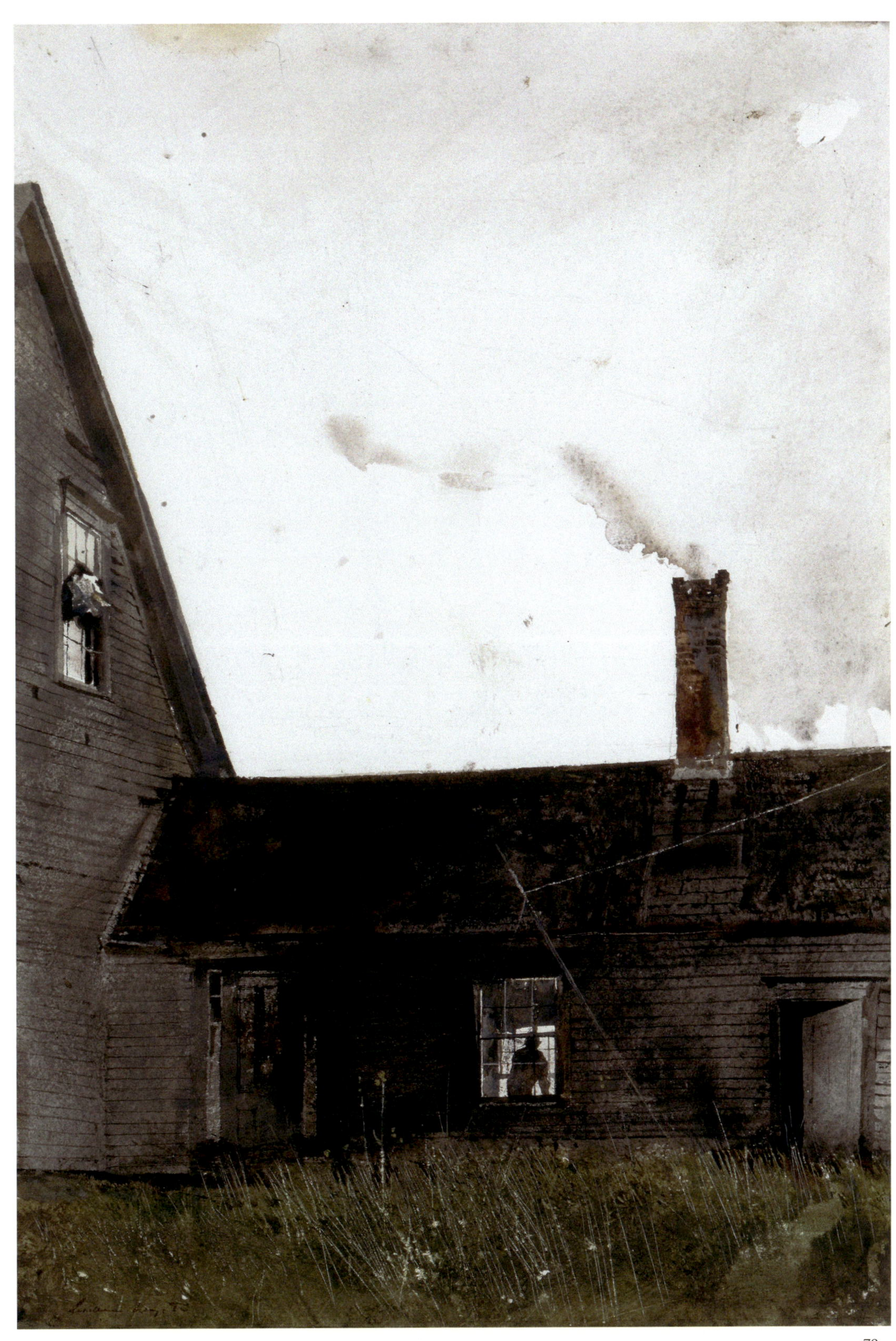

Breakfast at Olsons, 1967;
watercolor on paper; 23 3/4 x 16 in.;
©Andrew Wyeth; collection of
Marunuma Art Park, cat. 26

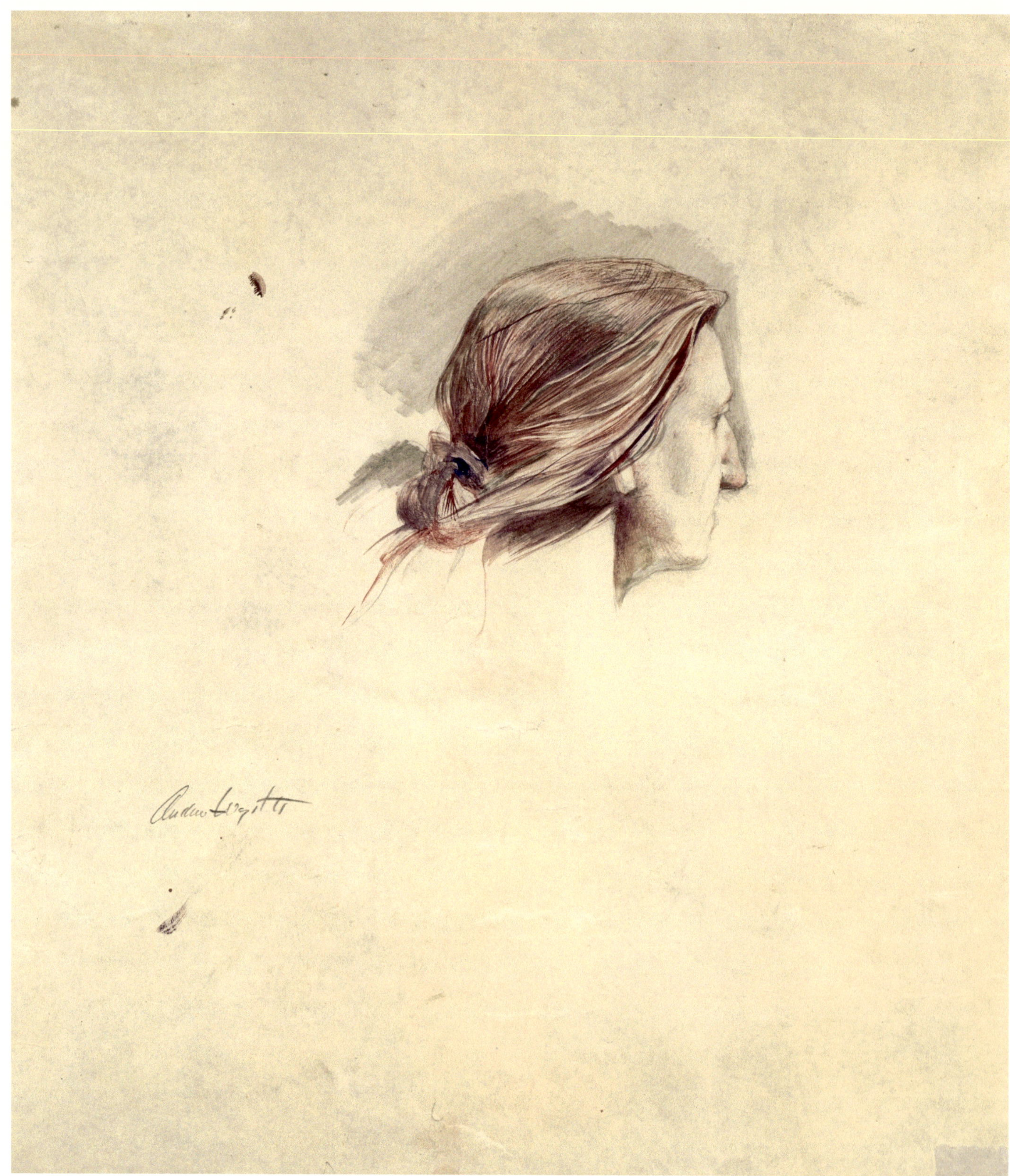

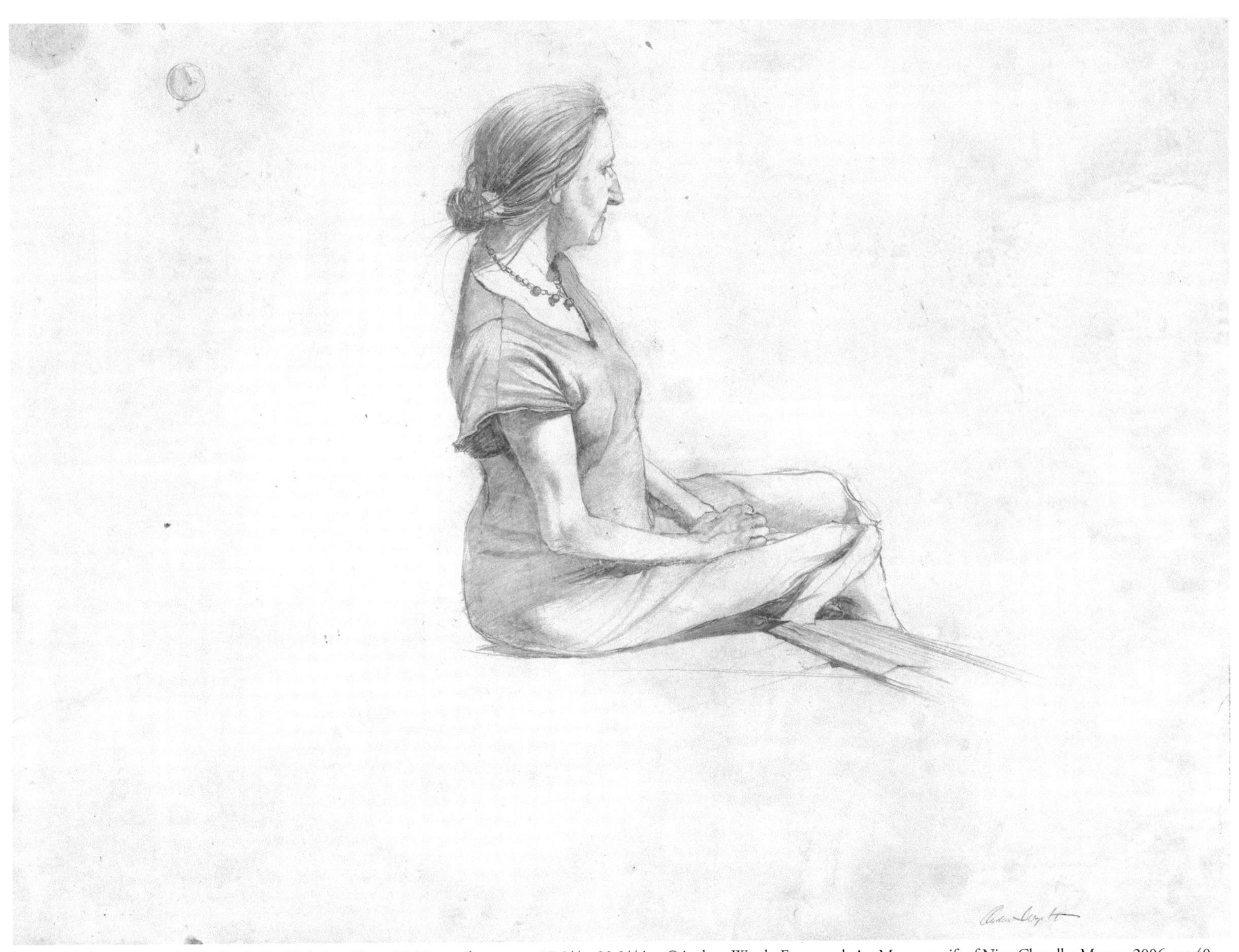

Above: **Christina with Beads, Study for Christina Olson**, 1947; pencil on paper; 17 3/4 x 23 3/4 in.; ©Andrew Wyeth; Farnsworth Art Museum: gift of Nina Chandler Murray, 2006, cat 40
Left: **Christina's Head, Study for Christina Olson**, 1947; watercolor on paper; 12 1/4 x 10 5/16 in.; ©Andrew Wyeth; Farnsworth Art Museum: gift of Nina Chandler Murray, 2006, cat. 39

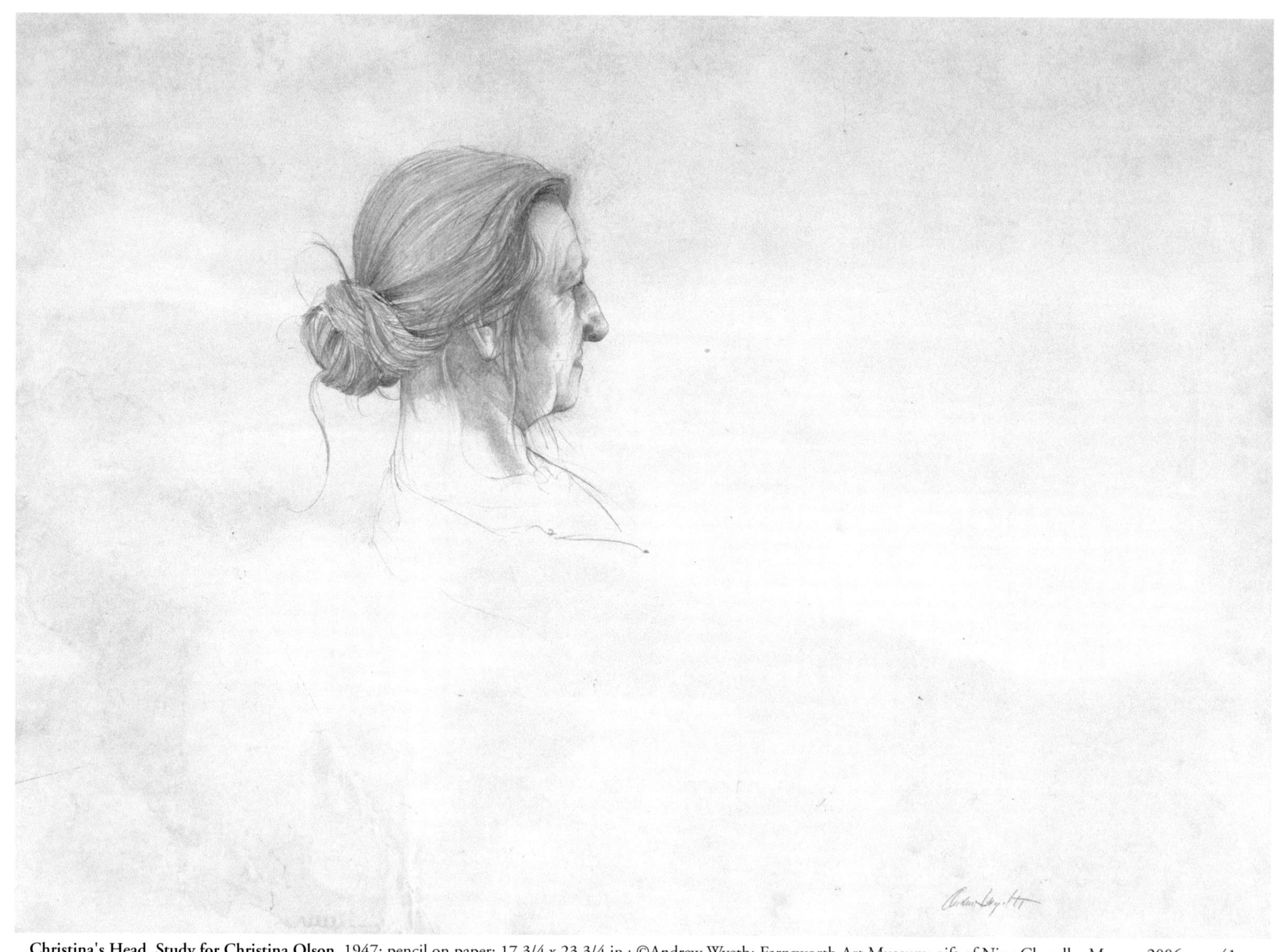

Christina's Head, Study for Christina Olson, 1947; pencil on paper; 17 3/4 x 23 3/4 in.; ©Andrew Wyeth; Farnsworth Art Museum: gift of Nina Chandler Murray, 2006, cat. 41

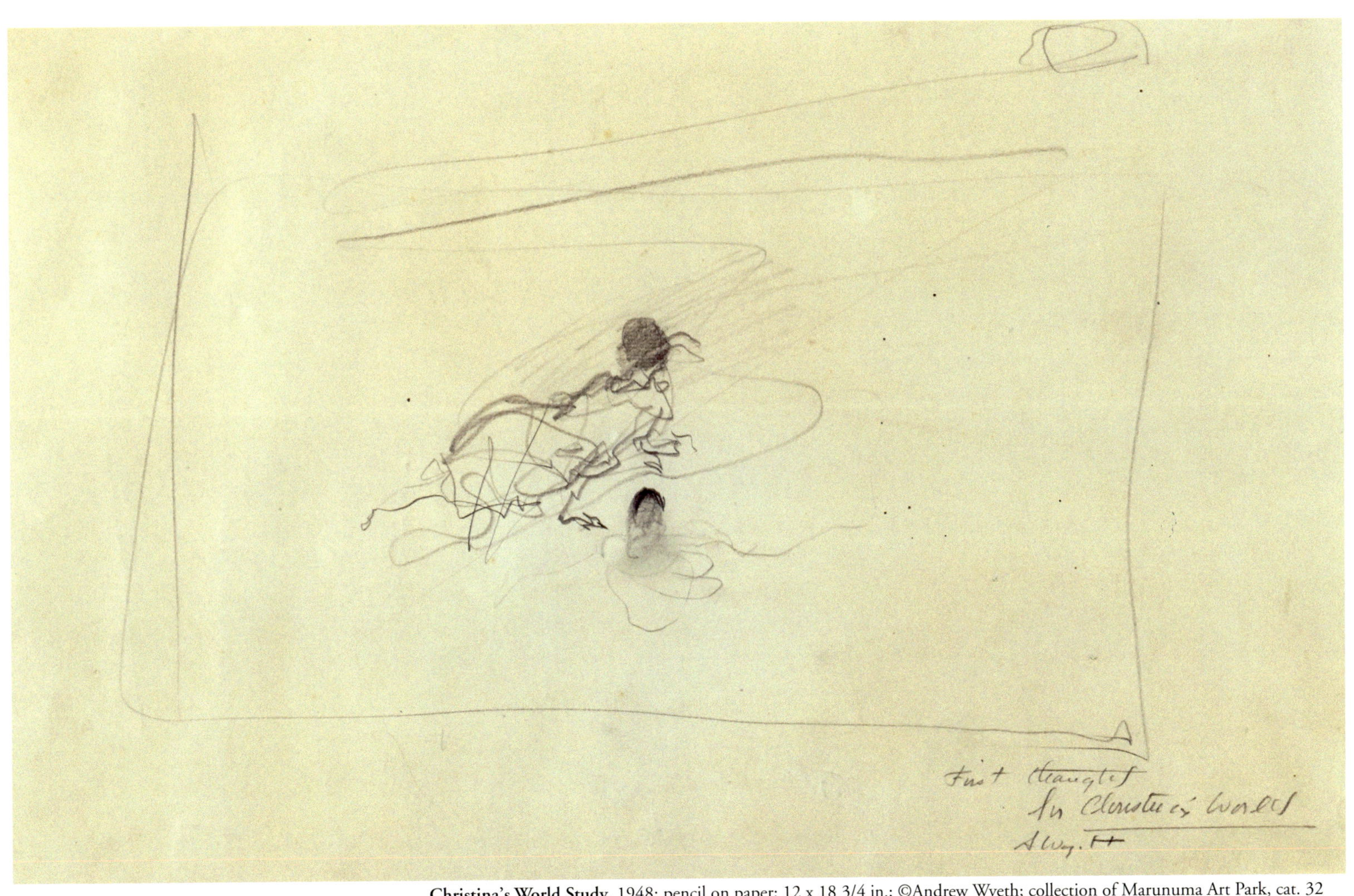

Christina's World Study, 1948; pencil on paper; 12 x 18 3/4 in.; ©Andrew Wyeth; collection of Marunuma Art Park, cat. 32

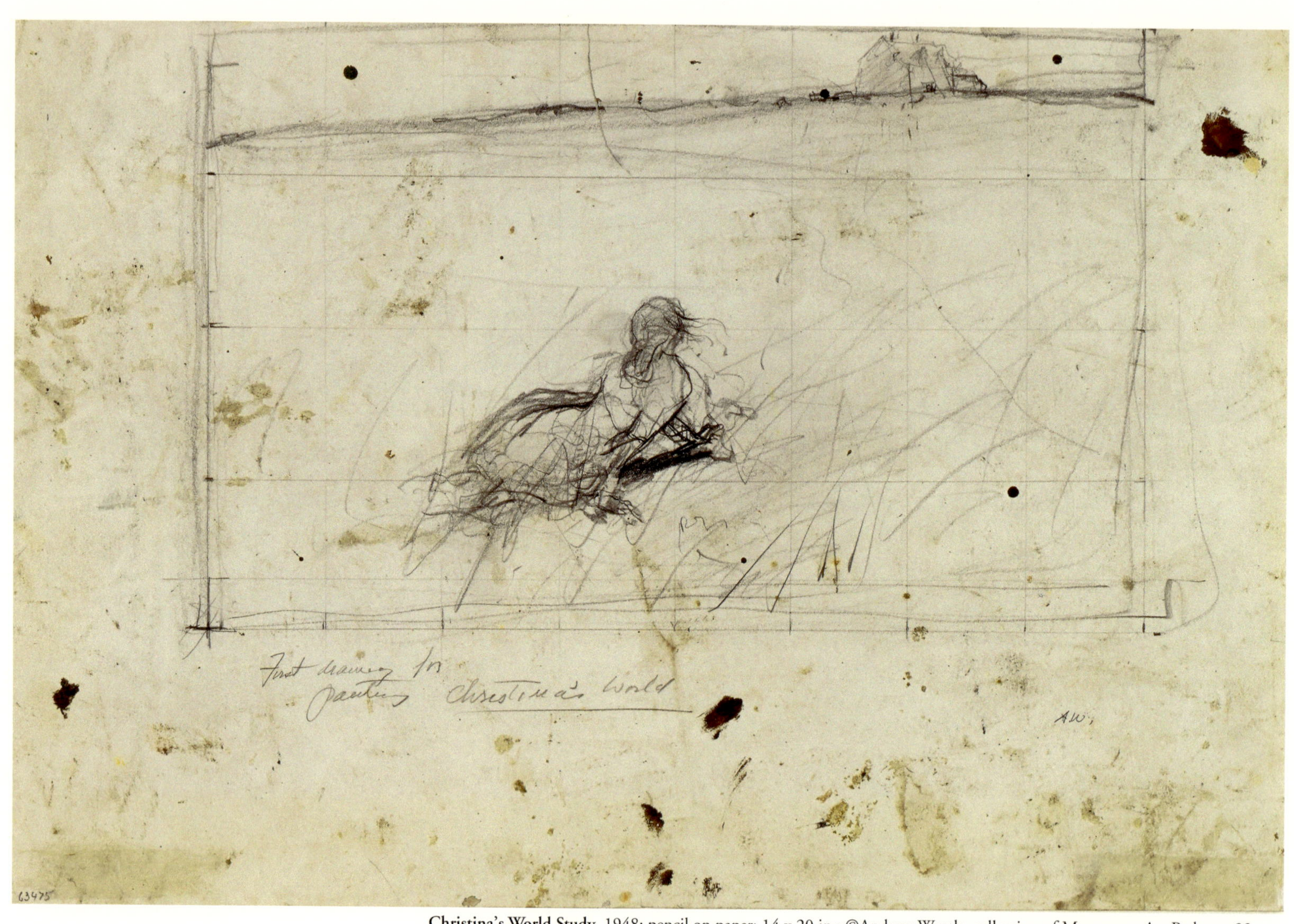

Christina's World Study, 1948; pencil on paper; 14 x 20 in.; ©Andrew Wyeth; collection of Marunuma Art Park,cat. 33

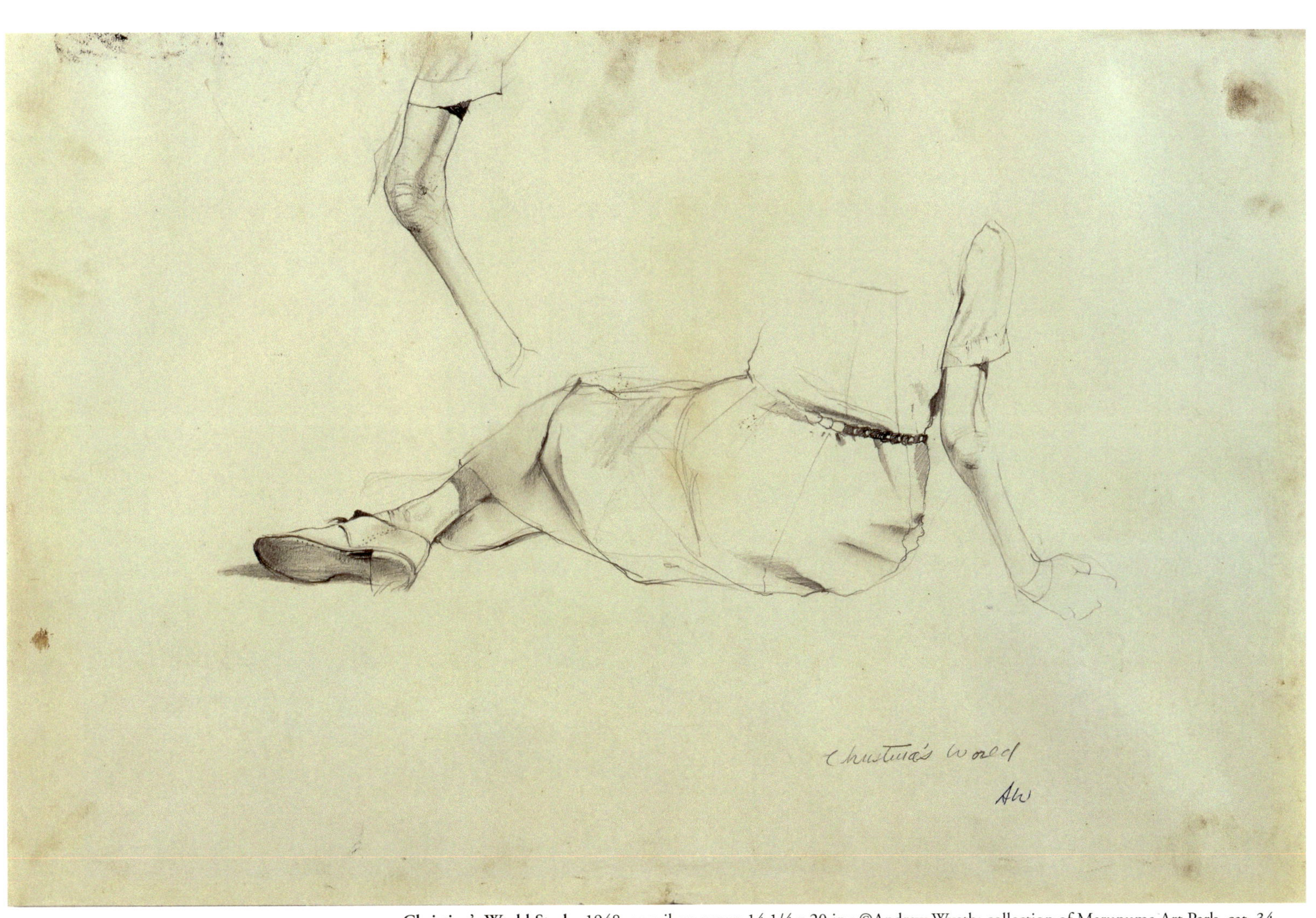

Christina's World Study, 1948; pencil on paper; 14 1/4 x 20 in.; ©Andrew Wyeth; collection of Marunuma Art Park, cat. 34

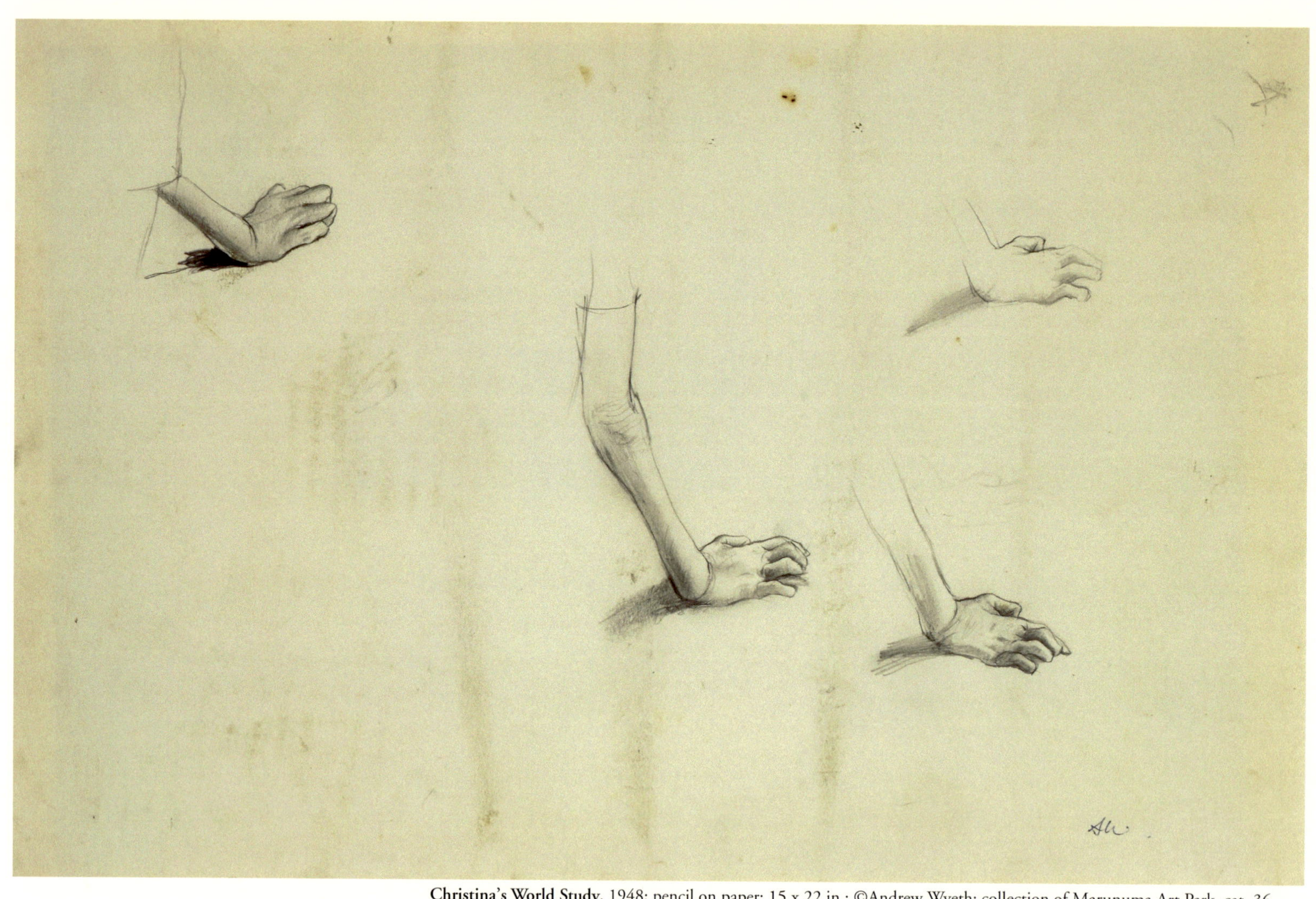

Christina's World Study, 1948; pencil on paper; 15 x 22 in.; ©Andrew Wyeth; collection of Marunuma Art Park, cat. 36

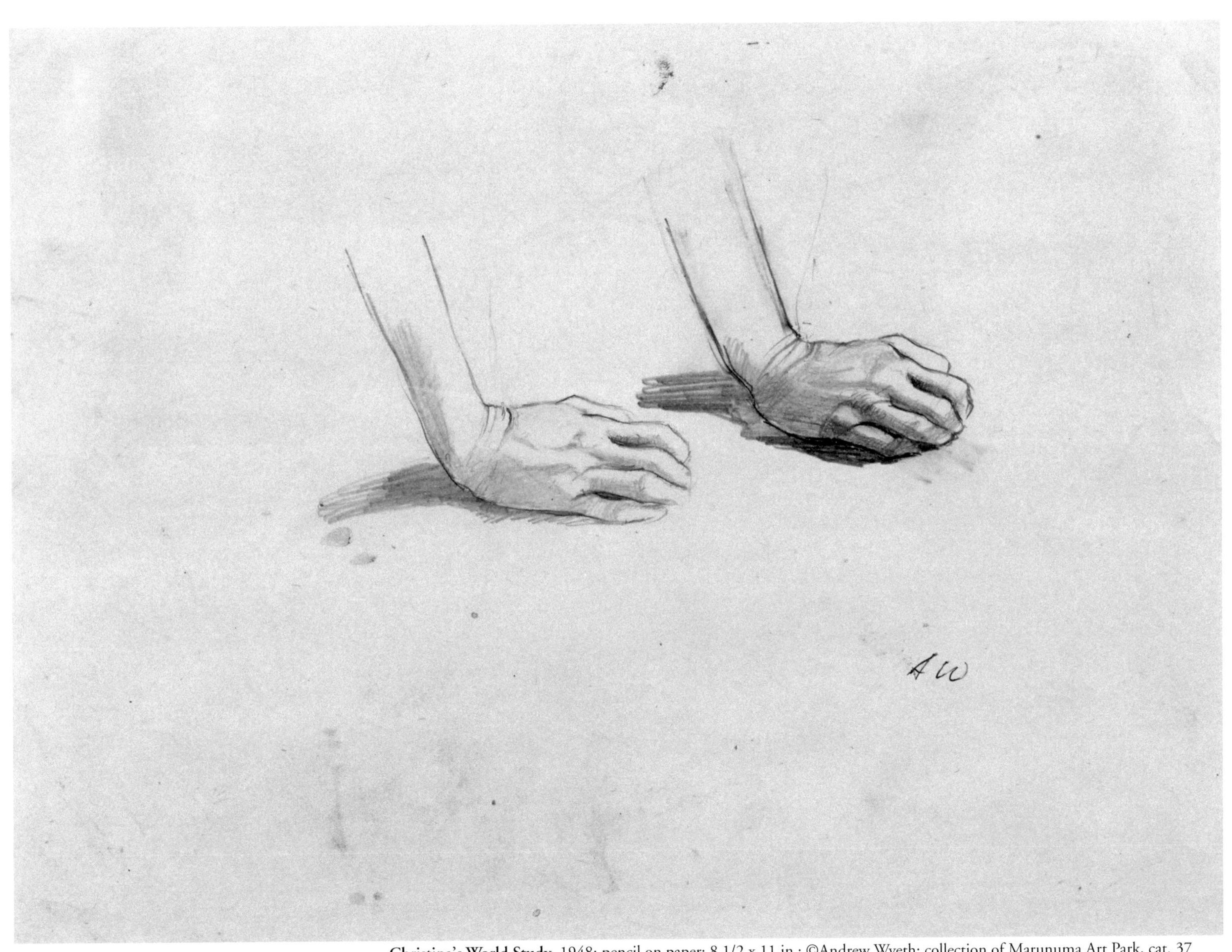

Christina's World Study, 1948; pencil on paper; 8 1/2 x 11 in.; ©Andrew Wyeth; collection of Marunuma Art Park, cat. 37

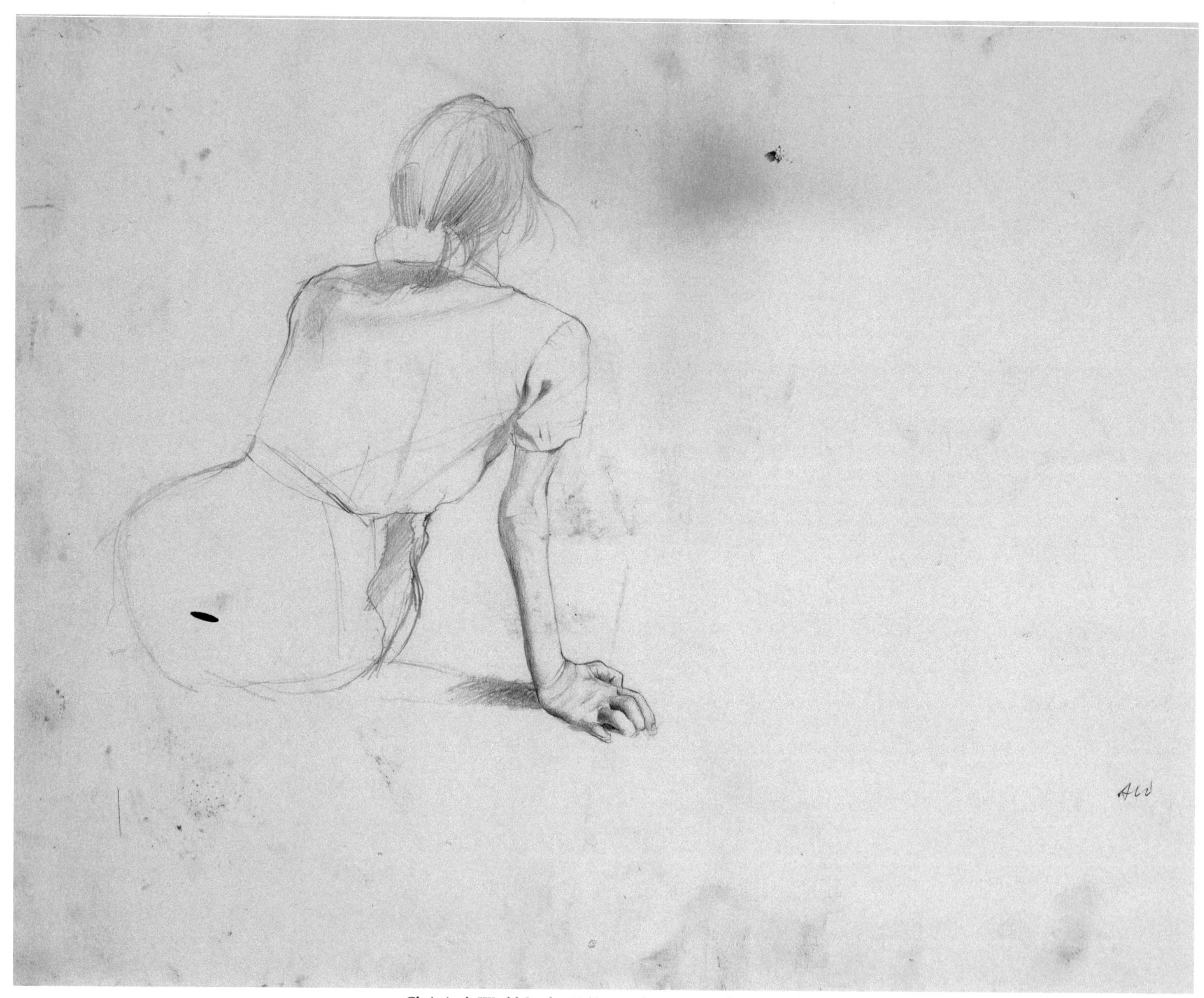

Christina's World Study, 1948; pencil on paper; 14 x 18 in.; ©Andrew Wyeth; collection of Marunuma Art Park, cat. 35

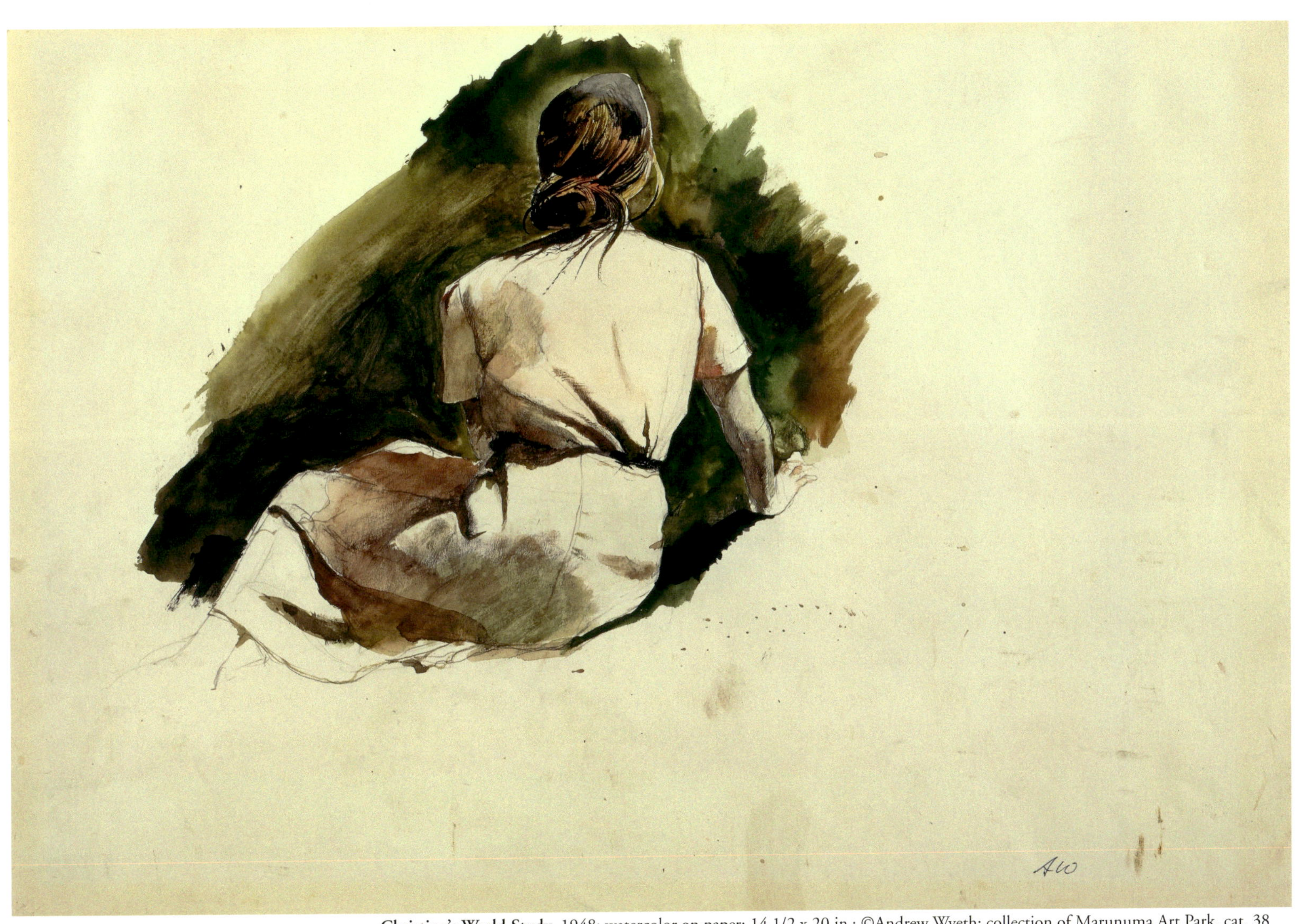

Christina's World Study, 1948; watercolor on paper; 14 1/2 x 20 in.; ©Andrew Wyeth; collection of Marunuma Art Park, cat. 38

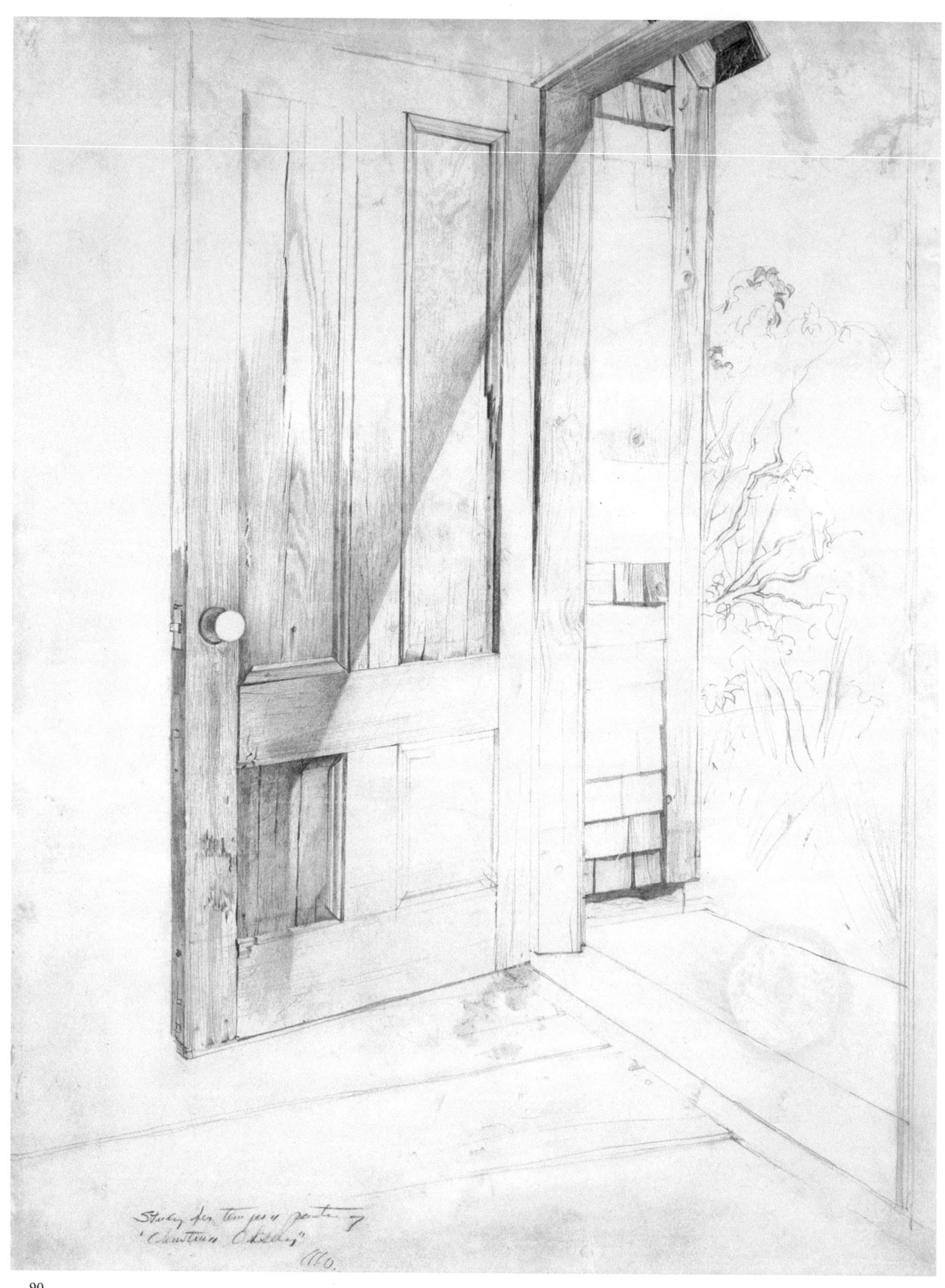

Doorway, Study for Christina Olson, 1947; pencil on paper; 23 3/4 x 17 3/4 in.; ©Andrew Wyeth; Farnsworth Art Museum: gift of Nina Chandler Murray, 2006, cat. 42

the OLSON HOUSE

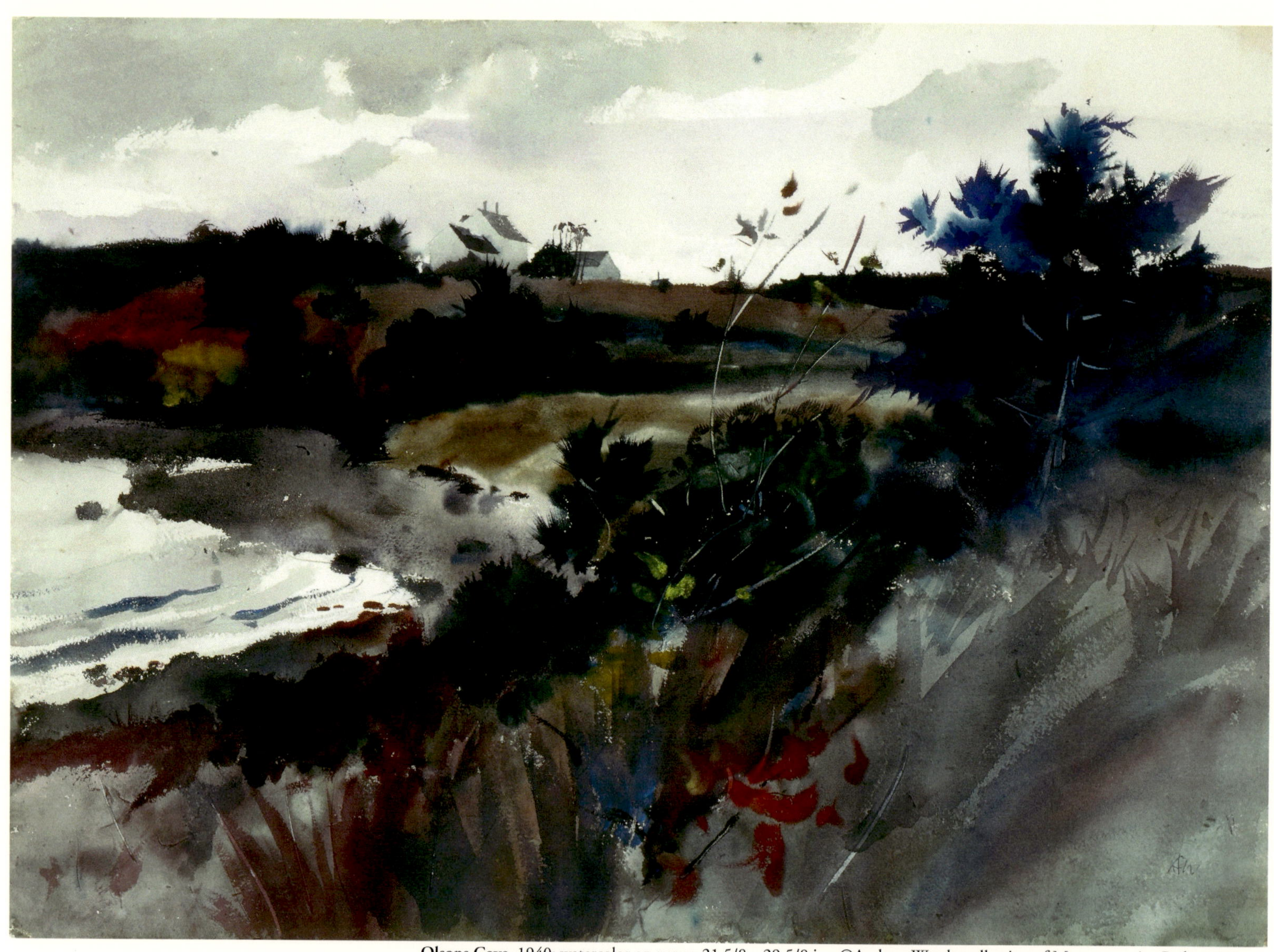

Olsons Cove, 1940; watercolor on paper; 21 5/8 x 29 5/8 in.; ©Andrew Wyeth; collection of Marunuma Art Park, cat. 1

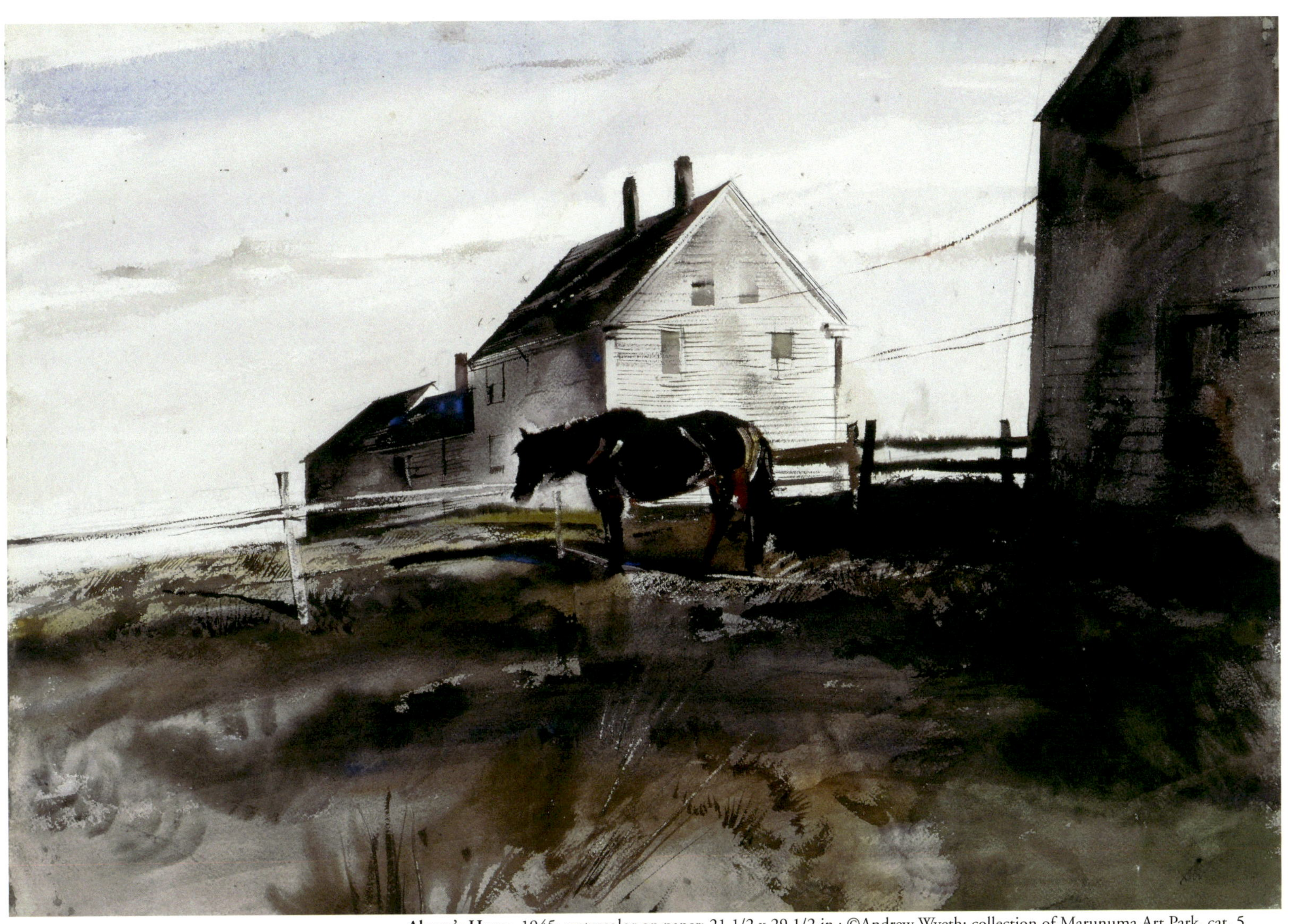

Alvaro's Horse, 1945; watercolor on paper; 21 1/2 x 29 1/2 in.; ©Andrew Wyeth; collection of Marunuma Art Park, cat. 5

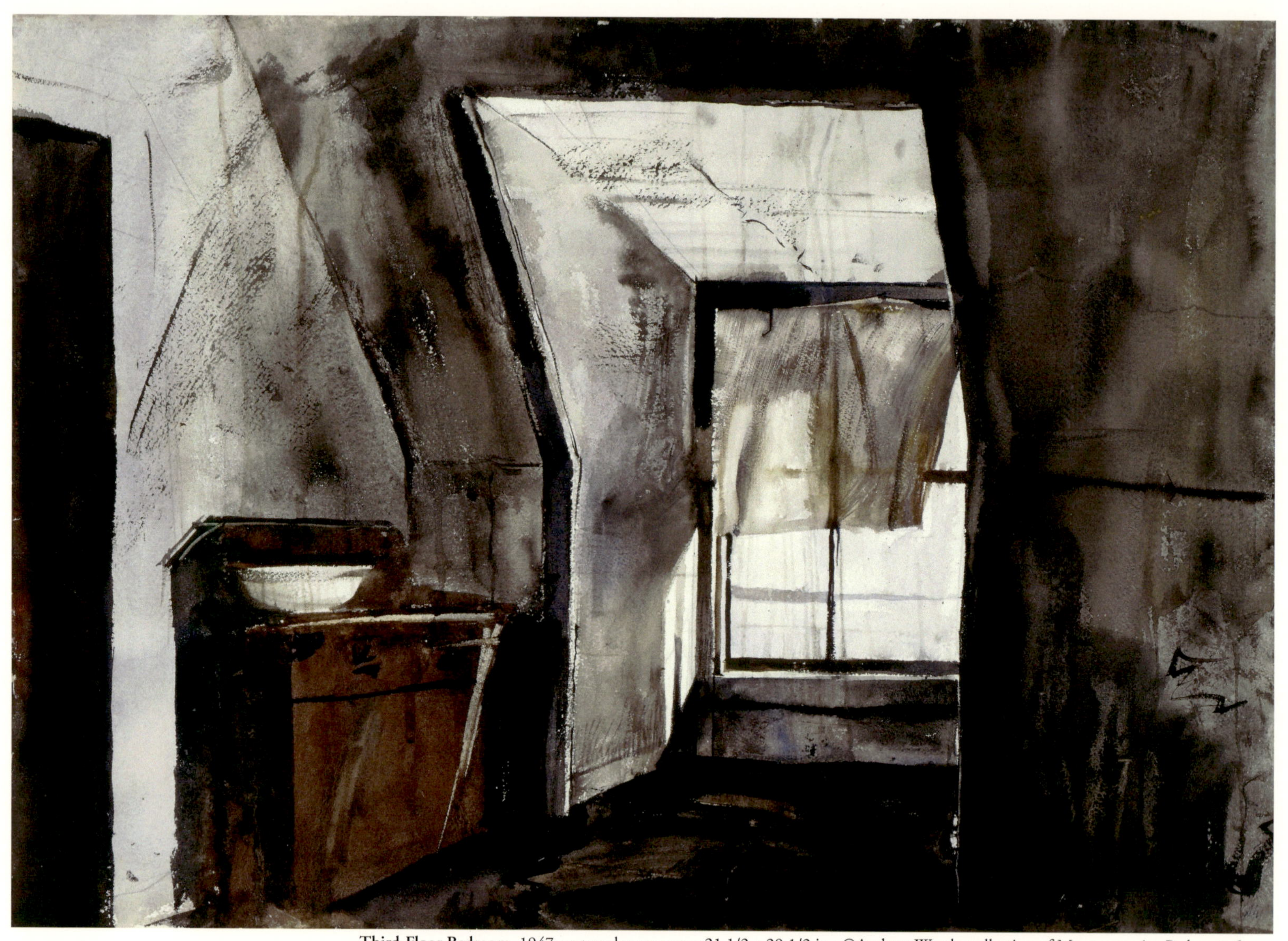

Third-Floor Bedroom, 1947; watercolor on paper; 21 1/2 x 29 1/2 in.; ©Andrew Wyeth; collection of Marunuma Art Park, cat. 6

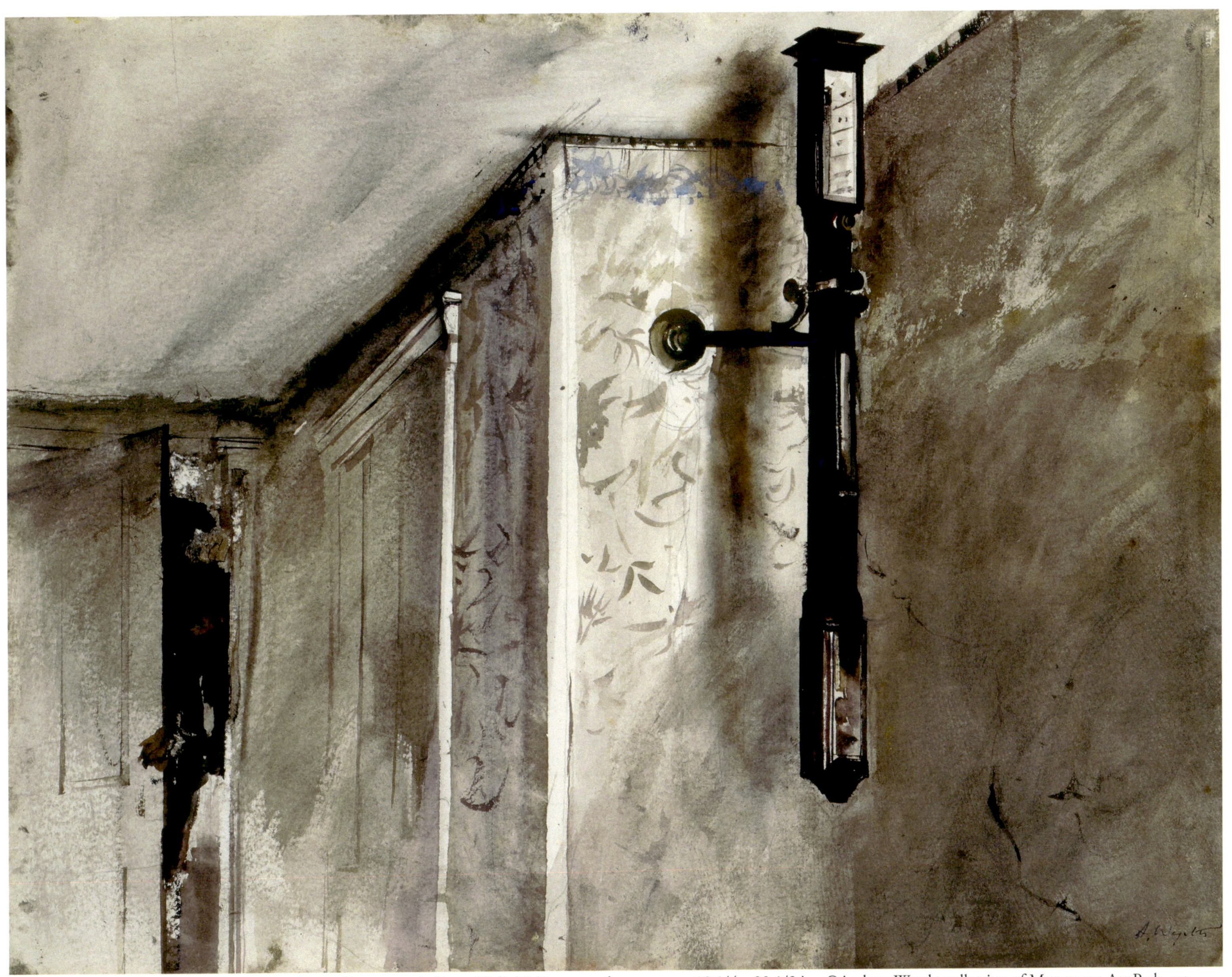

Barometer in Front Hall, 1949; watercolor on paper; 18 1/4 x 23 1/2 in.; ©Andrew Wyeth; collection of Marunuma Art Park, cat. 10

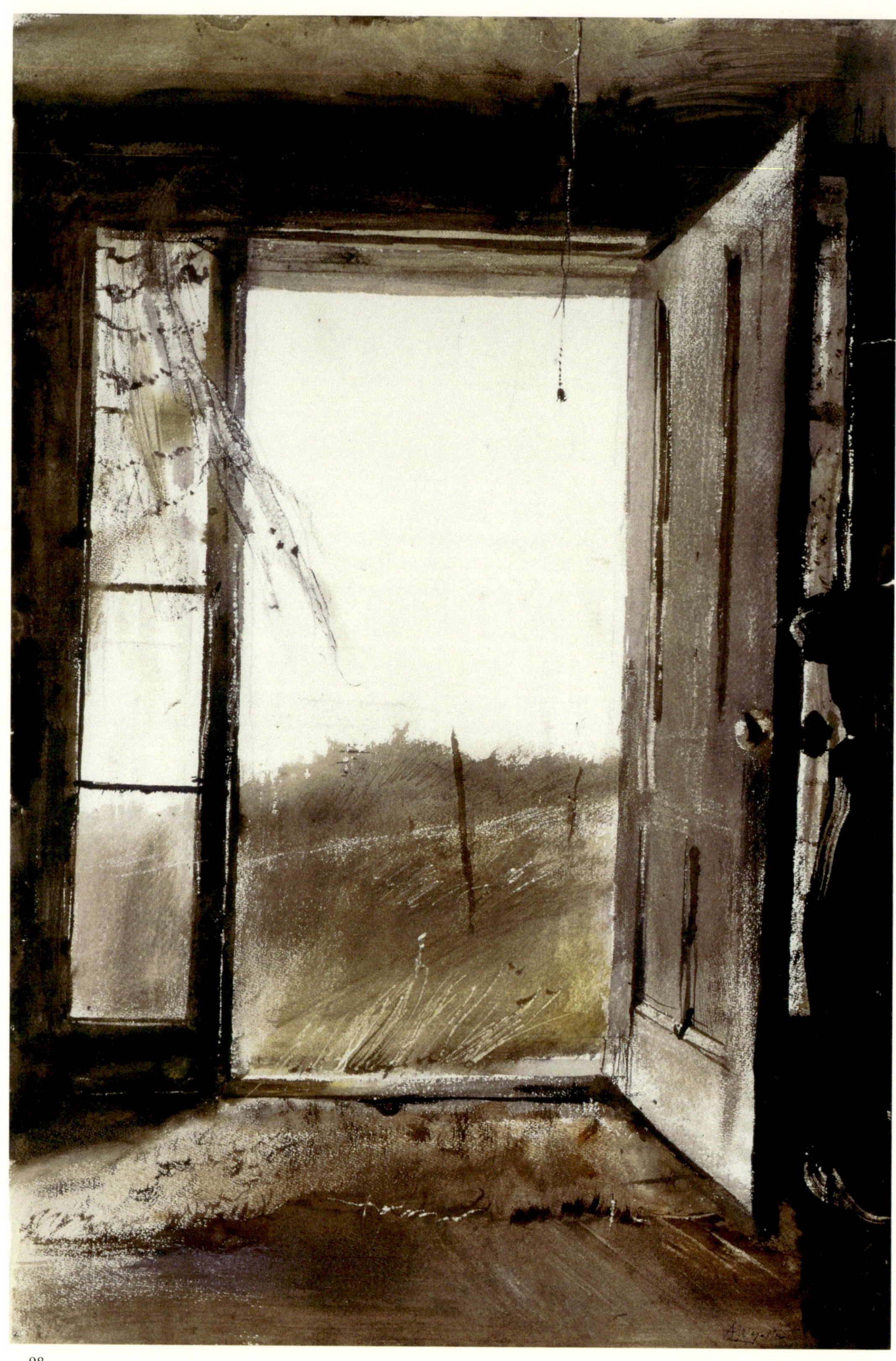

Olsons Front Door, 1957; watercolor on paper;
30 x 20 in.; ©Andrew Wyeth;
collection of Marunuma Art Park, cat. 12

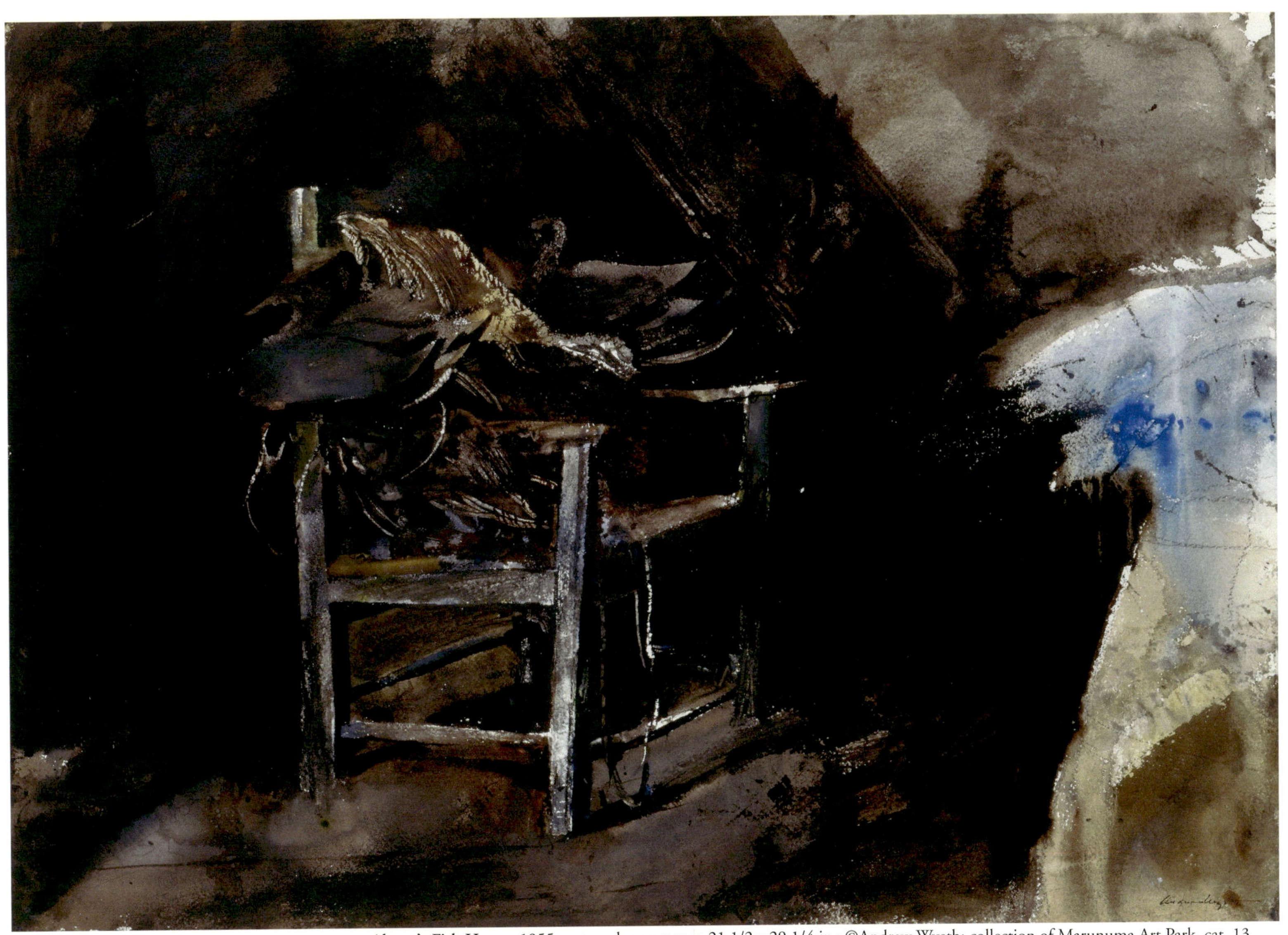

Alvaro's Fish House, 1955; watercolor on paper; 21 1/2 x 29 1/4 in.; ©Andrew Wyeth; collection of Marunuma Art Park, cat. 13

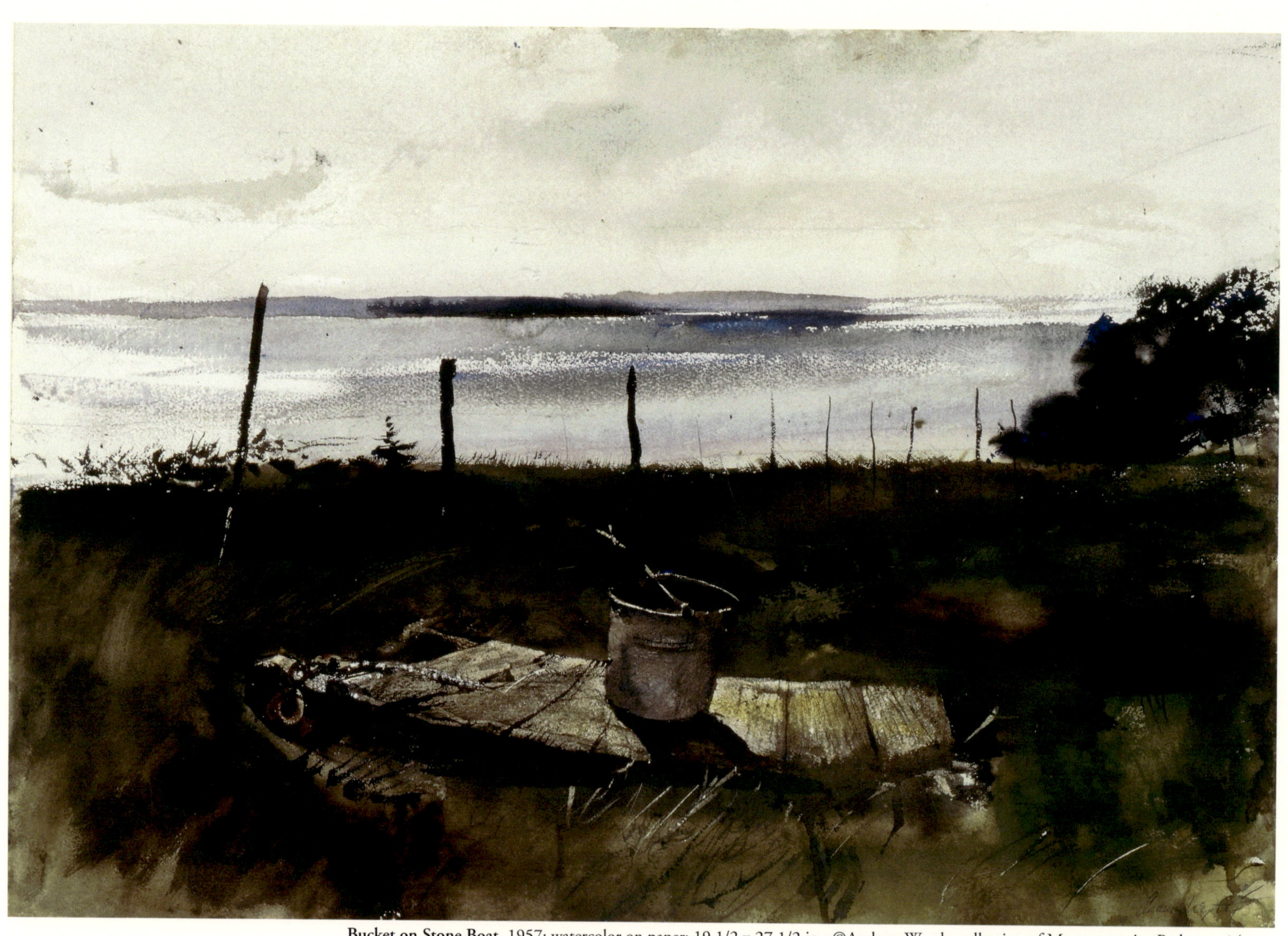

Bucket on Stone Boat, 1957; watercolor on paper; 19 1/2 x 27 1/2 in.; ©Andrew Wyeth; collection of Marunuma Art Park, cat. 14

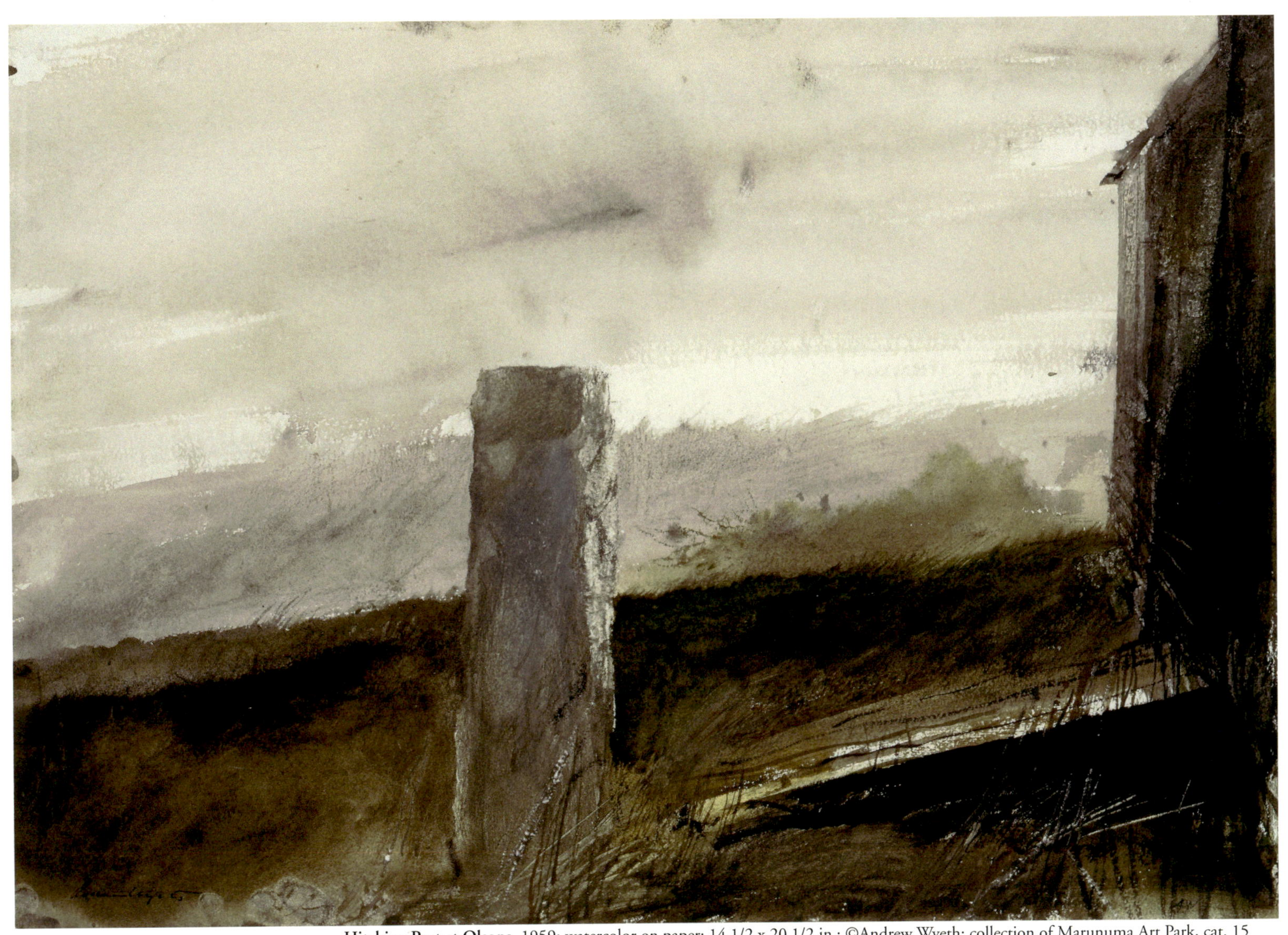

Hitching Post at Olsons, 1959; watercolor on paper; 14 1/2 x 20 1/2 in.; ©Andrew Wyeth; collection of Marunuma Art Park, cat. 15

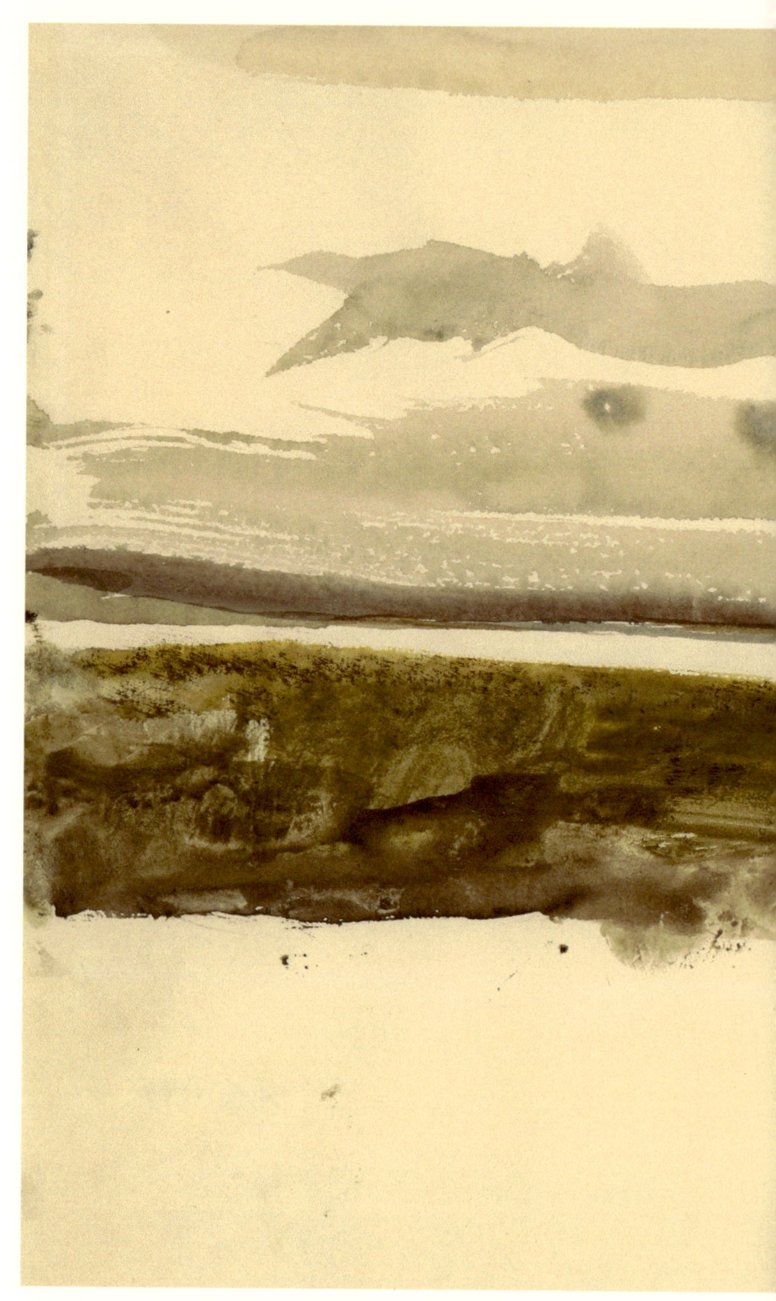

Alvaro's Hayrack, 1958; watercolor on paper; 9 x 23 in.;
©Andrew Wyeth; Farnsworth Art Museum:
gift of Mr. and Mrs. Andrew Wyeth, 1960, cat. 43

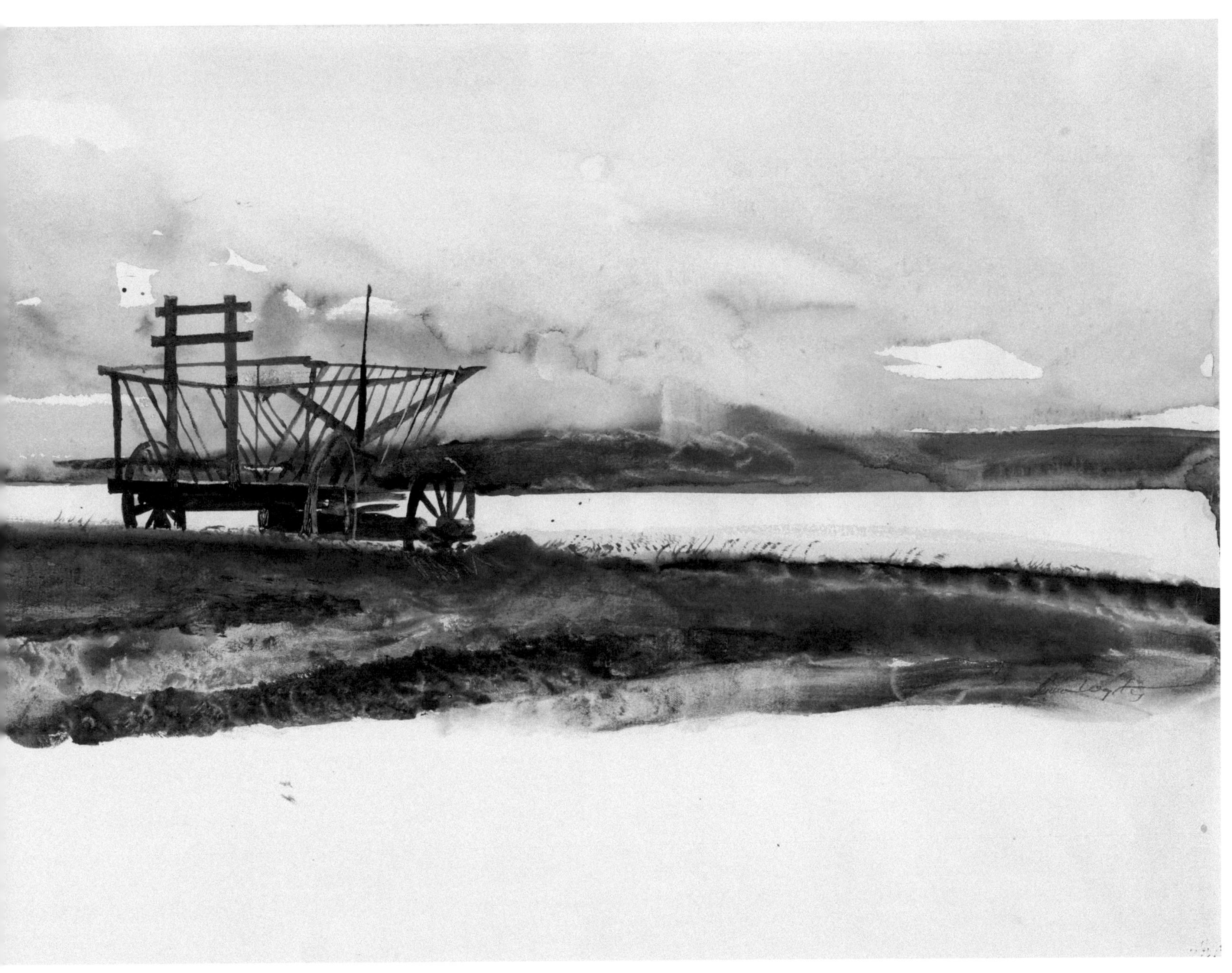

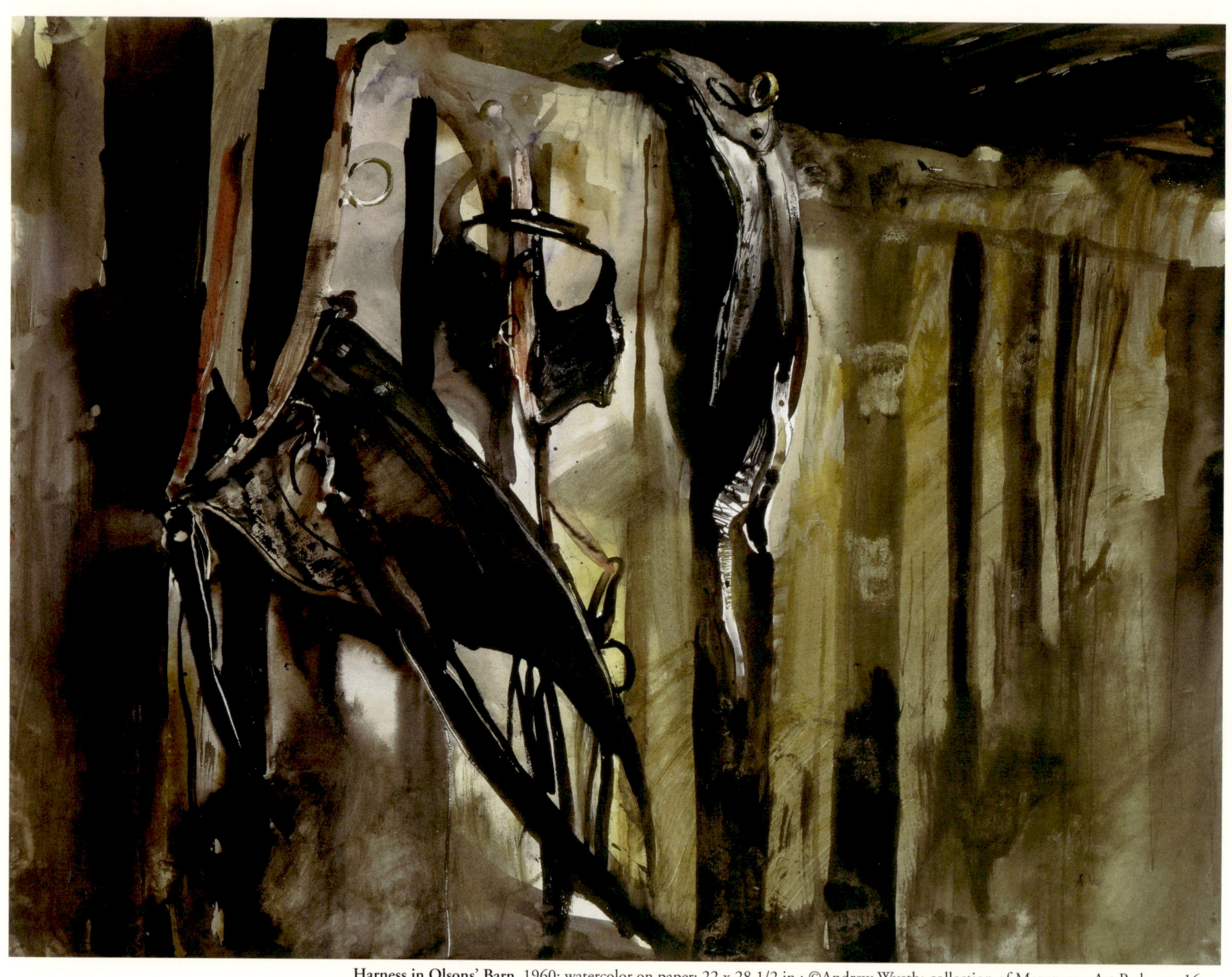

Harness in Olsons' Barn, 1960; watercolor on paper; 22 x 28 1/2 in.; ©Andrew Wyeth; collection of Marunuma Art Park, cat. 16

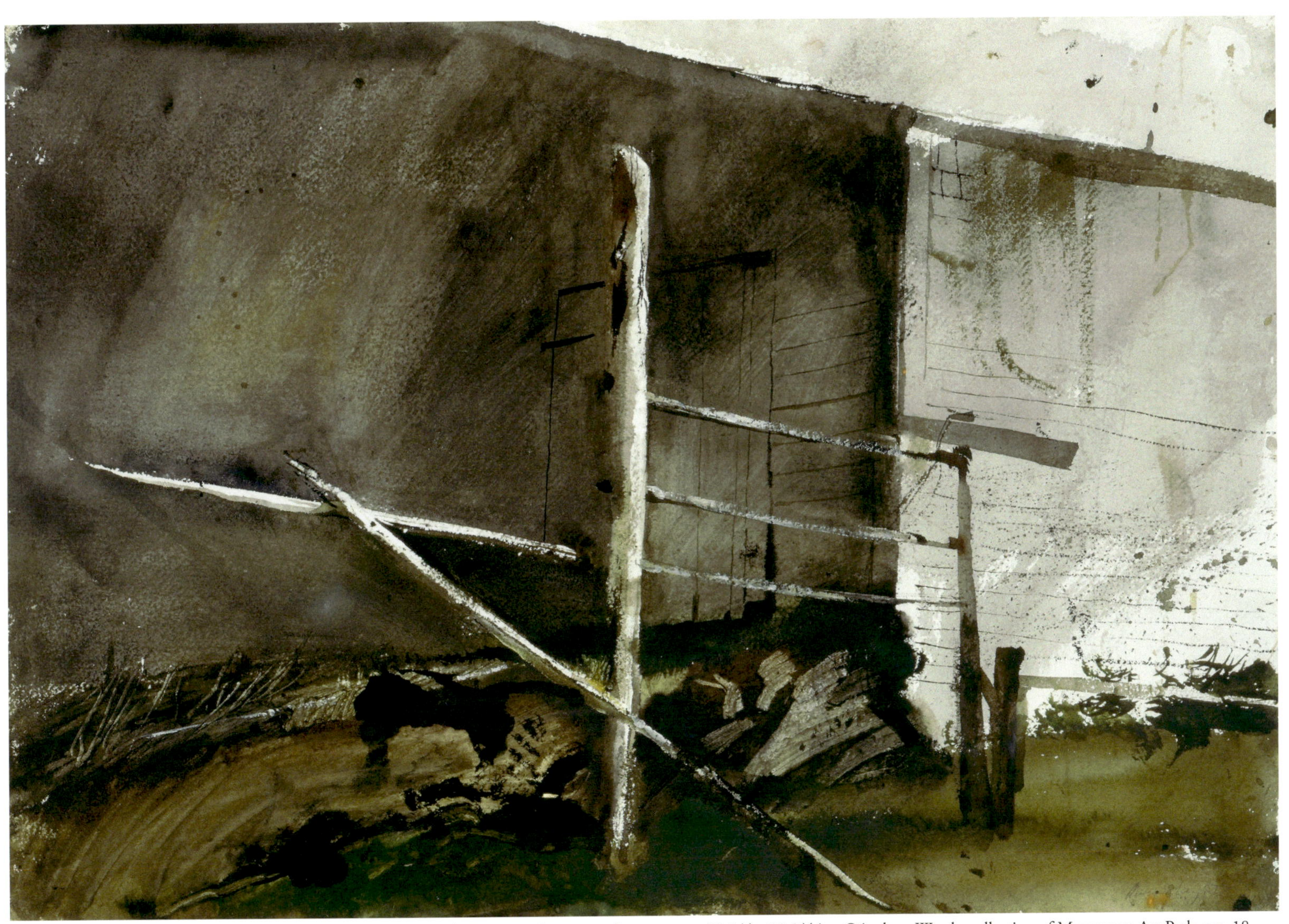

Pole Fence, 1961; watercolor on paper; 21 1/4 x 29 3/4 in.; ©Andrew Wyeth; collection of Marunuma Art Park, cat. 18

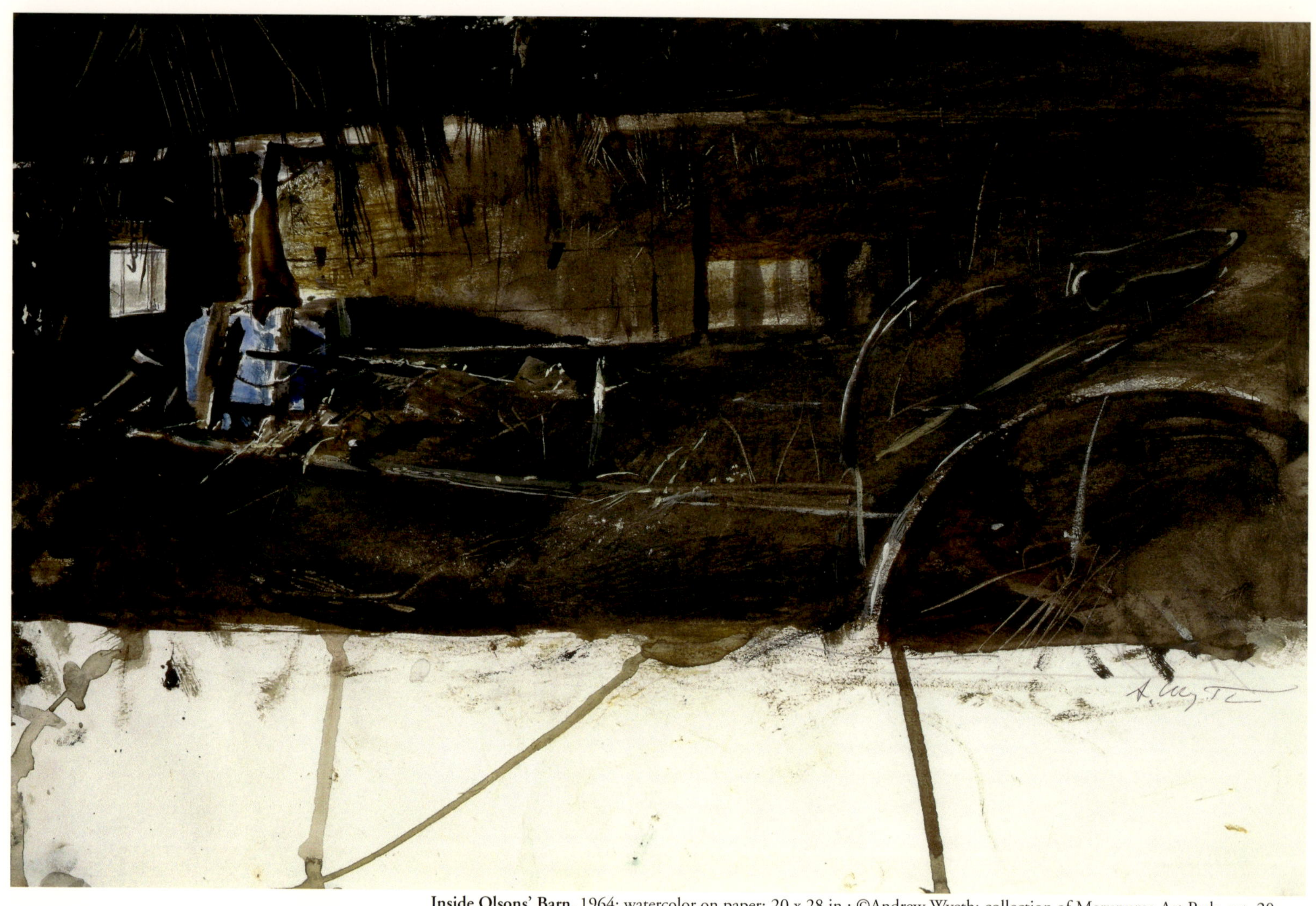

Inside Olsons' Barn, 1964; watercolor on paper; 20 x 28 in.; ©Andrew Wyeth; collection of Marunuma Art Park, cat. 20

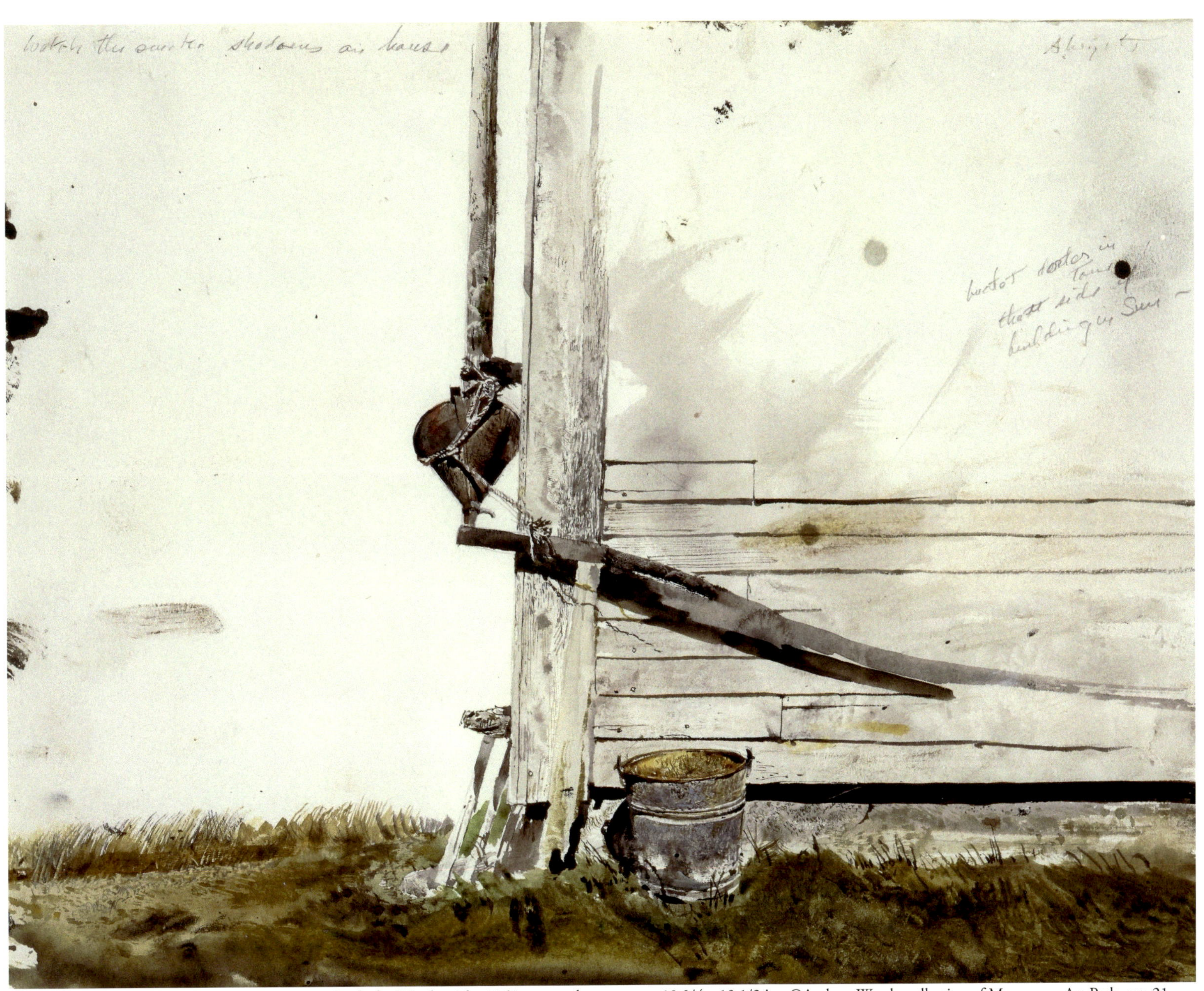

Downspout, Study for Weatherside, 1965; watercolor on paper; 10 3/4 x 13 1/2 in.; ©Andrew Wyeth; collection of Marunuma Art Park, cat. 21

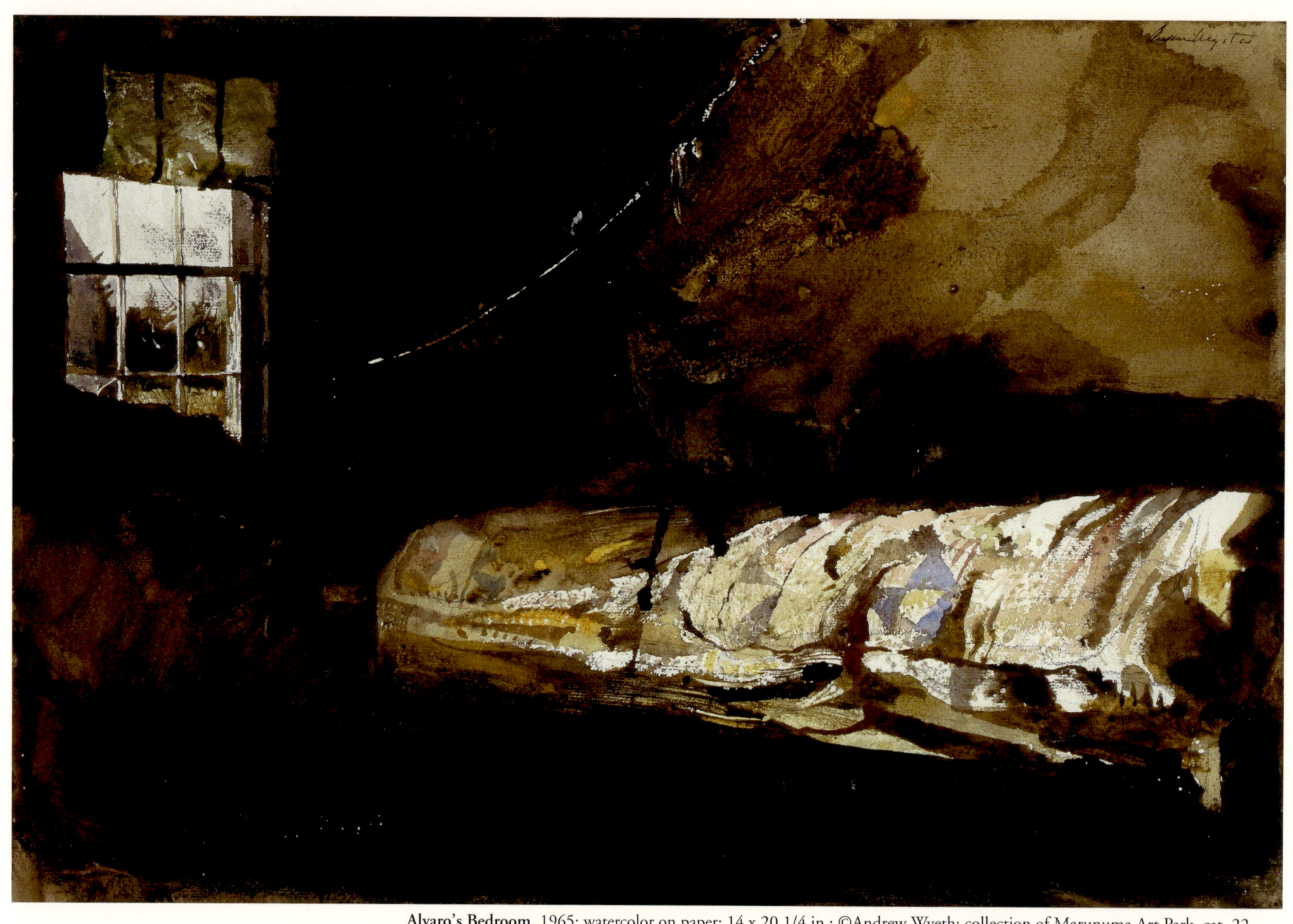

Alvaro's Bedroom, 1965; watercolor on paper; 14 x 20 1/4 in.; ©Andrew Wyeth; collection of Marunuma Art Park, cat. 22

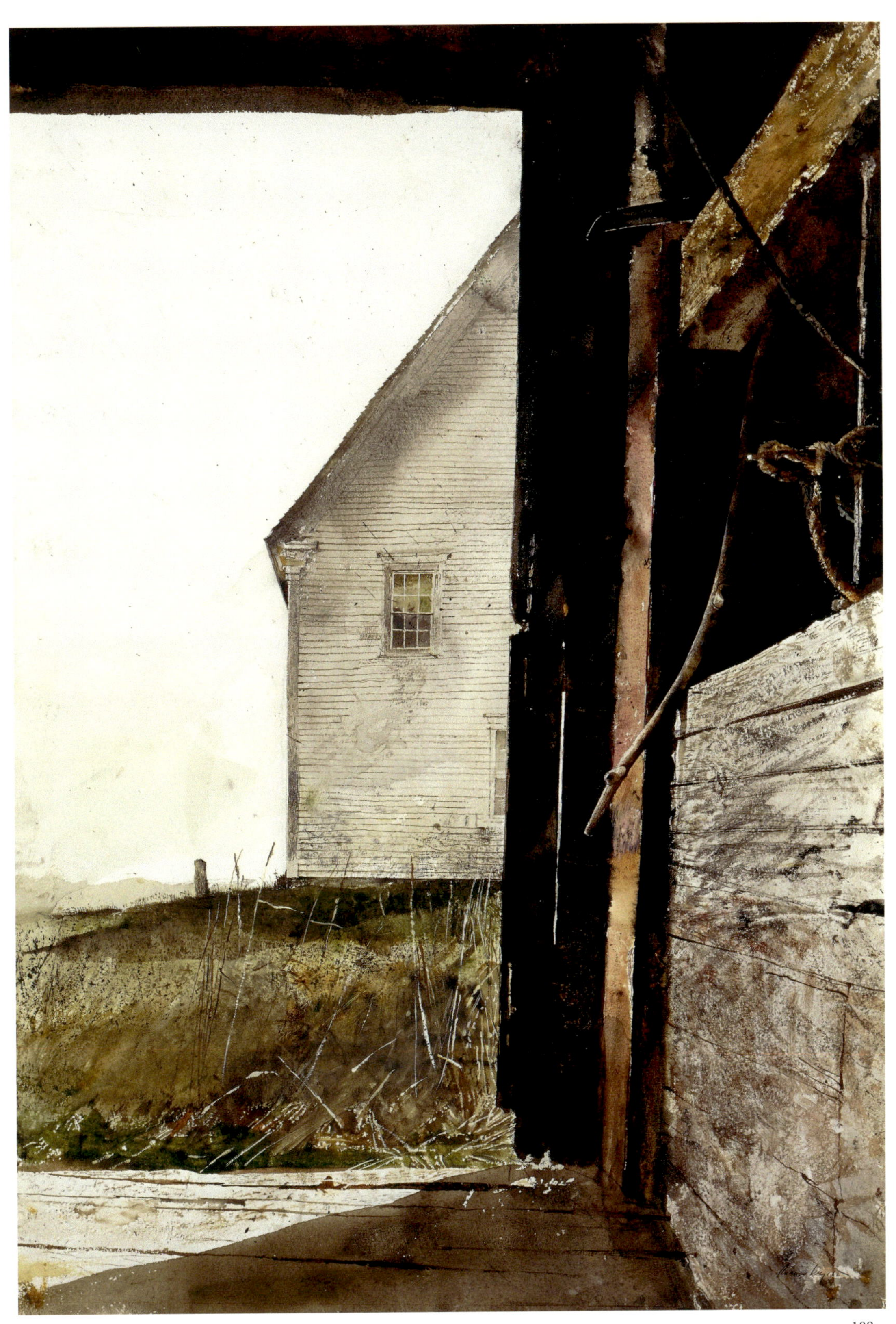

Olson House, 1966; watercolor on paper; 27 1/4 x 18 1/2 in.; ©Andrew Wyeth; collection of Marunuma Art Park, cat. 23

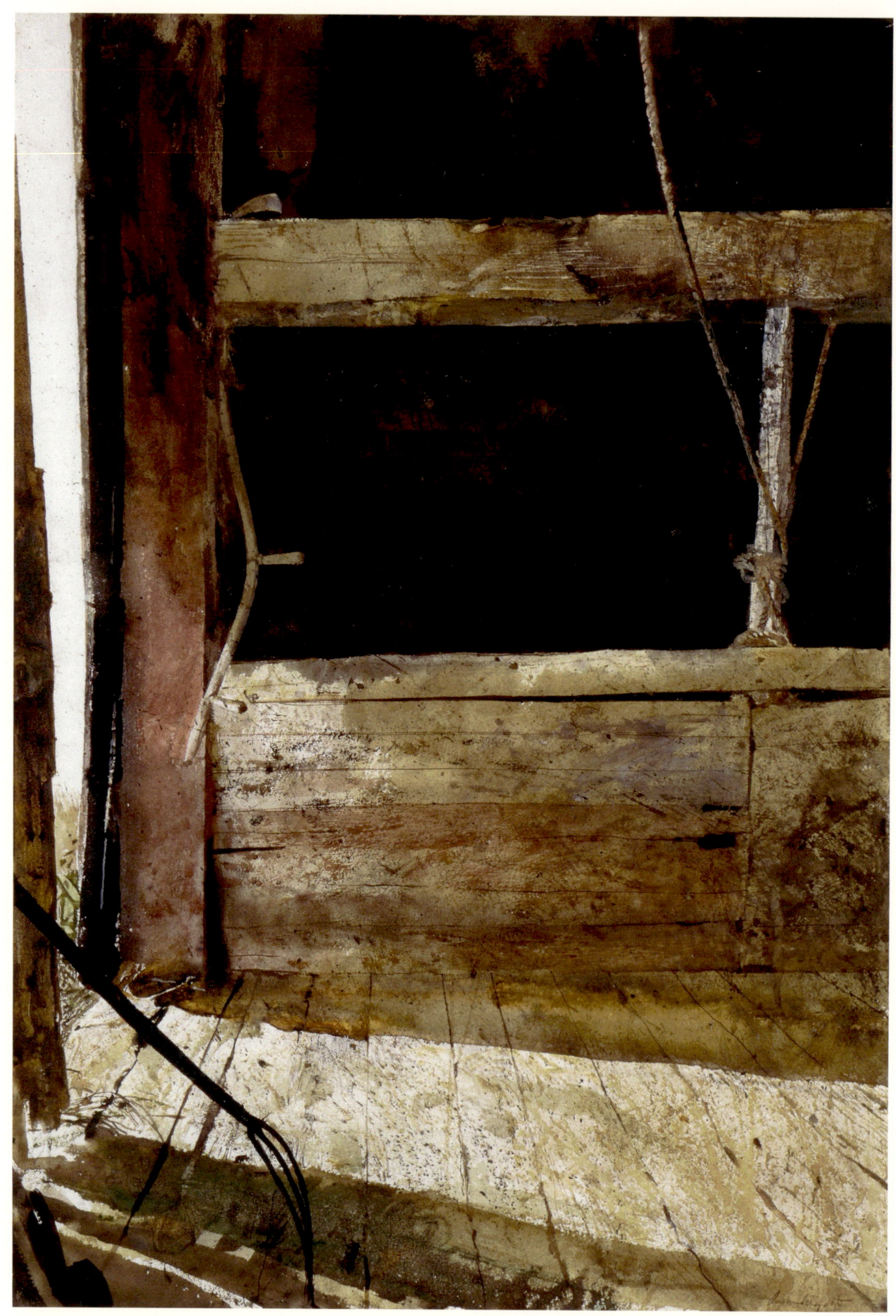

Hayloft in Olsons' Barn, 1966; watercolor on paper; 27 1/4 x 18 1/2 in.; ©Andrew Wyeth; collection of Marunuma Art Park, cat. 24

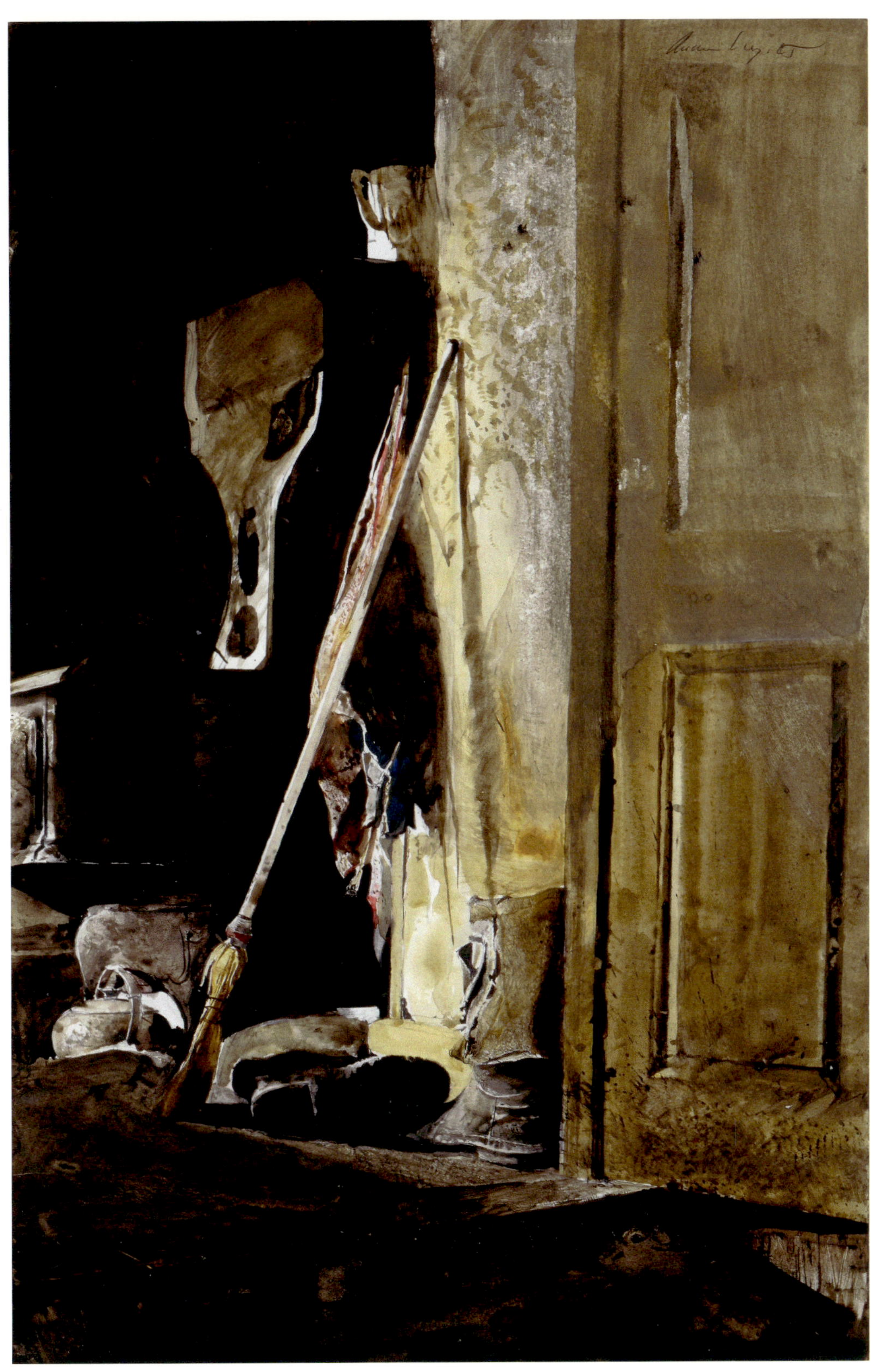

Kitchen at Olsons, 1967; watercolor on paper; 21 1/2 x 13 3/4 in.; ©Andrew Wyeth; collection of Marunuma Art Park, cat. 27

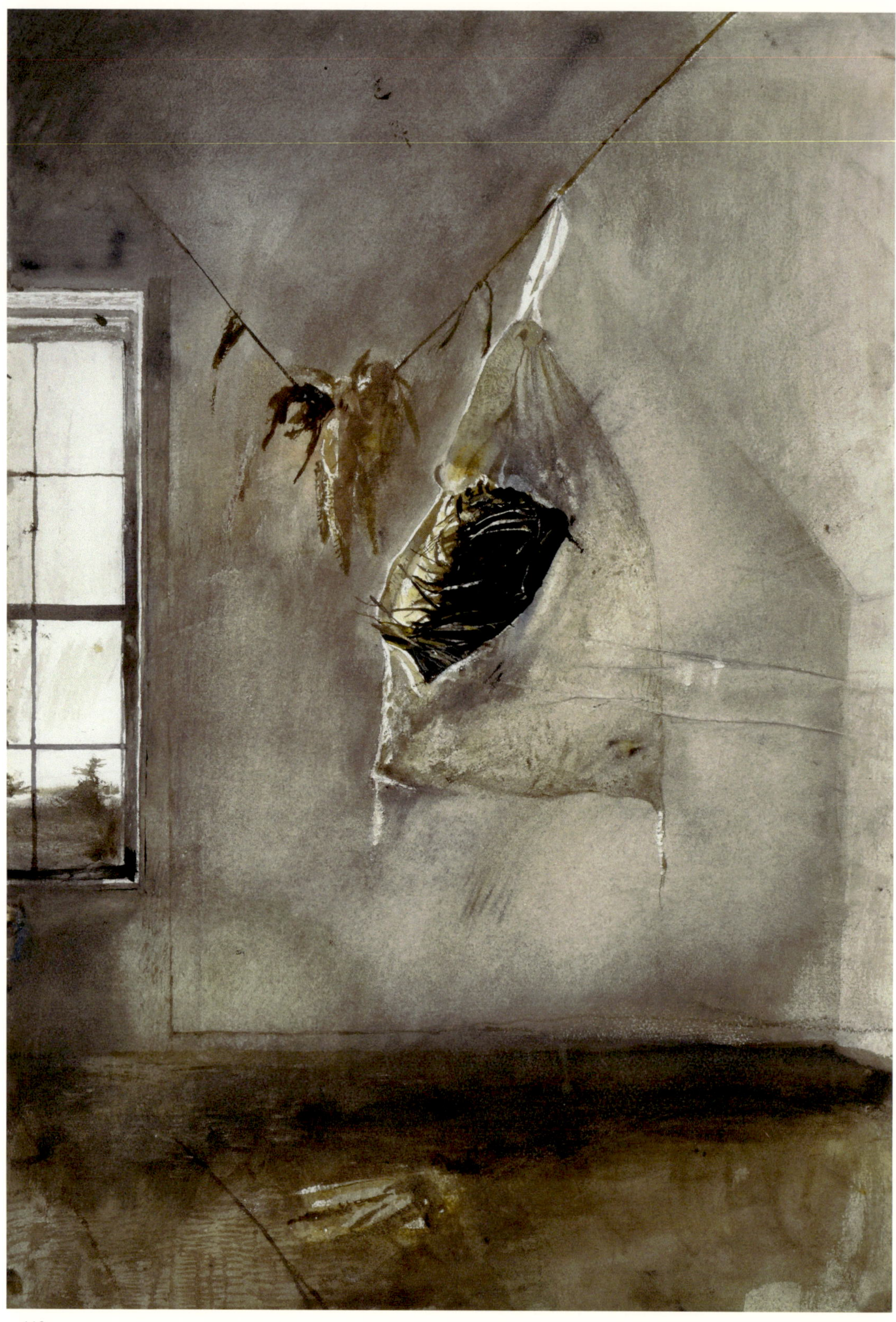

Beans Drying, 1968; watercolor on paper; 27 1/2 x 18 1/2 in.; ©Andrew Wyeth; collection of Marunuma Art Park, cat. 28

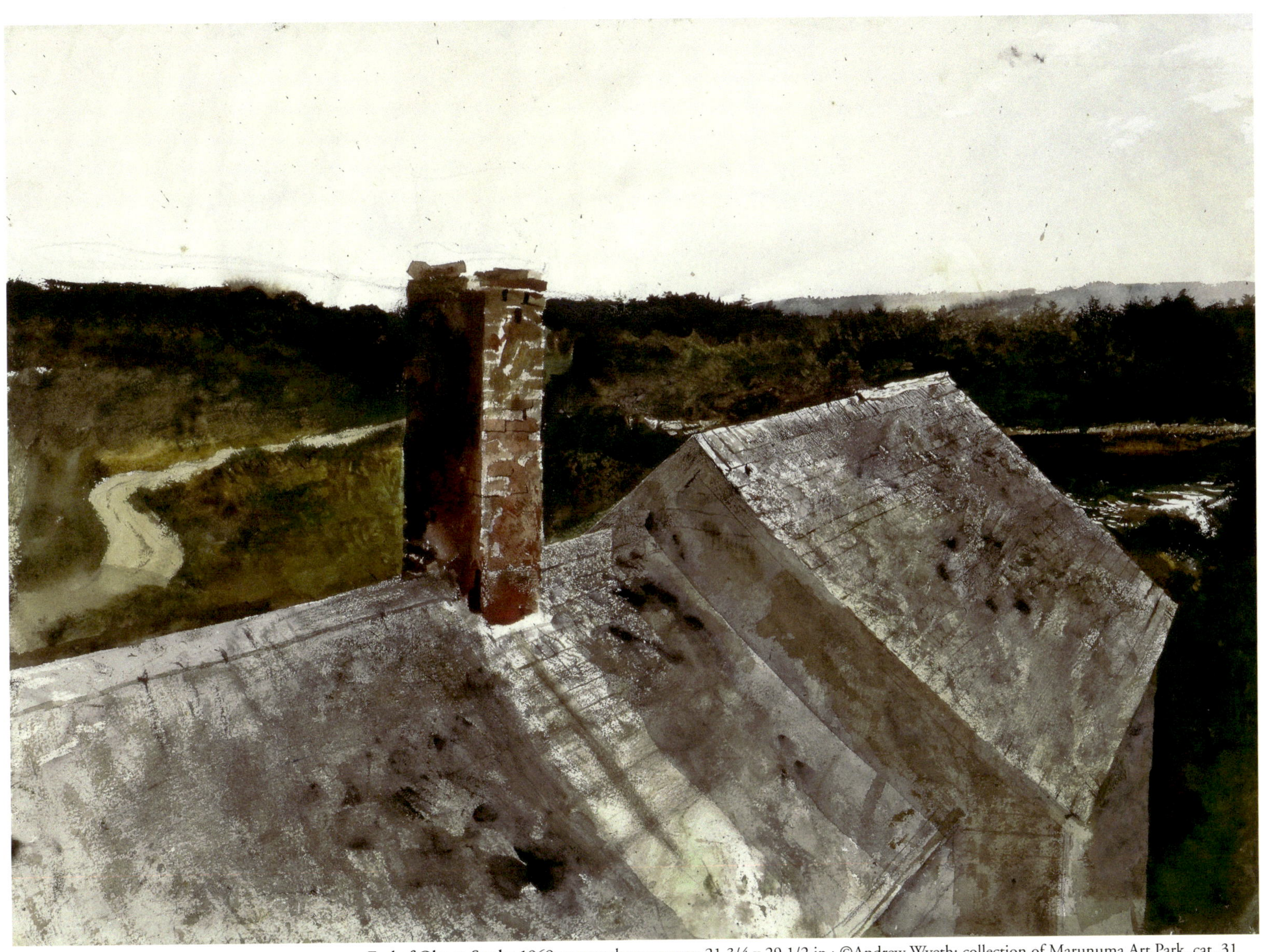

End of Olsons Study, 1969; watercolor on paper; 21 3/4 x 29 1/2 in.; ©Andrew Wyeth; collection of Marunuma Art Park, cat. 31

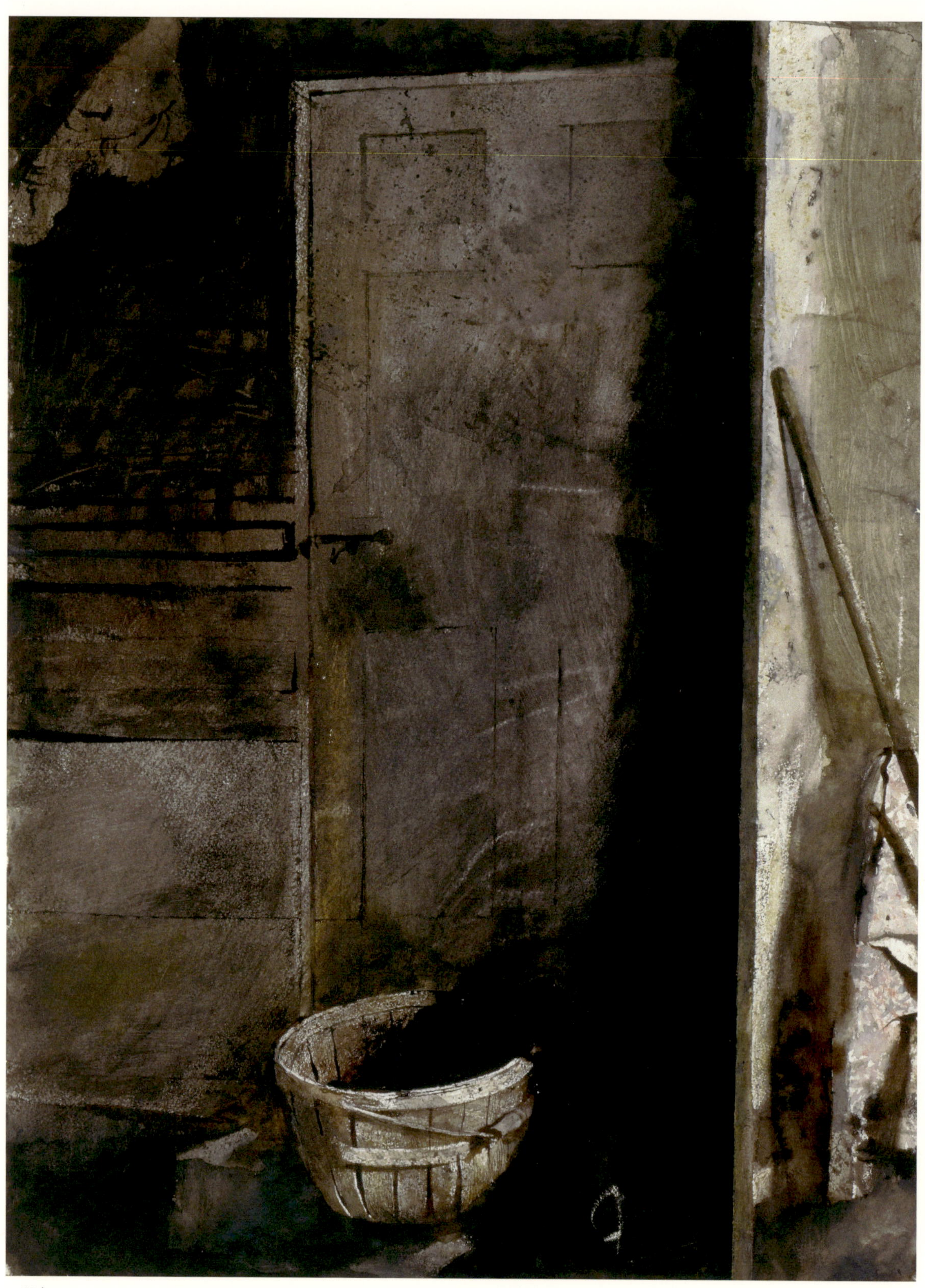

Alvaro and Christina Study, 1968; watercolor on paper; 29 1/4 x 21 in. ©Andrew Wyeth; collection of Marunuma Art Park, cat. 29

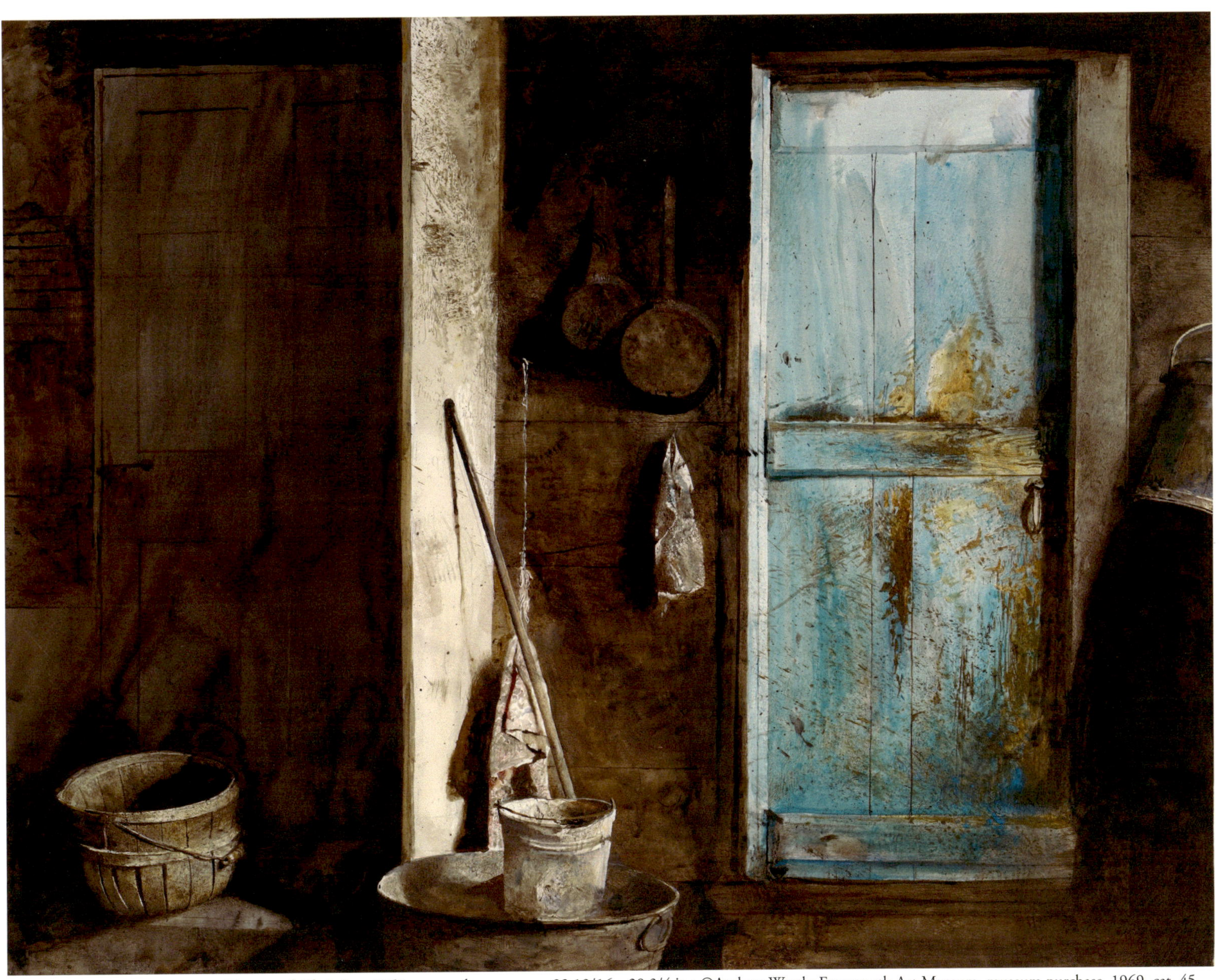

Alvaro and Christina, 1968; watercolor on paper; 22 13/16 x 28 3/4 in.; ©Andrew Wyeth; Farnsworth Art Museum: museum purchase, 1969, cat. 45

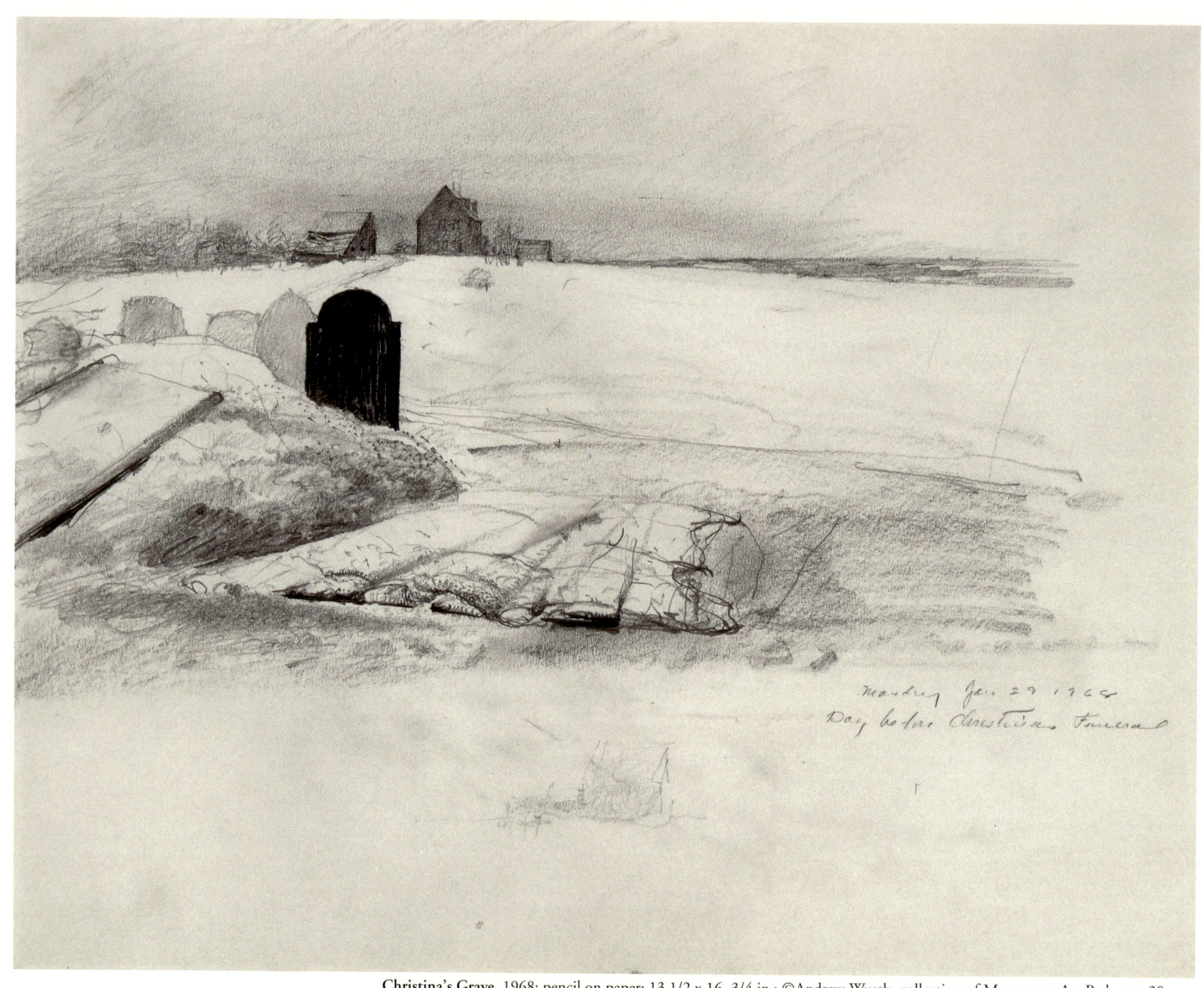

Christina's Grave, 1968; pencil on paper; 13 1/2 x 16. 3/4 in.; ©Andrew Wyeth; collection of Marunuma Art Park, cat. 30

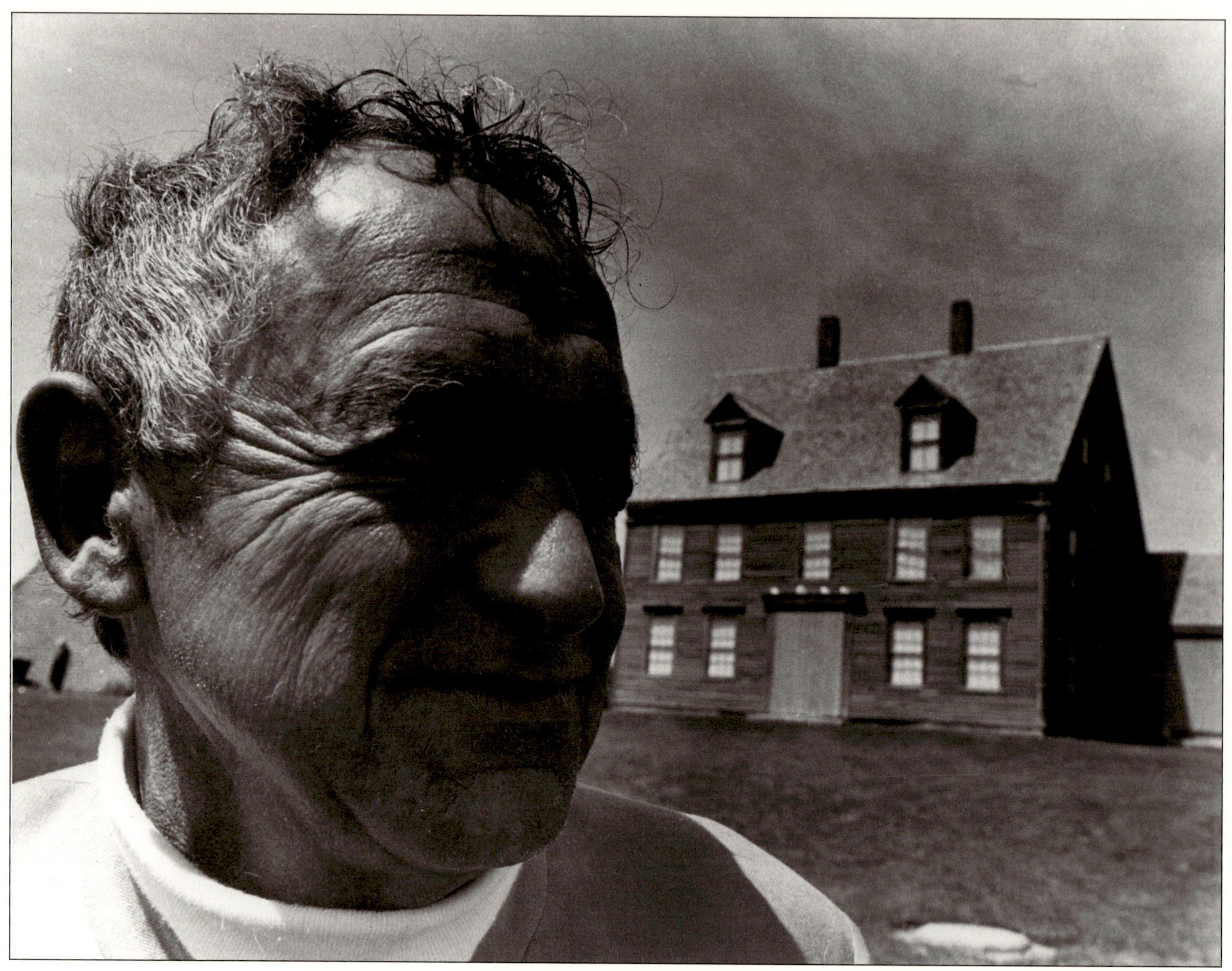

Andrew Wyeth at the Olson House, c. 1980

CHECKLIST

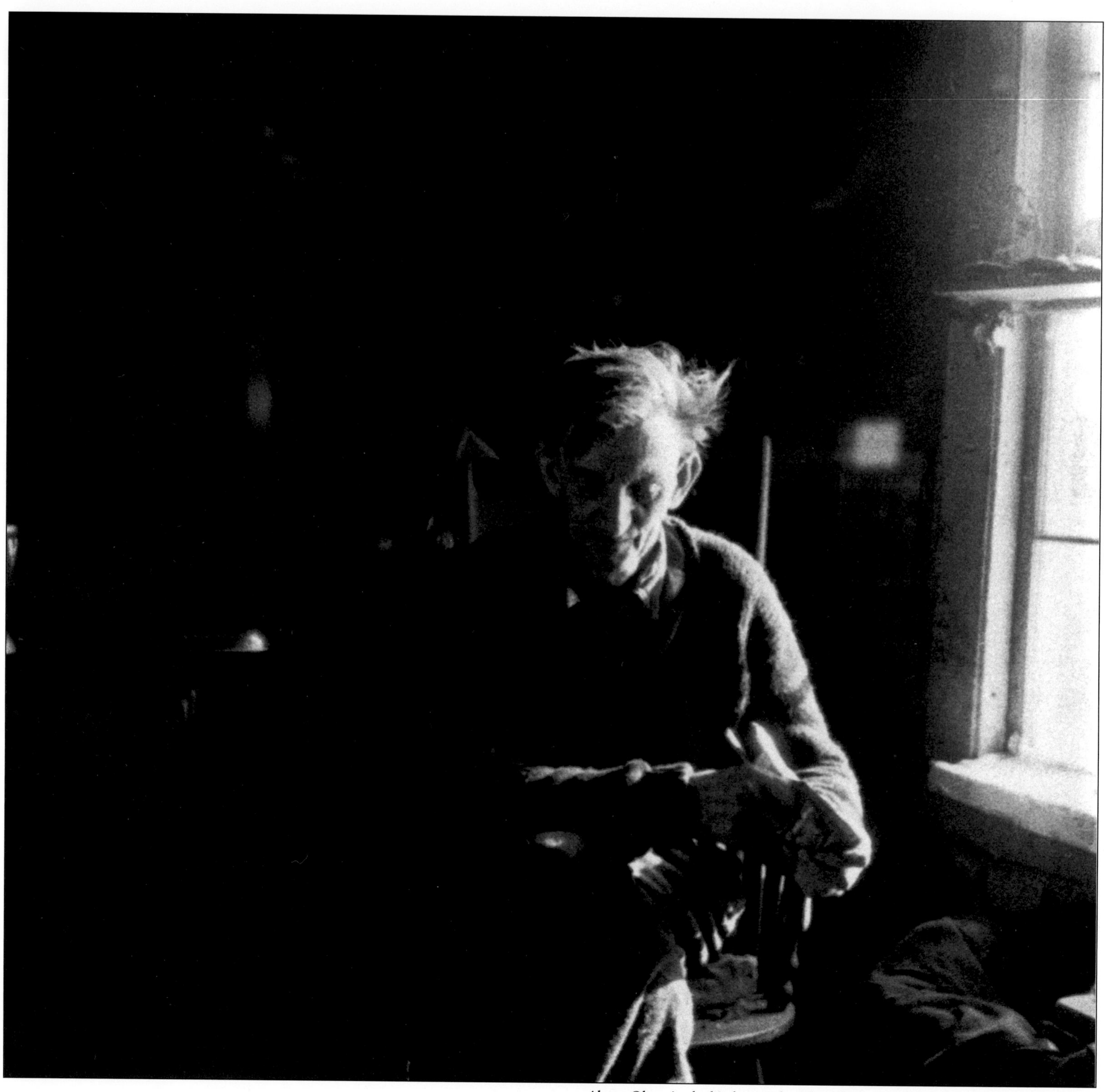

Alvaro Olson in the kitchen at the Olson House, 1963; photograph by Jim Moore

From Marunuma Art Park

1. *Olsons Cove,* 1940
Watercolor on paper
21 5/8 x 29 5/8 in.
©Andrew Wyeth
Collection of Marunuma Art Park

2. *Alvaro in His Garden*, 1940
Pencil on paper
10 x 15 1/2 in.
©Andrew Wyeth
Collection of the Marunuma Art Park

3. *Alvaro and Others, Raking Blueberries*, 1942
Watercolor on paper
21 1/2 x 29. 3/8 in.
©Andrew Wyeth
Collection of the Marunuma Art Park

4. *Alvaro on Front Doorstep*, 1942
Watercolor on paper
21 1/2 x 29 1/2 in.
©Andrew Wyeth
Collection of the Marunuma Art Park

5. *Alvaro's Horse*, 1945
Watercolor on paper
21 1/2 x 29 1/2 in.
©Andrew Wyeth
Collection of the Marunuma Art Park

6. *Third-Floor Bedroom*, 1947
Watercolor on paper
21 1/2 x 29 1/2 in.
©Andrew Wyeth
Collection of the Marunuma Art Park

7. *Alvaro Painting His Dory*, 1947
Watercolor on paper
20 3/4 x 29 1/4 in.
©Andrew Wyeth
Collection of the Marunuma Art Park

8. *Alvaro Raking Hay*, 1949
Watercolor on paper
20 3/4 x 29 in.
©Andrew Wyeth
Collection of the Marunuma Art Park

9. *Stairway and Front Door,* 1948
Watercolor on paper
19 1/2 x 13 1/2 in.
©Andrew Wyeth
Collection of the Marunuma Art Park

10. *Barometer in Front Hall,* 1949
Watercolor on paper
18 1/4 x 23 1/2 in.
©Andrew Wyeth
Collection of the Marunuma Art Park

11. *Reshingling the Roof,* 1952
Watercolor on paper
21 1/2 x 29 1/2 in.
©Andrew Wyeth
Collection of the Marunuma Art Park

12. *Olsons' Front Door*, 1957
Watercolor on paper
30 x 20 in.
©Andrew Wyeth
Collection of the Marunuma Art Park

13. *Alvaro's Fish House*, 1955
Watercolor on paper
21 1/2 x 29 1/4 in.
©Andrew Wyeth
Collection of the Marunuma Art Park

14. *Bucket on Stone Boat*, 1957
Watercolor on paper
19 1/2 x 27 1/2 in.
©Andrew Wyeth
Collection of the Marunuma Art Park

15. *Hitching Post at Olsons*, 1959
Watercolor on paper
14 1/2 x 20 1/2 in.
©Andrew Wyeth
Collection of the Marunuma Art Park

16. *Harness in Olsons' Barn*, 1960
Watercolor on paper
22 x 28 1/2 in.
©Andrew Wyeth
Collection of the Marunuma Art Park

17. *Grain Bag*, 1959
Watercolor on paper
22 1/2 x 14 in.
©Andrew Wyeth
Collection of the Marunuma Art Park

18. *Pole Fence*, 1961
Watercolor on paper
21 1/4 x 29 3/4 in.
©Andrew Wyeth
Collection of the Marunuma Art Park

19. *Wood Stove Study*, 1962
Watercolor on paper
20 3/4 x 29 1/4 in.
©Andrew Wyeth
Collection of the Marunuma Art Park

20. *Inside Olsons' Barn*, 1964
Watercolor on paper
20 x 28 in.
©Andrew Wyeth
Collection of the Marunuma Art Park

21. *Downspout, Study for Weatherside,* 1965
Watercolor on paper
10 3/4 x 13 1/2 in.
©Andrew Wyeth
Collection of the Marunuma Art Park

22. *Alvaro's Bedroom*, 1965
Watercolor on paper
14 x 20 1/4 in.
©Andrew Wyeth
Collection of the Marunuma Art Park

23. *Olson House*, 1966
Watercolor on paper
27 1/4 x 18 1/2 in.
©Andrew Wyeth
Collection of the Marunuma Art Park

24. *Hayloft in Olsons' Barn,* 1966
Watercolor on paper
27 1/4 x 18 1/2 in.
©Andrew Wyeth
Collection of the Marunuma Art Park

25. *Anna Christina Study,* 1967
Watercolor on paper
29 x 21 1/4 in.
©Andrew Wyeth
Collection of the Marunuma Art Park

26. *Breakfast at Olsons,* 1967
Watercolor on paper
23 3/4 x 16 in.
©Andrew Wyeth
Collection of the Marunuma Art Park

27. *Kitchen at Olsons,* 1967
Watercolor on paper
21 1/2 x 13 3/4 in.
©Andrew Wyeth
Collection of the Marunuma Art Park

28. *Beans Drying,* 1968
Watercolor on paper
27 1/2 x 18 1/2 in.
©Andrew Wyeth
Collection of the Marunuma Art Park

29. *Alvaro and Christina Study,* 1968
Watercolor on paper
22 1/4 x 21 in.
©Andrew Wyeth
Collection of the Marunuma Art Park

30. *Christina's Grave,* 1968
Pencil on paper
13 1/2 x 16. 3/4 in.
©Andrew Wyeth
Collection of the Marunuma Art Park

31. *End of Olsons Study,* 1969
Watercolor on paper
21 3/4 x 29 1/2 in.
©Andrew Wyeth
Collection of the Marunuma Art Park

32. *Christina's World Study,* 1948
Pencil on paper
12 x 18 3/4 in.
©Andrew Wyeth
Collection of the Marunuma Art Park

33. *Christina's World Study,* 1948
Pencil on paper
14 x 20 in.
©Andrew Wyeth
Collection of the Marunuma Art Park

34. *Christina's World Study,* 1948
Pencil on paper
14 1/4 x 20 in.
©Andrew Wyeth
Collection of the Marunuma Art Park

35. *Christina's World Study,* 1948
Pencil on paper
14 x 18 in.
©Andrew Wyeth
Collection of the Marunuma Art Park

36. *Christina's World Study,* 1948
Pencil on paper
15 x 22 in.
©Andrew Wyeth
Collection of the Marunuma Art Park

37. *Christina's World Study,* 1948
Pencil on paper
8 1/2 x 11 in.
©Andrew Wyeth
Collection of the Marunuma Art Park

38. *Christina's World Study,* 1948
Watercolor on paper
14 1/2 x 20 in.
©Andrew Wyeth
Collection of the Marunuma Art Park

From the Farnsworth Art Museum

39. *Christina's Head, Study for Christina Olson,* 1947
Watercolor on paper
12 1/4 x 10 5/16 in.
©Andrew Wyeth
Gift of Nina Chandler Murray, 2006

40. *Christina with Beads, Study for Christina Olson,* 1947
Pencil on paper
17 3/4 x 23 3/4 in.
©Andrew Wyeth
Gift of Nina Chandler Murray, 2006

41. *Christina's Head, Study for Christina Olson,* 1947
Pencil on paper
17 3/4 x 23 3/4 in.
©Andrew Wyeth
Gift of Nina Chandler Murray, 2006

42. *Doorway, Study for Christina Olson,* 1947
Pencil on paper
23 3/4 x 17 3/4 in.
©Andrew Wyeth
Gift of Nina Chandler Murray, 2006

43. *Alvaro's Hayrack,* 1958
Watercolor on paper
9 x 23 in.
©Andrew Wyeth
Gift of Mr. and Mrs. Andrew Wyeth, 1960

44. *Wood Stove,* 1962
Drybrush watercolor on paper
13 3/8 x 26 ¼ in.
©Andrew Wyeth
Museum purchase, 1962

45. *Alvaro and Christina,* 1968
Watercolor on paper
22 13/16 x 28 3/4 in.
©Andrew Wyeth
Museum purchase, 1969

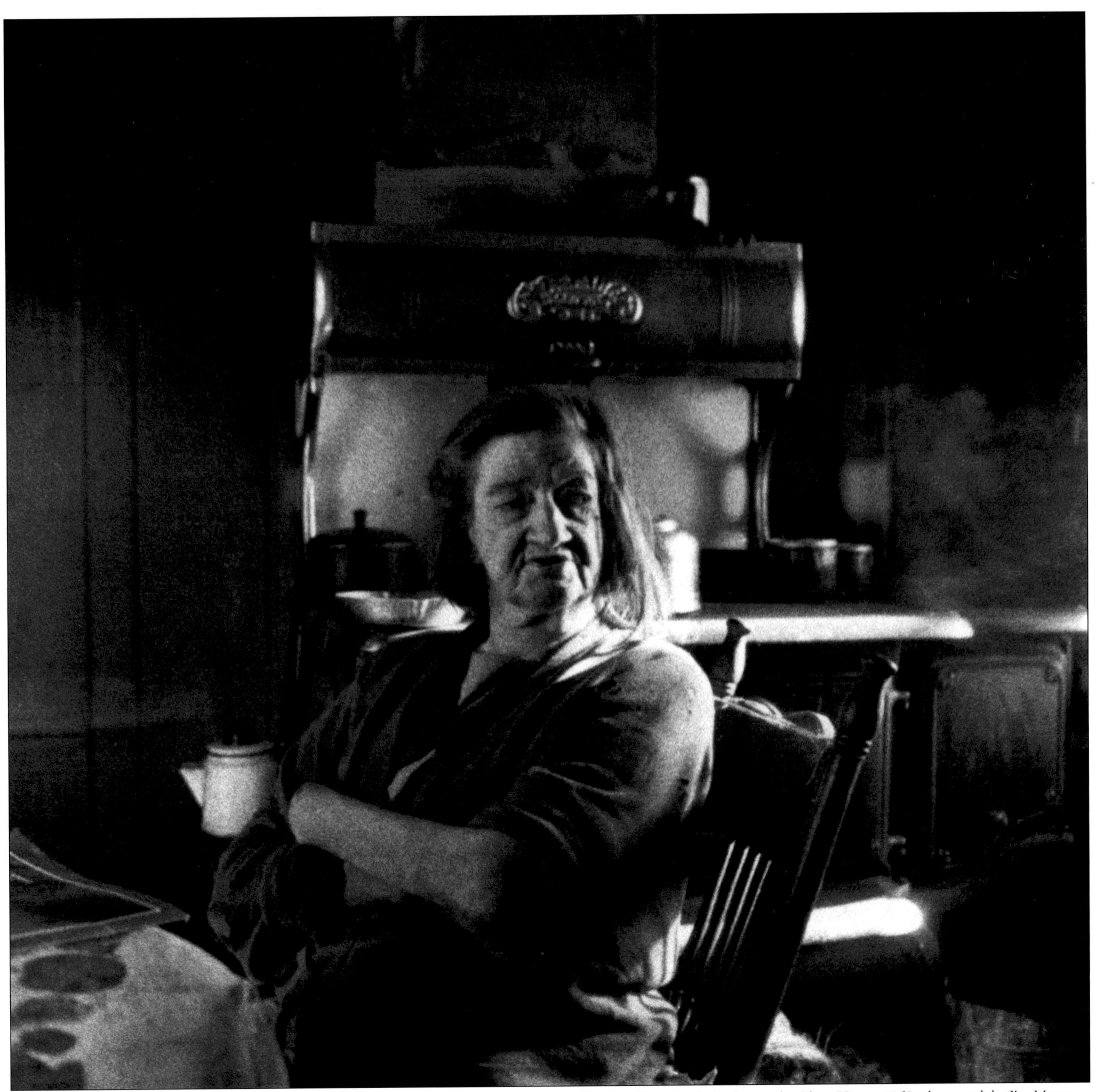

Christina Olson in the kitchen at the Olson House, 1963; photograph by Jim Moore

PUBLISHED ON THE OCCASION OF THE EXHIBITION AT
THE FARNSWORTH ART MUSEUM, ROCKLAND MAINE
JUNE 11—OCTOBER 30, 2011

Funded in part by a grant from the Maine Arts Commission, an independent state agency supported by the National Endowment for the Arts.

Distributed in the U.S. trade by Random House, New York

IN CONJUNCTION WITH
Skira Rizzoli Publications, Inc.
300 Park Avenue South
New York, NY 10010
www.rizzoliusa.com

2011 2012 1013 1014 / 10 9 8 7 6 5 4 3 2 1
Library of Congress Catalog Control Number: 2011930035
ISBN 2011930035

DESIGNER: Mary Margaret Sesak, Farnsworth Art Museum
PRINTER: J.S. McCarthy Printers, Augusta, Maine

Fonts: ITC Usherwood, Adobe Garamond
Paper: Chorus Art Gloss 100 lb. text and 63 lb. cover